THE PERFECT SEASON

THE PERFECT SEASON

How Penn State Came to Stop a Hurricane and
Win a National Football Championship

M. G. MISSANELLI

The Pennsylvania State University Press
University Park, Pennsylvania

Library of Congress Cataloging-in-Publication Data

Missanelli, M. G., 1955-
   The perfect season : how Penn State came to stop a
   hurricane and win a National Championship /
   M.G. Missanelli.
      p.   cm.
Includes bibliographical references and index.
 ISBN-13: 978-0-271-03282-5 (cloth : alk. paper)
 1. Pennsylvania State University-Football-History.
 2. Penn State Nittany Lions (Football team)-History.
 3. Fiesta Bowl (Football game) (1987 : Tempe, Ariz.)
 I. Title.

GV958.P46M57 2007
796.332'630974853-dc22
 2007010235

Book design/typesetting by Garet Markvoort/zijn digital

CONTENTS

FOREWORD

I REMEMBER FEELING LIKE SOMEBODY HAD HIT ME over the head with a blunt object. My mouth was wide open. I was stunned into silence.

It was the night before the Fiesta Bowl, January 2, 1987. Hours before we went out to break heads in the game for the national championship, Penn State's players and coaches broke bread with Miami's players and coaches at a barbeque given by bowl organizers. College football, after all, is about sportsmanship.

Or so we thought.

John Bruno, our punter and team crack-up, had just finished what we thought was a hilarious parody of Miami coach Jimmy Johnson and his stiff, sprayed-up hair. No one from Miami—whose players mostly wore battle fatigue clothing to the shindig—cracked a smile.

All of a sudden, Jerome Brown, the Hurricanes' All-American defensive tackle, got up and made a loud statement.

"Did the Japanese sit down and eat with Pearl Harbor before they bombed them?!" Brown screamed. "We're out of here!"

And with that, the entire Miami team got up and walked out.

I followed them with my eyes all the way out the door, thinking that this was their comedy routine. I figured they would soon do an about-face, come back into the room, and say, "Just kidding." When they didn't, I looked at Bucky Conlin, one of our mammoth offensive linemen. Bucky had barely looked up from his plate, despite the mayhem that surrounded us, and continued cutting into a big steak.

"Let 'em go," Conlin said. "That's just more food for us."

Conlin's cavalier reaction spoke volumes. As a team, we were covered with this quiet confidence, and Miami's disrespect only heightened our intensity about three or four times what it already had been.

They have no idea what they just did, I remember thinking to myself.

We were a heavy underdog to Miami that night, but we had come to Tempe on a mission. College football experts had called the 1986 Nittany Lions frauds—and that was the nicest word they called us—with no legitimate claim to a national championship. We came into the Fiesta Bowl undefeated. But our schedule was soft, they said, and we had a hard time even overcoming that during the season. Our quarterback, John Shaffer, was said to be a no-name and a no-talent—even though he had lost only one game since seventh grade as a starting quarterback.

But we knew better.

The die had been cast for a Fiesta Bowl triumph the year before, almost to the day, after we took an undefeated record into the '86 Orange Bowl and promptly got smoked by Oklahoma, 25–10. We were embarrassed that night by a team whose image was brashly similar to Miami's. A freshman quarterback named Jamielle Holloway had said during the week leading up to that game that all Oklahoma had to do to beat us was "put seven points on the board." The Sooners coach, Barry Switzer, was about as rebellious as our coach, Joe Paterno, was conservative. We knew Joe didn't much like Switzer and liked losing to him a lot less. After that loss, the part of the sporting public that derided the Penn State program for being "too squeaky clean" reveled in our misfortune. So we were determined not to let that happen again.

In the locker room after the Oklahoma loss, a collection of guys who would be fifth-year seniors said they were coming back for another year rather than leave for the NFL draft. We were already an experienced team because most of the juniors—guys like Shaffer, Tim Manoa, Steve Smith, Shane Conlan, Trey Bauer, and myself—had gotten playing time our freshman year. We didn't have to start over after that Orange Bowl loss; we merely had to take it up one more notch.

Knowing that, we started our workouts for the next season literally the next day when we returned home to State College. A bunch of us decided to go out and take a jog through campus. All of a sudden, almost everybody on the team was running on a daily basis—despite the frozen snow that is Penn State University in the winter.

By the time the season began that September, we were fueled for something really special. Our goal was simple: another undefeated season, and this time, to win that final game and the national championship.

Through the eyes of several of the key players who helped make the '86 championship season, this is the story of how we did it.

D.J. Dozier

PREFACE AND ACKNOWLEDGMENTS

I WAS IN THE STADIUM THE NIGHT PENN STATE pulled off its greatest football triumph.

I was sitting in the south end zone of Sun Devil Stadium, my heart in my throat, watching, perhaps, a national championship go up in flames, when linebacker Pete Giftopoulos stepped in the way of a Vinny Testaverde pass. Giftopoulos, the kid from Canada whose parents had emigrated some twenty years ago from Greece, cradled the ball like a big stuffed grape leaf, milled around for a bit, then dropped to his knees. Seconds later, John Shaffer, Penn State's quarterback, fell on the ball and the Nittany Lions had pulled off the unthinkable—beating big, bad Miami to win the 1986 national championship.

After the game my brother, John, and I had to run for a taxi so we could catch our commuter flight back to San Diego. We were running on air, carried on a magic carpet from the energy of Penn State's win. It had been such a struggle. Miami's offense was on the field for what seemed like 200 plays, moving the ball up and down the field on Penn State. They had about twelve future pros on their roster. All week long in the buildup to the game they had worn combat fatigues, talked trash about what they were going to do to the Nittany Lions, and thumbed their noses at anything that resembled the establishment. And Penn State had beaten them, 14–10.

To be a Penn State football fan is to be a little "off." Folks not connected with Penn State seem to think of us as a little cultist, a little too elitist, and a little too weird. Autumn springs eternal for Penn State fans as we measure up how the squad stacks up against the rest of the nation and what surprises our ageless legend, Joe Paterno, has in store for us this season. It's a Happy Valley thing. You wouldn't understand.

I didn't buy into any of that for a long time. I was one of those rare Penn Staters too cynical to be consumed by the *goodness* of Nittany Lion football. I had graduated from Penn State in the late 1970s, when the football program was going through somewhat of a lull. My freshman year, I got to share in the excitement of John Cappelletti and his run to the Heisman Trophy. But the next three years brought just average success. The quarterbacks were decent guys, but just average players. I wasn't compelled to walk around campus in a John Andress or Dayle Tate jersey (with all due respect to John Andress and Dayle Tate). I couldn't understand how a team like Iowa could come into Beaver Stadium and beat Penn State, 7–6. And adding to a Penn Stater's misery was the fact that the University of Pittsburgh, thanks to a guy named Tony Dorsett, had usurped the role of best college program in the state.

But I also had another reason to be cynical. I was jealous.

I was a varsity baseball player, which is to say, in the Penn State athletic hierarchy I was lower than third class. Penn State football ran the show, devouring anything else in its wake. Playing baseball at Penn State is like playing baseball in Alaska. By the time the spring weather finally takes root, the season and semester are over. We practiced and played in conditions better suited for polar bears. The university had just built a lavish Astroturf field in the east part of campus, across the way from Beaver Stadium and the adjacent Penn State baseball field. One day we petitioned the athletic department to use the Astroturf so we wouldn't have to practice on our muddy and/or frozen infield. We were denied.

What's more, we never got to eat as much as the football team. All Penn State athletes get to enjoy what's called "training table." Because practice schedules took us beyond the normal dinner hour, we athletes would congregate to a specially designated dining hall where the food was prepared specifically for us. Penn State footballers got to eat as much as they wanted. The baseball team was allowed to spend only $2.50 per person on its meal, which even back then was not a lot. In other words, we'd take our tray through the line and a cashier with a hairnet would add up what we had. *Okay, that's one piece of meatloaf at 75 cents, a potato, a quarter, a side of string beans, 50 cents, two half-pints of milk at 25 cents each,* and so on. Meanwhile, some offensive lineman right next to you had a pile of food bigger than Mt. Nittany, and he was whisked right through. It was unnerving, to say the least.

But there is something about a national championship that bonds even the most rabid cynic.

In December 1982 I took a flight to New Orleans to spend some time with my college roommate, Bill, who was going to graduate school at Tulane. I arranged the visit for the same time of the year when Penn State was to play Georgia in the Sugar Bowl for what would turn out to be a national title. Georgia had Herschel Walker and other stars such as quarterback Buck Beleu and safety Terry Hoage. Our tickets were right in the middle of a Georgia fan section and we were serenaded throughout with Bulldog chants. "Go Hush-all!" "Terr-ray Hoag!" "Hunker down, you hairy dawgs!" Then Todd Blackledge hit Gregg Garrity with a fifty-yard pass to begin the game, the Penn State defense cracked down on Herschel Walker like he stole something, and running Curt Warner danced on the Superdome turf as if it was Mardi Gras right there on the field. Penn State won the game, and at the end Georgia fans turned to us and said, "Y'all kicked our ass." It was such a source of pride.

Just four years later, we Penn Staters would get to experience that feeling again in Tempe, Arizona. But this time, because of all the subplots of this game with Miami—because it was like taking on the bully in the schoolyard and winning—it was even better.

I MUST FIRST THANK my two main colleagues on this project, D.J. Dozier and Kevin Courter. It was Courter, a Penn State alum and rabid devotee of all things Nittany Lion football, who first came to me with the idea of writing a book about the '86 team, reminding me that it has been twenty years since PSU won its last national championship. I have always been fascinated with "Where are they now?" stories about people whose lives we followed from afar—members of a rock band who had a couple of hits, athletes who had brief moments of fame in either college or pro ball. How do they turn out? What do they do when the games are finally over?

Courter, who would provide me with some tireless research on the subject, then put me in touch with D.J. Dozier, whom he had gotten to know while working with Jerry Sandusky's Second Mile charity. I drove to Norfolk, Virginia, where I found Dozier working in an impressive high-rise office as a big-time financial adviser. He looked as slick and polished as ever and, I thought, in good enough shape to resume his football career on the spot. We started talking about his '86 Penn State team and where some other of his teammates had ended up. As I tracked down a lot of the 1986 Nittany Lions, I discovered many interesting stories about that national championship year—stories that I felt would make a pretty good book.

I met up with Shane Conlan on the Jersey shore. He vacations there every year, where he delights in bodysurfing for hours with his young sons. He was twenty pounds lighter than his playing weight as an All-Pro linebacker with the Buffalo Bills and Los Angeles Rams and looked terrific. I located John Shaffer on Wall Street, where he uses the same leadership skills and fierce determination as a corporate bondsman that he used as the Penn State quarterback who never lost.

I found Pete Giftopoulos back in his hometown of Hamilton, Ontario. Gifto told me specifically to call *him*. When I did, we talked for about an hour and a half as if old friends. When I looked at my telephone bill the next month, I saw that the call to Gifto had cost me $147. Giftopoulos, the kid who thought $8 for a haircut in State College was way too expensive and instead waited until he returned to Canada after a school term so his barber father could cut it for free, had fleeced me good. But it was the best $147 I ever spent.

I tracked down Trey Bauer, Ray Isom, Tim Johnson, and Bob White. Bauer is a bond trader in North Jersey, Isom an insurance agent in Harrisburg, Johnson a pastor in Nashville, and White an assistant athletic director back at Penn State. All of them shared themselves with me willingly. These guys *wanted* to look back to 1986. It was one of the greatest times of their lives.

The story you are about to read is the story of the 1986 Penn State Nittany Lions through the eyes of the people who made that year special. It takes us through the entire 1986 football season and then the wondrous 1987 Fiesta Bowl, where the

Nittany Lions pulled off what many thought was impossible—a win over Miami. The book is written through the eyes of the people who made that victory happen. It was the perfect season—an undefeated team that won a national championship in the one-hundredth year of Penn State football.

While what you are about to read is a tale of triumph, it is also a story that exposes for us the human condition. John Bruno, Penn State's brilliant punter who was one of the Miami game's most valuable players, died just a little more than five years after that game of skin cancer, a cheating death that came too sudden and swift. Steve Smith, the Nittany Lions' fullback who went on to achieve great success in the NFL with the Los Angeles Raiders and who shared the same backfield with the likes of Marcus Allen and Bo Jackson, suffers from amyotrophic lateral sclerosis (ALS, or Lou Gehrig's disease). It is a horrible disease, one that has robbed Smith of his once-muscular frame, taken away his normal bodily functions, and made him a prisoner of his own body.

I thank all of the players and coaches who allowed me to take up some of their time. But I especially thank the Brunos and the Smiths.

John Bruno's dad and mom, John Sr. and Alfrieda; sister Cheryl Bruno Gamber; and good friends, Joe Johns and Mark Arnold, opened up their hearts and scrapbooks to me so I could truly know their son, brother, and friend. In the end, I felt cheated that I never got the chance to meet John Bruno.

Of all the time I spent in the research of this book, my visit with Steve Smith, his wife, Chie, and their beautiful children, Dante and Jazmin, at their Texas home will live with me forever. I am inspired by their courage and I thank them for opening their home to me.

Also my heartfelt thanks to Joe Bodkin, the man who provided me many of the photos in this book. A metallurgist engineer who settled in State College in the 1960s, Bodkin combined his love for photography and Penn State football into a gig as chief photographer for the famed *Penn State Football Letter*, a weekly report on the season. A kindly man, Bodkin passed away in March 2007 after a long illness. His generosity will never be forgotten and my sympathies go out to his wife and family.

Penn State football will live on for future generations. The pomp and circumstance of the tailgates, the dancing drum major, the mad charge through the stadium tunnel, the prowling Lion mascot, and the soothing, sound-enhanced growl of the Nittany Lion—everything about game day is special. The hope for another national championship remains fervent and, certainly, is possible most every year the Blue and White suit up.

But there may never be another season like 1986, the season Penn State beat Miami in the Fiesta Bowl.

HOW THEY FINISHED 12–0: THE SEASON IN REVIEW

The following is a game-by-game account of Penn State's 12–0 season.

1. September 6 (Beaver Stadium): Penn State 45, Temple 15

In the first night game ever played at Beaver Stadium, quarterback John Shaffer connected on 12 of 18 passes for 194 yards and three touchdowns. It was the first three-touchdown game of Shaffer's career. The Lions scored the first three times they had the ball and led 21–0 after only 9:21 of the first quarter. Shaffer tossed TD passes of 10, 14, and 12 yards to Steve Smith, Eric Hamilton, and Jim Coates, respectively. Tim Manoa led Penn State rushers with 89 yards on just six carries, including a 51-yard run. D.J. Dozier, who came into the season as a candidate to win the Heisman Trophy, ran for 54 yards and a touchdown and caught four passes for 73 yards. Temple's Paul Palmer, who had gained 206 yards on Penn State the year before, was held to 96 yards on 24 carries.

2. September 20 (at Foxboro, Mass.): Penn State 26, Boston College 14

With the issue in doubt, two of the Lions' big-play people, Dozier and linebacker Shane Conlan, stepped forward to secure the win in a nationally televised night game. Dozier, who led all rushers with 78 yards, caught a 17-yard TD pass from Shaffer after Boston College drew within 12–7 and later added a seven-yard scoring run that pushed the score to 26–7. Conlan made 11 tackles, had a quarterback sack, and intercepted a BC halfback pass in the end zone to turn aside an Eagles drive that had reached the Penn State two-yard line with the Lions in front, 19–7. The Penn State defense held BC to just 33 rushing yards and had seven takeaways, including five interceptions.

3. September 27 (Beaver Stadium): Penn State 42, East Carolina 17

Ray Isom intercepted an East Carolina pass on the second play of the game, and the offense quickly capitalized to get Penn State rolling. The Lions put the game out of reach in the second quarter, scoring 21 points to take a 35–0 lead into half-time. Shaffer completed 11 of 16 passes for 157 yards and hit Ray Roundtree and

Eric Hamilton for touchdown passes. Dozier finished with 71 yards on 12 carries. Sophomore Blair Thomas, getting significant playing time, gained 67 yards on nine carries. Backup quarterback Matt Knizner played, completing 5 of 10 passes for 33 yards. Coates returned seven punts for 75 yards. The Penn State defense dominated, limiting East Carolina to minus-17 yards rushing in the first half.

4. October 4 (Beaver Stadium): Penn State 31, Rutgers 6

In an early showdown of undefeated eastern teams, Penn State disposed of Rutgers, rolling up nearly 500 yards of offense and holding the Scarlet Knights to just 45 yards rushing. Eleven rushers for Penn State contributed to 287 yards on the ground. Dozier had 54 yards on 15 carries and moved ahead of John Cappelletti into fourth place on the all-time Penn State rushing list. Smith had 50 yards on seven carries, moving over the 1,000-yard rushing plateau for his career. Shaffer was 13-of-23, passing for 187 yards, and he also rushed six times for 33 yards. The Penn State quarterback engineered a 14-play, 82-yard drive that gobbled up 6:51 off the clock and resulted in a seven-yard touchdown pass from Shaffer to Hamilton. Roundtree scored on a 34-yard end-around play. The Penn State defense limited Rutgers to just 1-for-16 on third down conversions, and the Scarlet Knights had to punt ten times.

5. October 11 (Beaver Stadium): Penn State 23, Cincinnati 17

Penn State survived a scare when Thomas came up with a pair of clutch plays in the fourth quarter. Facing a third-and-10 on the Penn State 25 with Cincinnati, a 24-point underdog, leading 17–14, Shaffer found Thomas coming out of the backfield for a 32-yard completion. Thomas followed up that catch with a five-yard run and a 27-yard run that moved the ball to the Bearcats' 11. Two plays later, David Clark carried tacklers the final six yards to score the winning touchdown with 3:07 remaining. Shane Conlan blocked a punt for a safety in the final minute to seal the deal. Dozier gained a season-high 87 yards on 14 carries, but was nursing a groin pull and was not in the game in the final frantic moments. The Penn State defense got gashed by Cincinnati quarterback Danny McCoin, who completed 25 of 38 passes for 254 yards.

6. October 18 (Beaver Stadium): Penn State 42, Syracuse 3

Penn State used an overpowering running attack that included the longest run from scrimmage in Nittany Lion history to crush the Orangemen. PSU gained 434 yards on the ground as Thomas collected 132 yards on just three carries (for an average of 44 yards per rush), one of them being a record 92-yard run that brought the ball from the Penn State seven to the Syracuse one. He also had a 38-yard touchdown run. Manoa, the bruising fullback, added 96 yards and two touchdowns on 12 carries. The Nittany Lions' defense sacked Syracuse's mobile quarterback, Don McPherson, six times and held Scott Schwedes, the Orangemen's dangerous receiver, to just three catches for 13 yards. Kicker Massimo Manca kicked his fifty-fifth straight extra point to break a record previously held by Herb Menhardt.

7. October 25 (at Tuscaloosa, Ala.): Penn State 23, Alabama 3

Shaffer had another big game and the Penn State defense was stifling as the Lions surprised previously unbeaten and second-ranked Alabama. It was only the thirteenth home loss ever for the Crimson Tide since Bryant-Denny Stadium opened in 1929. Shaffer had the best single-game completion percentage of his Penn State career (76.4), completing 13 of 17 passes for 168 yards with no interceptions. Dozier and Thomas scored the Lions' touchdowns on runs of 19 and 3 yards, respectively. Dozier finished with 63 yards on 15 carries, and Thomas added 57 yards on eight carries. Manca had three field goals. The Lions defense, led by linebacker Trey Bauer, held Alabama's tenth-ranked rushing attack to just 44 yards and harried quarterback Mike Shula into a 14-for-30 day that included two interceptions. Penn State sacked Shula five times and recovered three Tide fumbles.

8. November 1 (at Morgantown, W.V.): Penn State 19, West Virginia 0

For the third straight game, the Penn State defense didn't surrender a touchdown, holding West Virginia to 134 net offensive yards and just 8 rushing. The Mountaineers could only manage nine first downs in the game and turned the ball over three times. Penn State generated more than 400 yards total offense but could only score one touchdown, a 23-yard pass from Shaffer to Dozier. Dozier had 67 yards on 12 carries and moved into second place on the all-time Penn State rushing list. Manca tied a school record by attempting six field goals, hitting on four of them—42, 37, 22, and 27 yards. Shaffer completed 11 of 20 passes for 171 yards but got sacked five times.

9. November 8 (Beaver Stadium): Penn State 17, Maryland 15

Defensive tackle Pete Curkendall returned an interception 82 yards to turn what looked like a sure Maryland scoring drive into a Penn State touchdown opportunity as the Lions survived another threat to their undefeated season. With the Lions leading only 7–3 in the fourth quarter and Maryland at the Penn State seven, Curkendall picked off an errant Dan Henning pass forced by a Bob White hit at the moment of delivery and lumbered 82 yards to the Terrapin nine. One play later, Dozier made it a 14-point swing with a nine-yard TD run that made the score 14–3. Still, Penn State's defense had to ward off a late Maryland charge as the Terps scored two late touchdowns. Maryland closed within 17–9 with a TD but missed a two-point conversion. They then scored again and attempted another two-point conversion that would have tied the game in the final fourteen seconds. But Duffy Cobbs had good coverage on Maryland receiver James Milling and the pass for two went incomplete. It was Penn State's twentieth straight regular-season victory over Maryland, dating to 1961. Dozier had his first 100-plus-yard rushing game of the season, finishing with 111 yards on 25 carries.

10. November 15 (at South Bend, Ind.): Penn State 24, Notre Dame 19

Pushed into the shadow of its own goal posts, the Penn State defense staged a dramatic fourth-quarter stand to preserve a victory over the feisty Irish. Camped at the Penn State six-yard line with just over a minute to play, Notre Dame was thrown for a three-yard loss by Isom on first down, and quarterback Steve Beuerlein was sacked for a nine-yard loss by White and linebacker Don Graham on second down. Backup corner Gary Wilkerson then broke up an end-zone pass intended for tight end Joel Williams on third down before the Lions chased Beuerlein into a harmless incompletion on fourth. Shaffer completed nine of only thirteen pass attempts but hooked up with Roundtree for a 37-yard TD pass. Dozier, who had been injured during the week of practice, got 77 yards on 17 carries. The Lions defense had trouble curtailing Beuerlein, who completed 24 of 39 passes for a career-high 311 yards and two TDs. But Penn State did extend its streak of not allowing a rushing touchdown to twenty-one quarters.

11. November 22 (Beaver Stadium): Penn State 34, Pittsburgh 14
Thomas's 91-yard first-quarter kickoff return destroyed Pitt's momentum and Penn State survived another aggressive backyard battle with the upset-minded Panthers that all but assured the Nittany Lions a matchup with Miami to decide the national championship. Pitt's Craig "Ironhead" Heyward gave the Panthers a 7–3 lead on a one-yard TD plunge. But Thomas took the ensuing kickoff 91 yards for a TD—the first kickoff-return touchdown since Curt Warner went 88 yards against West Virginia in 1980—to put PSU in the lead for good. Dozier gained 77 yards on 13 carries and had a 26-yard touchdown run. Thomas added 46 more on six rushes. The game was marred by several skirmishes; one led to the ejection of Graham and two Pitt players.

12. January 2, 1987 (at Tempe, Ariz.): Penn State 14, Miami 10
Pete Giftopoulos intercepted a Vinny Testaverde pass with nine seconds left to preserve Penn State's second national championship in four years with an upset win in the 1987 Fiesta Bowl. Testaverde, the 1986 Heisman Trophy winner, completed 26 of 50 passes in the game but was intercepted five times—two each by Conlan and Giftopoulos. Penn State managed only 162 total offensive yards (Dozier rushed for 99 in 20 carries and was voted the game's top offensive player) to Miami's 445. But Penn State scored a key touchdown in the fourth quarter—on a Dozier five-yard run—after Conlan intercepted a Testaverde pass and ran 38 yards to the Miami five-yard line. That put the Lions up 14–10, and then the defense staved off a final, frantic Miami drive. The Hurricanes had the ball at the Penn State six with less than a minute remaining. On second down, Tim Johnson sacked Testaverde for a six-yard loss. Then, on fourth and goal at the 12, Giftopoulos stepped in front of a final Testaverde pass for an interception.

THE PERFECT SEASON

1

DEKE

"EVERY TIME WE CALLED that play that year, we scored," Dozier later recalled.

He had even scored with a singed hand. A couple of minutes earlier, D.J. carried a sweep toward the left sideline. After being run out of bounds, he inadvertently bumped into NBC sideline broadcaster Ahmad Rashad, who held a hot cup of coffee that spilled on Dozier.

"I screamed, 'Man, that's hot!'" Dozier said. "Ahmad looked at me with this blank stare as if I just spoiled him enjoying a cup of coffee. Sometimes you remember moments like that more than you do a good carry."

D.J. Dozier looked out from the large window of his Norfolk, Virginia, office, a window that opens to a lovely view of the marinas of the Chesapeake Bay. He is a successful entrepreneur now, a broker in commercial real-estate ventures for Wex Trust, Inc.—far removed from his days as one of Penn State's all-time leading rushers, an NFL career with the Minnesota Vikings and Detroit Lions, and a brief foray as a professional baseball player with the New York Mets and San Diego Padres.

157 Power.

That play had been Penn State's bread and butter all season long with field position near the five-yard line. The Nittany Lions were at the Miami five with less than nine minutes to go in the game.

Shane Conlan had put them there when he picked off Vinny Testaverde with an over-the-shoulder grab at the Miami 43 for his second interception of the game and then rumbled 38 yards down the right sideline.

In the huddle, quarterback John Shaffer called 157 Power, a formation where the Nittany Lions spread the field with three wideouts and then power it inside with D.J. Dozier following the fullback off tackle. On first down in that formation, the quarterback fumbled the snap! But the Lions retained possession.

On second down, Shaffer called the same play. This time, the transfer went perfectly and Dozier rumbled untouched into the end zone to give Penn State a 14–10 lead with 8:13 left in the fourth quarter.

The years have been kind to Dozier. He is still strikingly handsome and, at only ten or so pounds over his playing weight, looks fit enough to carry the football tomorrow in an NFL game. He's also in good shape financially. Before taking the job at Wex Trust, he had enough money saved to be an investor in commercial real estate.

His Penn State football career was a meteor that flashed through the mountain air of the Nittany Valley. A sensation as a freshman, Dozier gained over 1,000 yards at State before he was old enough to shave. Then came a series of nagging injuries that limited his production and spoiled a legitimate candidacy for a Heisman Trophy. By the end of his college days, D.J. Dozier had become one of the best running backs in Penn State history. But his career also became a maddening tease to most Nittany Lion fans, who seemed to always want more. It would be a tease that continued to ride with Dozier in his professional days.

Following a heroic performance in the Fiesta Bowl, Dozier was drafted by the Minnesota Vikings fourteenth overall in a first round that would include the likes of Vinny Testaverde, Cornelius Bennett, Jerome Brown, and Rod Woodson. But he gained only 643 yards in four seasons as a Viking, mostly serving in a reserve role.

The year Dozier was finally supposed to be the Vikes' starting halfback, the team acquired Herschel Walker in a celebrated deal with the Dallas Cowboys—one that would shape the Cowboys' repeated Super Bowl runs under Jimmy Johnson and Jerry Jones. That year Dozier wound up being Walker's blocking fullback; the following year he was put on waivers. Acquired by the Detroit Lions for the 1991 season, Dozier carried the ball only nine times for 48 yards. After the season, he quit football for good.

In the spring of 1991, D.J. Dozier, who had been a highly regarded baseball prospect in high school, signed with the New York Mets. He zoomed through the Mets' farm system and, at the end of his second full year in baseball, made it to the major leagues, playing twenty-five games with the big club in 1992. But Dozier hit only .191 (9 for 47), while striking out nineteen times. The following year he was back with the Mets' triple-A team, the Tidewater Tides. That year he was traded to the San Diego Padres (with pitcher Wally Whitehurst for shortstop Tony Fernandez) and then was peddled to the St. Louis Cardinals organization. He never made the majors again and left baseball for good in 1993.

During that whirlwind athletic tour, D.J. Dozier also went through a painful divorce from his high school sweetheart. Today he is remarried, with three children, splitting time at residences in Lancaster, Pennsylvania, and Virginia Beach. The tailback who ended every one of his Penn State touchdowns with a kneeldown prayer remains devoutly religious. Following his athletic career, he served as the athletic director at Rock Church's Rock Academy in Virginia Beach. When baseball teams were clamoring for him to give the sport another try, Dozier turned them all down, saying that with the Rock Church job the Lord had provided him with a better calling.

William Henry Dozier Jr. was born in Virginia Beach, just up the road a piece from Norfolk. His dad, William Henry Dozier Sr., was known in the area as "Deke." And so William Henry Dozier Jr. became Deke Jr., or D.J.

Deke had been a well-regarded athlete in those parts himself and his first-born son would inherit those genes. Painfully shy as a kid, D.J. Dozier found refuge in sports. He was good at almost anything. But what he liked most of all was carrying a football and running either past or through anyone who tried to tackle him. He was a wispy 160-pound wide receiver on the Kempsville High varsity as a freshman considered too thin and too slight to play his preferred position, running back. But one day during his sophomore year, Dozier was thrown in at halfback for an injured upperclassman, slashed his way to a long, touchdown run, wound up gaining 84 yards on 13 carries as Kempsville won at Bayside High, and never saw the end position again.

That sophomore year Dozier gained 694 yards, including two 100-plus yard efforts. He had 110 yards on 11 carries against vaunted Princess Anne, then followed that with 108 yards the next week against Green Run. Virginia Beach, a smallish, predominately white community known more for its beachfront charm than its high school football prowess, suddenly had a star.

Dozier put together a monster junior year. In Kempsville's second game of the season, he exploded for 175 yards on just 15 carries, an average of 11.7 yards per play. He would finish the year with 1,306 yards, which included a 213-yard rushing effort in Kempsville's final game of the season against Norview.

Naturally, Dozier came into his senior year as one of the most sought-after high school running backs in the country. By then, he had tacked on about thirty pounds of muscle, topping out at 6′2″ and 190 pounds. His soft-spoken, almost shy demeanor made D.J. Dozier the all-American boy—a source of pride in the Virginia Beach community and perhaps a source of jealousy to some of his competitors.

In the first game of the 1982 season, Dozier's senior year, Virginia's defending class AAA high school champions, Hampton High, pounded Kempsville, 34–7. Hampton coach Mike Smith employed a defensive strategy that shadowed Dozier everywhere he went on the field. Battered and bruised, Dozier gained only 47 yards and sat out most of the second half with knee and wrist injuries. After the game, in an interview with reporters, Smith piled on:

Dozier's about the only black kid on a white team. He probably catches a lot of people by surprise with his quickness. But we see that kind of quickness all the time. That may be why he didn't run as well against us.

I think he's a fine back. He ran for 1,300 yards last season. We had a fine back who ran for 1,400 yards last year and didn't get near the publicity Dozier got.

The comments hadn't surprised Dozier. "I heard that some teams had a bounty on me that year," Dozier later recalled. "Coaches were dangling money to their players if they could take me out of the game."

But very few got a hand on Dozier his senior year, much less put him out of a game. He gained nearly 1,500 yards, putting his career total at Kempsville at well over 3,200. He was named Virginia's Player of the Year and feted at a banquet sponsored by Hertz Rent-A-Car. Hertz's spokesman at the time was O.J. Simpson, who had been Dozier's hero.

"We were both seated at the head table that night, so I walked up to him real slow, very shy, to shake his hand," Dozier remembered. "He said, 'How ya doin?' That was it. That's all I got. I walked back to my seat thinking, 'Gee, if I ever become some big football star, I hope I treat people better than that.'"

With NCAA regulations allowing five campus visits, Dozier locked in on Georgia, Notre Dame, North Carolina, and Virginia Tech. He compiled a four-school wild-card list for his final visit—Nebraska, UCLA, Alabama, and, at the bottom of the list, Penn State.

Georgia made the cut because one of his idols was Bulldogs' All-American Herschel Walker. Notre Dame had recruited Dozier hard, and he liked the style of current Irish running back Allen Pinkett. Dozier grew up a major Michael Jordan fan, so North Carolina would be a finalist. Ralph Gahagan, his coach at Kempsville High, urged him to consider an in-state school, which turned out to be Tech since the University of Virginia's program was in a down cycle at the time.

About the only thing Dozier knew about Penn State was that its campus was cold during the football season and so were its uniforms. Were it not for an invitation from the family of his school chum Mike West to come to the Wests' house on New Year's night to watch Penn State play Georgia for the national championship in the 1983 Sugar Bowl, D.J. Dozier may have left a legacy elsewhere. The Wests, a military family living in the military-laden Virginia Beach area, were huge Nittany Lions fans.

Dozier had already visited the Georgia campus, where his host was none other than Walker. "Herschel picked me up from the airport and rode me around campus in a brand-new Trans-Am," Dozier said. "I didn't ask him about the car. I'm thinking to myself, 'Are you kidding me? I'm hanging out with Herschel Walker!'"

Dozier parked in front of the Wests' television determined to root for Walker and the Bulldogs. But something about Penn State's resolve that day—they upset Georgia, 27–23, behind the passing of Todd Blackledge, the running of Curt Warner, and a defense that made life very difficult that day for Herschel Walker—made a lasting impression on Dozier.

In the end, his choice came down to Georgia or Penn State. Dozier found the racial dynamic of the Deep South troubling, the courtship by Walker notwithstanding. And then head coach Vince Dooley's disastrous visit with the Doziers —with a little help from Dooley's recruiting coordinator, Ray Goff—cinched it for PSU.

The night before the planned visit to Virginia Beach, Goff attended a high school football banquet in a town a few hours outside Atlanta. Afterward, the high school coaches wanted to play cards. Goff joined them, playing until 6:30 the next morning. He then drove to Atlanta, where the two coaches were recruiting another player, to meet Dooley. Goff and Dooley then returned to the Georgia campus in Athens intending to board a university plane that would fly them into Virginia Beach for a meeting with the Doziers. Bad weather grounded the small plane, so Dooley called an audible, telling Goff to book the first commercial flight out of Atlanta. Goff found a flight leaving in forty-five minutes. But it was an hour-and-a-half drive from Athens to Atlanta, so Dooley arranged for the university plane to fly the two coaches to Atlanta in time to board the commercial flight.

When they finally arrived at the Dozier home, Goff sat between D.J.'s parents on the sofa but was so exhausted he fell asleep during Dooley's pitch, bobbing his head off Mary Dozier's shoulder. If that weren't enough of a turnoff, Dooley, sitting on a chair across from the sofa, astonished the Doziers by propping his leg over the chair leg as if he was in a saloon.

"I don't know, maybe he did that with everybody," said Dozier. "Maybe he did it because he felt so comfortable around us. But it just seemed odd. When he did that, I looked at my mom, and you could tell she felt the same way."

By then, though, Dozier was already sold on Penn State after a February visit during which he stayed with team members at West Halls, a dormitory complex in the middle of campus. The closeness among team members he witnessed overrode his previous perceptions of the school's chilly climate and bland uniforms. On a visit to Joe Paterno's house, the coach offered him cookies and milk. Unhip, but so honest and simplistic, Dozier thought. Paterno told Dozier that no matter how good he thought he was, he was not going to start as a freshman. That only made Dozier want Penn State even more.

"Joe is a very smart man," said Dozier. "He was setting the bait. I think he wanted to find out if I was the type of kid who would back off or go after it. And as he is saying that, I remembered thinking, 'Oh, you have no idea.' One of Joe Paterno's greatest strengths as a coach is his ability to read people."

When Dozier arrived on campus for Penn State's preseason workouts, he was stunned to find himself in a mix of several running backs who would vie for playing time in the aftermath of Warner's graduation. Paterno had anointed senior John Williams—a tailback who had made a sacrifice to play fullback while Warner was the team's star—as the year's starting tailback. Several other running backs were coming off redshirt years—sitting out their freshman seasons in order to gain more strength and maturity and to preserve a year of eligibility—including highly touted Steve Smith. Meanwhile, Paterno had recruited several other backs along with Dozier, including a bruiser from Pittsburgh named Tim Manoa. Several walk-ons were there, too, trying to make the team.

"The one thing about Penn State is that they have absolutely no problem humbling you," Dozier said.

At Penn State, as with most college football programs, the depth chart is segregated by the color of the practice jersey. Blue jerseys signify first team. The second team wears green, the third team wears gold, and fourth team and walk-ons wear white. Dozier, Penn State's top freshman running-back recruit, was given a gold jersey, meaning he started his Nittany Lion career no better than a sixth running back on the 1983 season roster. The other two running backs behind him were walk-ons. If he listened hard enough, D.J. Dozier could hear Dooley and recruiters from all the other schools who had coveted him whispering, *I told you so.*

But Dozier was too good to keep down. Little by little, the freshman from Virginia Beach started to turn heads. Within two weeks, he was wearing a green jersey. He subsequently missed a couple of days of practice with a sprained ankle, but offensive assistant Bob Phillips made a point of telling Dozier how well he was progressing. To D.J., that meant he was impressing Paterno.

By the time Penn State played its first game in late August against Nebraska in the Kickoff Classic at the Meadowlands, D.J. Dozier was the second tailback on the depth chart behind Williams. He got two carries in the game—the Lions got bushwhacked, 44–6—then he ran for 41 yards the next week against Cincinnati, another loss. When Williams reinjured a knee in the Lions' game with Iowa, the seventeen-year-old freshman started the second half at tailback and never gave up the job from there. Dozier finished with 102 yards on just eight carries, including a memorable 58-yard burst. But Penn State lost to Iowa, 42–34, to begin the season 0–3. That week at practice, Paterno got hokey, breaking out a box of boxing-glove keychains.

"We've got our backs to the wall," the coach told his team, retreating toward a locker-room wall. "We've got to come out fighting."

Dozier, the naïve kid, sucked it all in.

The Nittany Lions rattled off five straight wins, and Dozier ran for 196 at Rutgers and 163 at home against Alabama. By season's end, Dozier had 1,002 yards as the Nittany Lions finished a respectable 8–4–1, beating Washington, 13–10, in the 1983 Aloha Bowl. None of Penn State's legendary running backs, not even John Cappelletti or Curt Warner, had been able to do that.

ELEVEN PENN STATE STARTERS from the 1987 Sunkist Fiesta Bowl were freshmen in 1982. All eleven were in uniform on the New Orleans Superdome sidelines on January 1, 1983, when Penn State defeated Georgia to win the national championship. That group would form the nucleus of the team that would play, four years later, for another national title.

For his part, Paterno sensed that his 1982 recruiting class was special. It was for that reason that the Penn State coach would ease them into the lineup over the next two years. Penn State lost three straight games in 1983. The following year in the final two games of the season, Notre Dame blasted the Lions, 44–7, and then so did Pitt, 31–11, to make their season an unremarkable 6–5. That put the press in a feeding frenzy. Midway through that '84 season, after some reporters began categorizing the "demise" of Penn State football, Paterno exploded.

"I'm trying to put together a team that some day can win the national championship," the coach snapped during a pregame press conference.

The following day, October 20, 1984, Penn State beat Syracuse, 21–3. Thirty-eight players who played in that game—Trey Bauer, Mike Beckish, John Bruno, Drew Bykoskie, Kurt Bernier, Dave Clark, Duffy Cobbs, Chris Collins, Shane Conlan, Chris Conlin, Pete Curkendall, Stephen Davis, Dwayne Downing, D.J. Dozier, Mitch Frerotte, Pete Giftopoulos, Darrell Giles, Don Graham, Eric Hamilton, Marcus Henderson, Ray Isom, Gregg Johns, Matt Johnson, Tim Johnson, Matt Knizner, Rich Kuzy, Sid Lewis, Massimo Manca, Tim Manoa, Dan Morgan, Paul Pomfret, Ray Roundtree, Mike Russo, John Shaffer, Mark Sickler, Brian Siverling, Steve Smith, and Bob White—would be on the team that would go on to beat Miami in 1987.

Shaffer started in place of the injured Doug Strang against Syracuse that day with Knizner as his backup. Dozier was already solidly entrenched at tailback with Clark behind him. Blair Thomas, a heralded tailback recruit from Philadelphia, would fill an important relief role in 1986. Chris Conlin was already the starter at offensive tackle as a sophomore. By 1986, Penn State had switched from a 4–3 defensive alignment to a 3–4, with White and Johnson as the starting ends flanking the nose guard, Russo. Graham, who had been an inside linebacker, was moved to an outside linebacker spot to team with Shane Conlan, giving the Lions a deadly blitzing combination.

The "hero" position in Jerry Sandusky's defense—a safety/linebacker combination position—belonged in 1984 to Michael Zordich. In 1986, Zordich would have been a fifth-year senior starter had he been redshirted with several other freshmen with whom he came to Penn State. But Paterno played him that freshman year and Zordich's eligibility was over. Fate had dealt Zordich a smarting blow. Although the former Nittany Lion would enjoy a lengthy NFL career, the college team he left ended up winning a national championship. Henderson wound up the starter at that position in '86. Isom and Cobbs would join him in the Nittany Lions defensive backfield.

AS PENN STATE ENTERED the 1986 season, the biggest issue was who would start at the most important position on the field—quarterback. Shaffer and Knizner were locked into a competitive duel for the starting position.

A high-profile recruit from Cincinnati's Moeller High (where he was coached by Gerry Faust), Shaffer had been Penn State's starting quarterback since his sophomore season. While showing a penchant for winning—Shaffer's only defeat as a starting quarterback since the seventh grade was Penn State's Orange Bowl loss to Oklahoma—Shaffer didn't seem to be dazzling enough for many Nittany Lions fans and was coming off a year in which he completed only 45 percent of his passes with eight touchdowns to ten interceptions. The more athletic Knizner had relieved Shaffer in the '86 Orange Bowl, completed eight of eleven passes for 90 yards, had a good spring practice, and was thought to have a bona-fide shot at winning the job in the fall.

Meanwhile, Dozier was in a tough spot. For the last two seasons the running back had shared a huddle with Shaffer. But his senior year, Dozier wound up renting a four-bedroom house—with one of the bedrooms a converted garage—just off campus with teammates Tim Johnson, Greg Truitt, Manoa, *and* Matt Knizner.

"I tried to stay as neutral as possible," Dozier recalled. "Most of the guys were used to John. But we all knew that Matt had a lot of talent. As far as we were all concerned, though, it didn't matter who Joe made the quarterback. We knew we had a good team and either guy would work."

Paterno went with the safe choice, though he waited long enough to do it. Just two days before the season opener against Temple, the Penn State coach announced he was giving the job back to Shaffer.

Meanwhile, Dozier came into the year as one of the favorites to win the Heisman Trophy. He had given away much of his sophomore and junior seasons to nagging injuries—groin pulls, a dislocated elbow, an injured neck, and a banged-up knee that required arthroscopic surgery. He carried only 125 times for 691 yards in 1984, though he did have three straight 100-yard-plus games that year, burning Syracuse for 159. He missed two games early in the 1985 season but ended strong, finishing with 723 yards as the Nittany Lions went 11–1 before losing that painful 1986 Orange Bowl to Oklahoma.

But now Dozier was finally healthy. And the ten pounds he had lost in hard summer workouts put him in the best shape of his life.

A few games into the season, when Dozier was only getting the ball a maximum of 15 times per game after sharing the load with other seniority-laden backs such as Smith and Manoa, the Heisman dream would fade. But as Shaffer would say later in consolation to Dozier, "You don't come to Penn State to win the Heisman Trophy, you come to win football games."

By the start of the 1986 season, Dozier had rededicated himself to Christianity. Raised in the Pentecostal Church, the running back was not averse to outwardly expressing his faith. But big-time college football had consumed him. His Sunday visits to church were not scripture absorbing. Instead, they had become vacant, daydreaming sessions. The spring of his junior year, he attended a sermon at the State College Assemblies of God, where former Penn State quarterback Todd Blackledge, also a devout Christian, delivered a guest sermon. Football could not be his God, Dozier thought. The two years' worth of injuries he had suffered his sophomore and junior years made him feel empty. Something was missing in his soul.

Later that spring, while Dozier was attending a service in his hometown, his pastor, the Reverend John Jimenez, noticed the running back in the last row of the balcony.

"D.J.," Reverend Jimenez said in front of the congregation, "God just spoke to me. He said if you put him first, he *will* take care of all of your desires. Honor him with the sport you play. All he wants is your heart."

Eerily, Dozier felt a strength he had never felt before.

THE LIONS OPENED THE SEASON against Temple on September 6 in the first night game in the history of Beaver Stadium, pasting the Owls, 45–15. Penn State scored the first three times it had the ball and led 21–0 with just five minutes gone in the first quarter. Shaffer, perhaps feeling reprieved, passed for a career-high three touchdowns, ran for a fourth, and finished 12 of 18 for 194 yards and no interceptions. Dozier added 54 yards and a touchdown and caught four passes for 73 yards. Manoa and Smith, sharing the fullback load, combined for 143 yards. The season was off and running. Dozier recounted, "It was like we busted through a brick wall. We felt this unbelievable pressure before that first game. We had no room for error. People were expecting this direct line to the national championship because we had come so close the year before. I remember sitting around our house that day, chewing my fingertips off, waiting for the night to come so finally we could play some football."

Dozier scored two touchdowns—one on a 17-yard pass reception from Shaffer—and set up another with a 35-yard run as Penn State won at Boston College the next week, 26–14. East Carolina was the next victim, 42–17, with Shaffer throwing for two more scores. The Lions gave no solace to Rutgers and its head coach, Dick Anderson, who had been a longtime Penn State assistant, spanking the Scarlet Knights the following week at home, 31–6.

Then Cincinnati came to town.

On October 12, 1986, the Bearcats arrived at Beaver Stadium as a 24-point underdog. But with just five minutes left in the game, Penn State trailed, 17–14, and faced a third down and 10 at its own 25. Paterno had decided against overusing Dozier, who had come into the game with a slight groin pull. He was on the sidelines in crunch time in favor of Blair Thomas, a sophomore from Philadelphia. Thomas pulled the Lions out of the fire. He slipped out of the backfield to catch a 32-yard pass from Shaffer to get the first down and then exploded for a 32-yard run to the Cincinnati 11-yard line. Two plays later David Clark scored, carrying what seemed like the entire Bearcats defense on his shoulders, to give Penn State a 21–17 lead.

Following a subsequent defensive stand, linebacker Shane Conlan busted through to block a Cincinnati punt for a safety, and the Nittany Lions escaped with a 23–17 win.

Dozier recalled the Penn State sideline being as quiet as a church prior to Thomas's reception and then like a fraternity party afterward. "We all breathed a collective sigh of relief. It was like a nightmare that suddenly turns into a happy ending. We were looking at a lost season had Blair not made those couple plays. But once we got through Cincinnati, we felt destiny was on our side."

There would be two more regular-season scares, though not until State made its biggest statement of the year at Bryant-Denny Stadium in Tuscaloosa, Alabama.

First, in a game that constituted nothing more than a scrimmage in preparation for 'Bama, Penn State crushed Syracuse, 42–3.

The Lions came to Alabama a six-point underdog, a circumstance that would reflect Penn State's lack of national respect. 'Bama came into the game undefeated and ranked No. 2 in the nation behind Miami. But Penn State, using the straight-ahead rushing of Dozier and Thomas, gobbled up the Crimson Tide's defense for a combined 210 rushing yards. Meanwhile, the much-maligned Shaffer enjoyed one of the best days of his Penn State career, completing 13 of 17 passes for 168 yards with no interceptions.

State's defense, led by their motorized linebackers Conlan and Trey Bauer, limited Alabama's supposed high-powered offense to just 44 yards rushing and 216 overall and picked off 'Bama quarterback Mike Shula twice.

In the end, Penn State won 23–3, handing the Tide their worst home loss in thirty-one years.

"There was no doubt from the third quarter on who was going to win this game," said Wes Neighbors, Alabama's All-American center after the contest. "They got after us."

IT WAS ONLY about a minute after State's win at Alabama that organizers of the Fiesta Bowl started posturing hard for a dream matchup pitting undefeated Penn State, which had vaulted to the No. 2 national ranking, against undefeated Miami. Needing Penn State and Miami to remain undefeated and in their same place in the polls—Penn State had four games left and Miami three—would churn up the insides of Fiesta Bowl chairman Bruce Skinner for the rest of the regular season. If Penn State and Miami followed suit, Skinner would preside over a New Year's Day bowl that rendered the bowl games with traditionally larger stature—Rose, Orange, Sugar, and Cotton—almost meaningless.

"For the next few Saturdays, I couldn't even eat," Skinner said.

Skinner and his crew had already taken the Fiesta Bowl out of the shadows four years earlier by moving the game—played in Tempe on the home field of Arizona State—to New Year's Day to compete with the Big Four. But in 1986, to lure the likes of Penn State and Miami, who as independents would have their pick of bowl games, Skinner embarked on a financial campaign to make the Fiesta's payout on a par with the other New Year's Day bowls: more than $2 million per team—more than double the amount the Fiesta Bowl had previously paid.

Clandestinely, Skinner attempted to pry a large chunk of that loot from NBC, which was thrilled to have such a marquee game on their network, and Sunkist, the game's corporate sponsor. He got another financial boost from a tony black-tie fundraising dinner—$500 a couple—at the Sheraton in Scottsdale. The sold-out dinner featured a comedy performance by Bob Hope. In light of his friendship with a Fiesta Bowl committee member, Hope cut his fee in half to $50,000. The Scottsdale Sheraton kicked in free food and booze. In the end, the Fiesta Bowl had about $2.6 million per team to offer its participants.

Still, it wasn't that simple.

Skinner decided to follow and lobby for Penn State, attending each of their games for the rest of the season. He assigned committee member Don Meyers to lure Miami. Meyers would have the more difficult assignment.

"When I asked Joe Paterno if he'd play in the Fiesta Bowl, he told me he'd play Miami in a parking lot in Brooklyn if that's what it took," Skinner recalled. "But getting Miami to us was a delicate situation."

The most natural landing place for the Hurricanes was their own Orange Bowl. But university executives saw a match with Oklahoma as unappealing—the Sooners were en route to winning the Big Eight, whose champion had an automatic berth in the Orange. Miami's business community preferred two out-of-town teams to fill the city's hotels and shops.

Southeastern Conference champ Tennessee had blasted Miami in the Sugar Bowl in New Orleans the year before. For Miami it turned out to be an experience so miserable that Hurricanes athletic director Sam Jankovich told friends he would not return there under any circumstances. By accepting a bid in the Cotton Bowl against an inferior opponent from the disheveled Southwest Conference, Miami would be seen as taking the easy way out to win a national championship—a circumstance that might adversely affect the final poll voters.

Instead, the wrench thrown into the Fiesta Bowl's machine came from the tiny Citrus Bowl, which was played each year—though not on New Year's Day—in Orlando, Florida. The Citrus had the financial backing of ABC, and for Miami it had an intangible: close enough to home to have Hurricanes fans potentially outnumber Penn State fans, which would not have been the case in Tempe. In addition, several influential members of the Citrus Bowl committee were Miami alums.

It seemed as if the Citrus was going to be a done deal except for one major circumstance: Orange Bowl executives cringed at the notion that a game four hours north in their home state was going to be bigger than their own traditional bowl game. They pressured the Hurricanes *not* to go there for the good of the city, a city that had contributed a lot of tax revenue to the school.

But on November 8, Penn State almost blew the whole deal.

One week after shutting out West Virginia, 19–0, and perhaps looking ahead to its game the following week at Notre Dame, Penn State eked out a 17–15 win over Maryland, a score that wasn't finalized until the game's final 14 seconds when the Terrapins couldn't convert on a two-point conversion to tie the game.

Lions tackle Pete Curkendall turned out to be the hero. In the fourth quarter, Maryland, trailing 7–3, had the ball inside the Lions' five-yard line when Curkendall intercepted a pass and rumbled 82 yards to set up a Dozier nine-yard TD run. Undaunted, Maryland came back to sandwich two touchdowns around a Massimo Manca field goal later in the quarter to give itself a chance to tie the game at the end.

Dozier gained 111 yards, his first 100-plus game of the season. But late in the contest, Dozier's frustration with Paterno—during a season in which the tailback felt he was severely underused—may have finally boiled over. In the game's waning minutes, with the Lions protecting their slim lead, the Penn State coach had Clark in the game at tailback. In full view of some 85,000 fans at Beaver Stadium, Dozier angrily gestured at his coach.

Paterno said later that he thought Dozier had told him he was tired. Dozier, meanwhile, told the press he had said no such thing. It was a rare intrateam public controversy between coach and player.

The following week the Lions defense rescued a 24–19 win over the Irish by stopping Notre Dame from scoring on four straight downs from the six-yard line. On first down, safety Ray Isom dragged down explosive receiver Tim Brown for a three-yard loss. On second, Bob White blew through the Notre Dame line and sacked quarterback Steve Beuerlein at the 18 for a nine-yard loss. On third, Beuerlein scrambled and passed to tight end Joel Williams. But Penn State cornerback Gary Wilkerson popped Williams from behind and the ball glanced off the receiver's fingertips at the goal line. Beuerlein's last-gasp effort was a complete pass to receiver Mark Green, who was surrounded and dropped at the 13. Penn State had survived.

In the game Dozier finished with 77 yards on 17 carries, a remarkable feat considering that just two days earlier he had hyperextended a knee in practice and had been ruled out of the Saturday game by team doctor James Whiteside. Whiteside, in fact, told Dozier it would take a miracle for his leg to heal enough by the Notre Dame game, which is exactly what the running back asked for.

When Dozier arrived back home that night from practice, he asked his roommate Johnson, also devoutly religious, to pray with him.

The Saturday morning of the game his knee was still giving him pain. Deke Dozier had made the trip to South Bend to see his son play. A few hours before kickoff he milled around the Notre Dame stadium tunnel and talked with a PSU booster.

"Hey, I hear that D.J. is hurt and isn't playing," said the booster.

"You heard what?" Deke Dozier replied. His son had told him nothing.

Before he caught the bus to the stadium that morning, D.J. flipped through the channels of his hotel television. He tuned into a religious show and noticed that the preacher on the screen was praying to heal the sick. He smiled at the irony. Minutes later in the trainer's room Whiteside examined Dozier, bending the knee back to measure its flexibility. The knee had good flexibility and gave Dozier only marginal pain. Whiteside sighed and D.J. smiled. The doctor told a trainer to wrap the knee tightly. He gave Dozier the okay to play.

Ironically, it wasn't the knee that most worried Dozier in the Notre Dame game—it was his head. Running toward the sideline at one point, he took a vicious shot to the helmet from an Irish linebacker and heard bells.

With Penn State's defense on the field, Dozier summoned Shaffer, saying, "John, it's possible I could start forgetting the plays. When you call the play in the huddle, make sure you tell me where I go."

Shaffer called the play. Penn State's offense broke its huddle. But as the quarterback walked toward his center, Radecic, Dozier trailed him, whispering in the helmet's earhole, "John, what is that play?"

"Just run this way," Shaffer said, pointing right.

The play was a 157-power handoff to Smith. Dozier and Manoa were to be the lead blockers. Protecting the left side of his head, Dozier missed the block. Smith got gang-tackled, twisting an ankle. On the sidelines after the play, Paterno ripped into his star running back, unaware that Dozier was still groggy.

On that same day, Minnesota upset Michigan, so the Nittany Lions moved up in the polls to No. 2 in the nation, behind No. 1 Miami. And the media began the frenzy—along with Fiesta Bowl organizers—lobbying for a national championship matchup between the two schools.

All that stood in Penn State's way was Pittsburgh, whom the Lions dispatched the following week, 34–14. The win made Penn State 11–0 and gave Paterno his sixth perfect season as the Nittany Lions' coach. But the game was not without controversy—among the players and between the coaches, Paterno and Pitt's Mike Gottfried. Gottfried had taken exception to Paterno running to the Pitt side of the field to help break up a players' scuffle where it appeared that the Penn State coach was lecturing several Panther players.

There were three fights and six personal fouls in the game. On one occasion, Paterno raced across the field to help separate the combatants. Dozier also nearly got into it with a Pitt cornerback when the Panther player tossed him by the jersey after Dozier scored.

"I wanted to rip that kid's head off," Dozier recalled. "And then I remembered to pray."

The following day the Fiesta Bowl extended an invitation to Penn State to play in the game, which was being moved from New Year's Day to January 2 to accommodate the importance of two undefeated teams playing for a national title. But Paterno delayed his acceptance of the Fiesta bid, pending Miami's final contest against East Carolina on Thanksgiving. Had East Carolina somehow found a way to win, Penn State's plan was to face off against Oklahoma, the No. 3 ranked team, in the Orange Bowl. Expectedly, Miami won in a blowout, 36–10, and the match race was on.

With their regular season ending on November 24, the Nittany Lions had to wait more than a month to play Miami, an eternity for players, but a necessary respite for Paterno and the Penn State coaching staff, which had to formulate perhaps their most difficult game plan of the season. With school out for the holiday break, Paterno could have implemented two-a-day practice sessions, as in preseason. But the Penn State coach stuck to his in-season routine, with one practice each day, beginning at the usual time of 3:30 P.M., keeping live contact between the players to a minimum.

Where Paterno monopolized the team's time was in the film room—daily matinees starring the Miami Hurricanes. The PSU coach wanted his team to absorb the full brunt of Miami's vaunted attack. He wanted them to know that many of the players they were seeing on film would be playing their next season in the NFL. He wanted them to understand how important it was to execute the game plan, to play the perfect game. He needed them to be intimidated by what they were seeing on film so they would work hard enough to overcome it.

"And we were unfazed by all of it," Dozier said. "We saw how explosive Miami was on film, but none of us had wide eyes. We were confident that no matter how much better they were supposed to be than us, we were going to win that game. No question about it."

THE GAME PLAN PATERNO SETTLED ON was brilliant in its simplicity.

Defensive coordinator Jerry Sandusky wanted to confuse the Hurricanes' Heisman Trophy quarterback, Vinny Testaverde, by dropping as many players in coverage as possible. Sandusky felt that his defensive linemen, led by Johnson and Bob White, could put enough pressure on Testaverde—without help from linebackers and corners or safeties—to keep him honest. Meanwhile, linebackers Shane Conlan, Trey Bauer, and Don Graham would drift to take the middle away from Testaverde. Sandusky also urged defensive backs such as Duffy Cobbs and Ray Isom to lower the boom on anybody who got into the middle of the field beyond Conlan and company and make the Miami receivers hear footsteps.

On offense, the Lions planned to take advantage of Miami's aggressive defensive front with counters and misdirection plays utilizing the slashing Dozier.

Penn State's basic running plays would be spiced up by a series of different, wide-set formations, spreading Miami's defense in order to clear out space between the tackles. By game time, though, Paterno's brain had done an end around.

That's what Miami is going to expect us to do, the coach thought. *They're not going to expect John Shaffer to throw the football. Let's come out and throw it early.*

That strategy would turn out to be a dreadful mistake.

Meanwhile, the long days of anticipation for the game became canvas for controversial quotes from several Miami Hurricanes.

Dan Sileo, a rowdy starting Miami defensive tackle who had grown up in Stamford, Connecticut, vented his dislike for anything Penn State in an interview with a Philadelphia newspaper:

They recruited me, but they told me I wasn't a Penn State–type player. I guess I didn't have a 5.0 grade-point average. I probably would have gotten kicked out the first semester. A lot of our guys wouldn't have fit in at Penn State. I was never a big Penn State fan. I didn't root for them as a kid. I'm tired of hearing about their goody-goody image. We intimidate.

Sileo, while admitting his hero was professional wrestler Rowdy Roddy Piper, was asked whether anyone in particular from Penn State could be intimidated. He said, referring to the Nittany Lions' quarterback,

Shaffer. He was intimidated in the Oklahoma game. I think their weakness is Shaffer, because he can't make the big play to his wide receivers. They don't have a diversified offense. To me, it's the same Penn State team that played in 1975.

Then Sileo went for the big finish:

Like a prize fighter, you try to build up a hatred for your opponent. We, as a team, are sick and tired of hearing Penn State this and Penn State that. We have a definite hatred of Penn State.

Miami came into the national title game ranked second in the country in give-aways/takeaways. The Hurricanes forced 44 turnovers while giving the ball away only 23 times during the season—an incredible plus-23 in the important give-away-takeaway statistic. In addition, they had collected 49 sacks—17 by defensive end Daniel Stubbs. Jerome Brown, Miami's 300-pound defensive tackle, was the collegiate lineman of the year. The middle linebacker, George Mira Jr., had 117 tackles during the regular season, including an incredible 17-tackle performance against Oklahoma. And, finally, safety Bennie Blades led the nation with ten interceptions.

Once the teams arrived in Tempe, the verbal sparring continued. Jerome Brown, fatigues covering his ample frame, led the Hurricanes in a walkout at a bowl-related barbeque. The night of the game, Miami arrived first at Sun Devil Stadium. But instead of going straight inside to their locker room, the Hurricanes loitered in the parking lot near the players' entrance and hooted at the Penn State players as their bus arrived. And then if that weren't enough, Stubbs and Brown crept from the Miami tunnel to heckle the Penn State players as they were performing pregame calisthenics.

That the University of Miami football team was even *in* Arizona was a mild upset. Miami was considered the prohibitive No. 1 team in the country, with no other college football team—not even the No. 2 ranked Penn State Nittany Lions—considered in their *league*. The Hurricanes made it clear that they would have preferred staying closer to home, even if it took playing a lesser quality opponent than Penn State. The implication was that they would rather take an easy win to secure their national championship than risk it by traveling three thousand miles across the country. It had taken a concerted effort from NBC, the network that would televise the Fiesta Bowl, and the Fiesta Bowl people themselves to get Miami to Tempe.

As the Hurricanes continued their overzealous pregame act, Bruce Skinner, the Fiesta Bowl executive whose tireless efforts helped lure them there, started to think he had made a mistake. "When Miami finally arrived, their demeanor said, clearly, that they didn't want to be here; and, ultimately, I think that was a significant factor in the game. They just weren't happy," Skinner said.

"Before the season, I remember, Rick Reilly of *Sports Illustrated* had written a story that just blistered the Miami program. And they played that whole season with a sort of persecution complex, as if everybody was out to get them. The president of Miami wasn't very happy with the way Jimmy Johnson was running the program. Meanwhile, Jimmy was miserable the whole week. The team felt like it was forced to play in a bowl game it really didn't want to play in.

"Knowing that, we tried to accommodate them as best we could. Whatever they needed, whatever they wanted, we tried to give it to them."

Skinner had arranged for the Hurricanes to practice at a brand-new practice facility used by the Arizona Outlaws of the United States Football League (USFL). But even that attempt at appeasement backfired. Penn State had been given Arizona State's practice field for its workouts. The Sun Devils were in Pasadena, preparing to play in their first-ever Rose Bowl. Arizona State athletic officials told Fiesta Bowl executives that its field could be used for practice, but not its locker rooms. Subsequently, Penn State was forced to dress for practice at Sun Devil Stadium and then walk two blocks to the ASU practice field. Skinner asked Miami officials for permission to have Penn State use the bigger locker room at the stadium—the home-team locker room—while Miami, technically the home team in the game, used the visiting locker room. Skinner's committee even paid to have the visiting room carpeted.

"They agreed to switch, but they weren't happy about it," Skinner remembered. "It just seemed like we could never satisfy them."

WHEN THE GAME FINALLY BEGAN Miami came out angry, as if on cue. The Lions looked overmatched on their first series. Shaffer tried a play-action pass on first down, hoping to catch Miami in a run defense. Instead, Stubbs bore through on Shaffer from right end and Sileo, the brash pregame talker, finished off the Penn

State quarterback for a 15-yard loss. On third down, Brown sacked Shaffer to set up a fourth and 26 for the Nittany Lions before most fans got into their seats.

And it went like that for most of the first half, with only Penn State's defense keeping the team in it. Miami got to the PSU 30-yard line on its first possession. Instead of having kicker Mark Seelig attempt a 47-yard field goal, Miami coach Jimmy Johnson went for it only to have Testaverde's fourth-and-four pass to tight end Charles Henry go incomplete.

The Penn State defense was succeeding in two major areas. First, it had managed to keep Michael Irvin, the All-American receiver, from being a factor. Irvin caught a 15-yard pass near the sidelines on Miami's first offensive play of the game. But after getting cracked over the middle by Isom on a subsequent possession, Irvin seemed a more docile sort. Testaverde, meanwhile, was having trouble deciphering Penn State's confusing zone alignment and unpredictable blitzes.

The Hurricanes needed a big play from their defense to get on the scoreboard. Midway through the second quarter, Dozier exploded for 19 yards off right tackle from his own 14-yard line to pull the Nittany Lions out of a deep hole. But on the next play, Shaffer, with his arm cocked in a throwing mode, was hit by Jerome Brown and fumbled the ball away. From the Penn State 20, Testaverde used an Alonzo Highsmith run and a quick pass to Henry to get the ball to the one-yard line. Then Melvin Bratton went airborne for the Miami touchdown and a 7–0 lead. By the time of the touchdown, the Hurricanes had run 40 offensive plays for 204 total yards to Penn State's 17 plays for 20 yards.

"The funny thing was, though, we never thought we were being outclassed," Dozier recalled. "We really thought it was a matter of time before things would come together. Our defense was making big plays. On offense, we knew we were going to catch Miami being overaggressive, and that was going to open it up for us."

With four minutes remaining in the half, Shaffer made his first significant completion—a third-and-12 to Eric Hamilton that gave Penn State a first down at the Miami 41. From there, Manoa, whom Dozier had nicknamed "Tonka Truck" for his aggressive, straight-on running style, burst through for 20 yards to the Miami 21. Shaffer then completed a swing pass to Manoa for 12 more and a first and goal at the Hurricanes' seven. Carrying on a straight off-tackle play, Manoa fumbled. But State's Darryl Giles recovered inside the Miami five. From there, Shaffer executed a perfect bootleg, rolled right, and dove into the end zone to complete a 74-yard drive to tie the game, 7–7, into halftime.

THE MIAMI GAME TURNED OUT to be a bittersweet night for Tim Manoa.

While Manoa had some brilliant moments for Penn State, contributing heartily to the Lions' touchdown drive toward the end of the first half, he also put the Nittany Lions in a couple of precarious spots. Not known as a fumbler, the Penn State fullback put the ball on the turf four times against Miami. His teammates recovered two of them and one was blown dead by an official's whistle. But the third, which came in the third quarter, was snared by Miami and was a huge momentum buster for Penn State. After that play, Paterno lambasted his fullback on the sidelines in front of his teammates and the national television audience and gave Manoa the football only once after that.

"I was so pissed off at myself after that play that anything Joe said to me was irrelevant," Manoa said later. "Tell you the truth, I don't even remember what he was saying to me. All I remember was that he was growling."

Tim Manoa had come to Penn State from Pittsburgh via Hawaii. Born on the island of Tonga, where he played rugby as a small boy, Manoa had the early physical gift of speed and power running with a football of any type. His dad, Tuuaki, moved the family from Tonga to Oahu, joining other relatives who had made the transition to live under a U.S. flag, where they settled in a small town on the north shore called Haula. Tim Manoa was seven years old at the time.

While in Hawaii, the Manoas quickly found a church of their denomination, where they met and befriended Ted and Mary Lou Tyler from Wexford, Pennsylvania, a small town just outside of the Steel City. The Tylers vacationed often in Oahu and, while there, attended the same church as the Manoas. Ted Tyler had an idea: Why not send one of the Manoa children back to live with the Tylers and experience the mainland? The Tylers had two daughters, so they asked to take Tim's sister, Sela. Tuuaki Manoa felt it better that the Tylers return with his rawboned son, Tim, for whom he desired a better education. That's how Tim Manoa got to be a star running back at North Allegheny High.

Tim Manoa had never seen snow. When his airplane touched down at Pittsburgh International, he was bewildered by the sight of a gray sky, a ground covered with white, frozen powder, and barren trees with no foliage anywhere. The kid who had spent much of his youth pulling coconuts off palm trees didn't know such a bleak world existed.

At first he was homesick on the mainland. He hated the food, was struggling to speak fluent English, and begged his father to let him return to Hawaii.

Tuuaki urged him to stick it out.

Encouraged by some school coaches who had a sense about the Tongan kid's athleticism, Tim joined the football team. In time, he started to make some good friends there—the North Allegheny jocks loved the kid with the island accent. There were also all these cute high school girls begging for his affection. All of a sudden, for Tim Manoa this mainland part of America wasn't such a bad place.

Manoa became a star at North Allegheny, so much so that coaches from neighboring high schools would soon curse their fate that he hadn't moved into their districts. When Penn State assistant Tom Bradley began recruiting Manoa, he often stopped in at North Hills High, which was close by, to visit with Jack McCurry, a friend and the North Hills football coach.

"One street," McCurry, shaking his head, would say to Bradley.

"What are you talking about?" Bradley replied.

"One street. The kid moves into a house one street over from where he is and he would have come here," McCurry said. He was talking about Manoa.

Tim was a "bull rusher"—6′3″, 230 pounds in high school, with great speed. It didn't take long for the American college football power schools to notice. USC and UCLA recruited him hard, figuring the kid from Tonga would like to be closer to the Pacific Ocean. But by then Manoa had grown to like the East Coast and its season changes. One of the Tyler girls had gone to Penn State, so he heard good things about the school. That made it a lot easier for Bradley. Manoa would become one of Paterno's most important recruits. He was a big fullback who could block and run, perfect for Penn State's offense. Bradley had to get him. And he did.

But when Tim Manoa got to Penn State, he gave Paterno nightmares. This was an athlete the Penn State coach would spend a lot of energy breaking down. After living on his own for the last several years under the somewhat diluted discipline of a guardian, Manoa had a fierce independent streak. He liked to drink a few beers from time to time and felt large and powerful enough to do whatever he wanted—even during his freshman year on campus. One night he and Knizner, his freshman roommate, were partying at a popular frat house. Knizner was engaged in a darts game with a couple of the frat brothers and was beating them out of some money when the brothers pulled rank and tried to run the young PSU quarterback out of the joint. He called for Manoa, who picked up a handful of darts and explained very calmly to the frat boys that if they messed with his friend Knizner again, the darts he held in his hand might soon be sticking from their torsos.

The following day Paterno called Manoa into his office to suggest, rather sternly, that this was not acceptable behavior for a Penn State football player.

But Tim Manoa was like a wild steed—there weren't that many efficient ways to tie him up. That summer Manoa stayed on campus to attend summer school, befriending a couple of fellow freshman players named Barry Buckman and Charlie Swenk. The original plan was to cut some of those boring summer classes and go to the Bahamas for a few days after Buckman had seen an advertisement for a $59 one-way flight. But none of them could come up with the scratch, so Swenk, who had a car, decided that their vacation would be to Virginia Beach. That's where the three players went, missing four days of summer school. A report got back to Paterno. He was furious. With the help of his secretary, the coach tracked them down *at* their hotel.

The phone in the room rang. *Who the hell knows we're here?* Swenk wondered. He answered.

It was Paterno's secretary. "Coach would like to speak with you," she said.

Swenk panicked. He handed the phone to Manoa. "*It's Joe!*"

Manoa held the receiver to his ear.

"Whose idea was it to leave summer school?!" Paterno barked.

"Uh . . . ," Manoa stammered.

"You guys had better be back here tomorrow, or you're finished," Paterno said. And he hung up. Abruptly.

When the players returned, Paterno immediately dismissed Buckman and told Swenk and Manoa to show up at a residence hall where, under the supervision of a couple of grad assistant coaches, they would have to run five miles per day for the next five days. Swenk didn't show and was also kicked off the team. Manoa showed up and ran. It pleased Paterno that Manoa had some desire after all. He would see his fullback as a kid who occasionally just needed a little kick in the butt and maybe a better example to follow.

Perhaps that's how Tim Manoa ended up with his buddy Knizner sharing a residence in 1986 with D.J. Dozier and Tim Johnson.

Coming into the season, Dozier had made no bones about his Christian conversion, and Johnson—who would become a church pastor after his NFL playing days—came to Penn State from Florida as already devoutly religious.

"Matt and I both liked to party," Manoa recalled. "D.J. and Timmy would have guys over for Bible study sessions. So what you had was a prayer meeting in one room and a party in the other."

Manoa was the guy Penn State teammates *had* to have with them as they perused the College Avenue bars just off campus. Manoa became the team's unofficial bodyguard, the guy they could always call on when they got in a little over their heads. He would put down his beer and suddenly emerge like Superman. *You pickin' on my boy here? Move along, Brudda.* The small toughs with beer muscles who would challenge Tim Manoa after midnight, the ones with the macho designs of taking down a big, bad Penn State football player, were usually defeated with just a little shove from the big kid from Tonga.

The years have mellowed Tim Manoa a little.

He is settled in a Cleveland suburb with his wife, Jill, and children Alexis and Morgan. The Cleveland Browns drafted Manoa after the Penn State season in the third round—one pick ahead of Steve Smith, his interchangeable fullback counterpart. He played three years with the Browns, signed with the Saints as a free agent but got cut before playing a down, and finished up with the Indianapolis Colts.

In Cleveland, there were always whispers of Manoa and some wild and crazy off-the-field activities. A few years later, after he had signed with the Indianapolis Colts, Manoa befriended a kindred spirit: a young and wild defensive tackle named Tony Siragusa. One night the two men got buzzed together and ended the night at the drive-through window of an Indianapolis fast-food joint. As a joke, Siragusa pulled out a handgun to scare the clerk into speeding up the order. Quietly, another employee alerted authorities and before their bag of food came out, Siragusa and Manoa were being ordered out of their car at police gunpoint. Both players were forced to make a court appearance. Siragusa had had a permit for the gun and after he explained that the caper was intended just to be a joke, the charges were dropped.

AT THE FIESTA BOWL, Tim Manoa studied all that Miami activity and thought maybe he had been better suited to be a Hurricane. But on the field that night in his black cleats and hefty shoulder pads, he watched Miami players walk right through where the Penn State running backs were doing their warmups. Some Miami player, walking right through Manoa and Dozier, said, "We're gonna kick your ass." Manoa jumped up and wanted to tear their heads off. An assistant coach stopped him. Being brash is one thing, Manoa thought. Doing that was disrespectful. He was glad he was on the plain-uniform side.

"I think Joe Paterno looked at me a little differently than he did some of the other guys," Tim Manoa said. "I think he thought, because I was so far away from home, that he had to watch over me, be more of a father figure. He knew he had to let me go a little, but he knew exactly when to reign me in. And I knew when to stop.

"One of the great things about our team is that we were all different. We all had different personalities. But we were all united for that one cause, and that was winning a national championship."

IN THE LOCKER ROOM AT HALFTIME of the Fiesta Bowl, Paterno was more resolute than rowdy. He knew that with all of Miami's offensive dominance, he had gotten a gift to be tied 7–7. The 'Canes had rattled off 244 total offensive yards in the first half, with twelve first downs to Penn State's six, and a whopping 17:10 in time of possession, five more minutes than the Nittany Lions. The Penn State coach huddled with his staff for several minutes as his players rested. He knew that the decision to come out passing instead of running in an attempt to throw off the Miami defense wasn't working that well. The Lions offense just couldn't stay on the field long enough. So he urged his offensive coordinator, Fran Ganter, to go back to the team's bread and butter—running the football with Dozier and the fullbacks. He also wanted to tweak his offensive line's blocking scheme to ward off Brown, Mr. Fatigues himself, who was wreaking havoc all night.

Then he came into the locker room to address the troops.

"Just be patient," he told them. "They're going to make yards. Don't let that defeat you. Just hang in there. We're in a good position."

Miami, on the other hand, felt more of a sense of urgency. They had talked the talk all week and now, before a big crowd and an even bigger national television audience, they were sputtering against a team the whole world had picked them to devour.

On the Hurricanes' first series of the third quarter, Testaverde threw a couple of lasers, first to Highsmith, who dropped it over the middle, then to Irvin, who dropped it in near the left sideline. Both receivers appeared to be looking over their shoulders before the ball was in their hands, waiting to be hit.

Toward the end of the third quarter, from the Penn State 31, Manoa took a handoff from Shaffer and the ball squirted out of his hands like a bar of soap. Miami recovered. The Hurricanes got to the Penn State 12 before Mark Seelig missed a 28-yard field goal. The Nittany Lions had dodged another bullet.

On the first play of the fourth quarter, Giftopoulos intercepted Testaverde and made a 24-yard return to give Penn State the ball at the Miami 36. On first down, Dozier swept right for three yards until he was pushed out of bounds and into Ahmad Rashad's cup of coffee. Dozier had never had a coffee injury. He made a note to put that on his dossier after the game.

But just a few minutes later, that singed hand would cradle a football long enough to reach the end zone for perhaps Penn State's most important touchdown ever.

2

LINEBACKER U

The defense Penn State was in on that play was not supposed to have Shane Conlan anywhere in that area. Sandusky and his Nittany Lion defensive assistants had debated whether to put Conlan in what they called "the curl," into the flanks where Miami sometimes curled their receivers. At the last second, they yelled for Conlan to stay in the middle. But when the ball was snapped, Conlan read correctly that Testaverde was going to throw to his left to Irvin, and the Penn State linebacker shifted that way naturally.

"Shane Conlan was smart enough to know that sometimes you just can't play like a robot," said Penn State assistant Tom Bradley. "That's what made him special. Some guys take coaching, which is good, but don't allow for their instincts to take over. Shane just made that play because of what he felt. That's what made him so special."

Trey Bauer thinks about the play often and he usually explains it with his tongue cemented inside his cheek. "Hey, I was a big part of that play. If Shane doesn't push me

Shane Conlan dropped into coverage and felt a man attached to his left hip: fellow linebacker Trey Bauer.

Penn State trailed 10–7 with less than ten minutes remaining in the fourth quarter. Miami was poised for a drive that the 'Canes hoped would put the game away—the Hurricanes were at their own 34-yard line. Conlan watched Vinny Testaverde drop back in the pocket, looking at his side of the field.

It was not a time for discussion or for two linebackers to be covering the same flank.

With his left arm, Conlan shoved Bauer toward the middle, never missing a stride. He looked up and saw a spiral in the air, about seven feet high and headed toward Michael Irvin, the receiver behind him. In a flash, Conlan turned his body and reached up, catching the ball over his right shoulder. He then whirled and followed a collection of blockers, the ball tucked tightly in the socket of his right arm, until a Miami tackler stopped him just five yards from a touchdown. As Conlan rose from the turf and calmly handed the ball to an official, the first person he encountered was Bauer, who was waiving his arms and jumping up and down as if he had just won the Lotto.

out of the way, maybe he doesn't have the momentum he needed to get up in the air to make that pick."

The years have taken them down different paths. Conlan forged a prosperous career in the NFL and now lives a calm and somewhat anonymous life with his wife and four children in tiny Sewickley, a Pittsburgh suburb. Trey Bauer never made it in pro ball, but his taste for the action never waned. With a partner, he founded a financial services firm after spending ten years as a Wall Street trader. His family life is no less sedate. Bauer and his wife, Maureen, welcomed a set of triplets and a set of twins all within an eight-year span.

Conlan and Bauer. The Stoic and The Excitable Boy. They were as different as Arizona sunshine and a winter day in State College.

IT WAS ABOUT 45 MINUTES before the national championship game. Penn State was at their end of the Fiesta Bowl field, working through calisthenics. The Hurricanes, who had come to Tempe dressed in fatigues, walked out of a pregame barbeque in defiance, and waited for the Penn State bus to arrive outside the stadium so they could pelt the Nittany Lions with insults, this time walked right into and through their opponents' calisthenics regimen.

Trey Bauer, the man who would take neither guff nor disrespect from anyone, picked up a football and winged it at Irvin.

"I missed him," Bauer recalled. "He turned around and started jawing at me, but he kept on walking toward his end.

"Michael Irvin was such a pussy. He dropped a ton of balls that night because he was scared of getting hit. And after the game, he used the excuse that the ball was wet. Hey, we were in Arizona. There wasn't any moisture in the whole state that night.

"About the only cool guy on the team was Stubbs," Bauer said. "I remember seeing him after I threw the ball at Irvin and I said, 'Hey, Dan, you should be with us. What the hell are you doing playing with those assholes?'"

Two days before the Fiesta Bowl, Bauer had been the last Penn State athlete scheduled for an individual press conference. School media relations officials shuddered. L. Budd Thalman, the Nittany Lions sports information director at the time, had been a public relations director with the Buffalo Bills in a previous life and knew the perils of published material the opponent could pin on its locker-room walls to use for motivation. He called Bauer over before the press conference was to begin and warned the linebacker to keep his comments generic. A Miami reporter asked Bauer his reaction to the game's point spread, which had the Hurricanes as a seven-point favorite. Bauer told the reporter that if the point spread was seven, people should bet the mortgage on Penn State. The next morning, the following headline blared atop the *Miami Herald*'s sports section: "State's Bauer Predicts Nittany Lion Victory."

Trey Bauer had been a precocious football talent at Paramus High in Bergen County, North Jersey, where his father, Charlie Bauer, was the head coach. The conference in which Paramus played was stocked with major college talent, so the scouts following their upper-class recruits also noticed Bauer, who was a starter at running back and linebacker at Paramus as a sophomore. When Fran Ganter, the Lions' offensive coordinator and chief recruiter, asked high school coaches who the top five players in the area were, Trey Bauer's name kept coming up.

The summer after his junior year, Bauer attended a three-day football camp at Penn State. The coaches saw a kid who was a plain terror on the football field. That was enough for them. On the last day of camp Ganter walked over to Bauer and offered the kid from Paramus a full scholarship right there on the spot. Ohio State, Pittsburgh, Boston College, and Rutgers had been actively recruiting Bauer. When the schools found out that Bauer, a linebacker, had been offered a scholarship at Linebacker U, they knew they had no chance. Trey Bauer would become a Nittany Lion.

In most every way, Trey Bauer was the antithesis of Joe Paterno's ideal student-athlete—the one who should be seen and rarely heard. And it was that way as soon as Bauer arrived on the Penn State campus. The kid was loud. He was brash. He was slightly obnoxious. He was the anti–Nittany Lion.

During his freshman year Bauer got thrown out of a study hall—a mortal sin with Paterno—for engaging a friend in horseplay.

"It really wasn't my fault. The other kid started it," Bauer recalled.

That same year, after Paterno was sure Bauer had learned his lesson from the study-hall caper, Bauer was at it again—arriving five minutes late to a team meeting.

"Joe screamed at me, I mean absolutely screamed at me in front of the whole team," Bauer said. "Everybody has heard him talk. His normal voice is kind of screechy. When he screams, it's like nails on a chalkboard. After he's done screaming, he tells me he'll talk to me after the meeting."

Paterno told his young linebacker to transfer immediately, that with an attitude like that, he'd never play at Penn State. Bauer called his dad, looking for a little sympathy. He didn't get it.

"My dad told me that he'd have thrown me off the team, too," Trey said.

Nobody could figure him out. He was just, as he says now, a Jersey punk with an attitude. But Bauer refused to go away. The kid loved playing football. And he loved the thought, especially, of playing football at Penn State. "At the end of the day, I think Joe figured out that on that football field, I'd always be there for him."

FOR THE FIRST TIME IN MANY YEARS, Shane Conlan sits to watch a DVD of the game that made television college football history. More people watched Penn State and Miami in the Fiesta Bowl—some 70 million—than any college football game then and ever since. It's as if Conlan is seeing it for the first time.

There is a play in the game's third quarter where Conlan is accidentally slammed in the knee by his own teammate, Duffy Cobbs, while pursuing a tackle. Penn State's All-American linebacker is on the ground for minutes, writhing in pain as the Penn State training staff surrounds him. Conlan doesn't remember the play or the pain ever happening.

A little earlier in the quarter, Miami's Irvin, spooked by several earlier hits from Penn State's attack-dog secondary, can't hold onto a third-down pass from Vinny Testaverde. Conlan, a player who mostly let his kamikaze style do the talking, is seen in Irvin's face, talking smack. He doesn't remember that either.

As a football player Shane Conlan was a caveman, a throwback. Even when he was an NFL star, it confused Conlan to see players celebrate after making a routine tackle. To Conlan, making great plays were something you were *supposed* to do; otherwise, the coaches would not have had you on the field in the first place. Conlan made a great play in perhaps the most famous game he's ever played in, and he can hardly remember it. He was a football player. It's what he did. To Shane Conlan, there never was a benefit to looking back and admiring. There was always another play to be made.

Of all the great linebackers who have played at Penn State, Shane Conlan may be the best. His combination of speed, intelligence, and tenacity helped make Penn State's defense in the 1986 season an art form every bit as enjoyable to watch as a D.J. Dozier touchdown run. Conlan parlayed his Penn State career into an early first-round draft pick. He was the AFC's Rookie of the Year with the Buffalo Bills in 1987. He was *Sports Illustrated*'s cover boy for the December 16, 1991, issue that featured a story on the Bills' torrid Super Bowl defense. He was elected the Los Angeles Rams' defensive MVP in 1994, the year he signed with the Rams as a free agent. Looking at Conlan today, examining his svelte 6′2″, 210-pound frame (some 35 pounds below his pro playing weight), salt-and-pepper-flaked hair, and quiet demeanor, one could get the impression that he never played football at all.

"Shane Conlan is the most unassuming famous guy I've ever known," admired Bauer.

Conlan's effort in the 1987 Fiesta Bowl may have been the finest game a college linebacker has ever played. Playing through intense pain all game long from a pair of banged-up knees and cramped-up legs, he was still a wrecking ball. That night Shane Conlan had eight tackles and two big interceptions, the last one being the one where he pushed Bauer away, the one that set up Penn State's game-winning touchdown with less than ten minutes remaining in the fourth quarter.

Like a lot of starters on Penn State's 1986 team, Conlan recalled having absolutely no fear of facing, and then defeating, Miami for the national championship. In fact, Conlan's air of confidence actually developed *before* the Lions began their month-long practice sessions for the game. When he ran into Testaverde on one of the two players' many All-American team junkets, Vinny told him that the Hurricanes preferred to stay at home and play in the Orange Bowl instead of going to the Fiesta Bowl. Conlan furrowed his brow.

Why would you not want to play your closest competitor head-up to prove that you're the best team in the nation? Conlan asked himself. "It was bizarre to me. That told me that either Miami was looking for the easy way out, or they were afraid to face us. Either way, they wouldn't be as focused as they should have been."

THAT SHANE CONLAN MORPHED INTO perhaps the finest linebacker to come out of Linebacker U drips with irony because Conlan almost didn't make it to Penn State in the first place. Paterno didn't think he was good enough. Conlan was a 180-pound all-purpose athlete at tiny Frewsburg Central High in Frewsburg, New York (pop. 1,908). He was a stud running back and linebacker for the football team, but that football team only had twenty-one players total and Conlan was playing against talent from small schools just like Frewsburg. How could anyone really evaluate him? Even townsfolk who worshipped Conlan like he was Jack Armstrong, the all-American boy, thought his best sport was baseball, for which the Pittsburgh Pirates were scouting him as a catcher.

Conlan, though, was determined to play major college football. His coach, Tom Sharpe, sent a tape to Tom Bradley. Impressed by the way Conlan moved on the field, Bradley showed the tape to Paterno, looking for a response.

"No," Joe said. And then he walked out of the room, leaving Bradley in a lurch.

By then, Ohio State and Syracuse, the only other Division I-A schools to show even a mild interest in Conlan, had bailed out. Edinboro, a small Division II school tucked in northwestern Pennsylvania and fairly close to Conlan's home, had a decent football reputation but didn't even want him. Sharpe knew that Paterno had been talking about adding more athleticism to his defense and tried Penn State again, urging Bradley on a Monday afternoon to come to Frewsburg to see Conlan play in a basketball game the next night.

The Penn State assistant told Sharpe he'd come out in a few days.

"That's not going to work," Sharpe said.

"Why?" Bradley asked.

"Because tomorrow is the last game of the season," said Sharpe.

With the national letter of intent signing date just eight days away and Bradley armpit-deep in locking down the jewels of Penn State's next recruiting class, the Penn State coach set his car on the road to Frewsburg.

"I get to the game and this tiny gymnasium had five row of bleachers; I sit on the fifth row," Bradley recalled. "First shot of the game goes up for Frewsburg, bangs off the rim, and Shane shoots through, catches it in the air, and dunks it. Now I move down to the first row of the bleachers.

"I'm watching this kid and he's all over the place. He's running the floor and jumping over people. My eyes are popping out of my head. He was a maniac out there."

Conlan, who was averaging 24 points a game for Frewsburg, scored only three points that night and fouled out early in the fourth quarter. But Bradley loved the kid's competitiveness. There was something about Shane Conlan that Bradley couldn't quite get a handle on, but he wanted him at Penn State.

Bradley went back to Paterno again.

"He's too skinny, Tommy," Paterno said. "You're crazy."

"Coach, you didn't see what I saw," Bradley said.

"All right, if you want him that badly, take him," Paterno said. "But you'd better be right."

Conlan took an official visit to State College that weekend. The Nittany Lions still had an available scholarship. Bradley called his new recruit Sunday night after Conlan returned to Frewsburg.

"Shane, we'd like to offer you a scholarship to come to Penn State," Bradley said.

"That would be great, Coach," Conlan replied softly.

"Listen, I have to be in Erie tomorrow. Do you want me to come by the house and talk with your dad?" Bradley asked.

"That's stupid; I just saw you," Conlan said.

"But, Shane, I can bring over the letter of intent and you can sign it right there," said Bradley.

"Coach, I'm coming to Penn State. I'll just mail it to you."

Years later it occurred to Tom Bradley that Shane Conlan was the greatest player he had the easiest time recruiting.

Conlan would run into Jim Tressel at a sports banquet years later. The head coach at Ohio State was an assistant at Syracuse when Conlan was a senior at Frewsburg High. Tressel scouted Conlan for a couple weeks, and then quickly lost interest.

"Boy, did I ever screw up with you," Tressel told Conlan at that banquet.

Penn State was perfect for Shane Conlan. It was no frills, just like he was. He *loved* the white uniforms, loved them much more even than Penn State's rich navy-blue home issue, which were *garish* by comparison. Penn State was straight plow-ahead football. It was steak and potatoes. The bling, that was for other guys. But Conlan also knew that actually *playing* at Penn State would not be easy. As a player from a tiny school, being offered a scholarship that was essentially a leftover, and thrown into a mix with some eighty high school All-Americans that could have had their pick of mostly any school they wanted, he had to get noticed.

Shane Conlan came to his first camp at Penn State 6′2″ and beefed up to all of 186 pounds after a summer of hard workouts following his high school graduation.

What position was he? No one knew.

Penn State coaches lined him up at cornerback for a day. No go. They moved him to safety. Not a fit. Finally they put him at outside linebacker, where he'd go against the Lions' massive, 6′5″, 250-pound tight end, Mike McCloskey. One practice, McCloskey ran a little out route. Conlan crashed into him with the force of a Hummer, separating McCloskey from the ball. The tight end got up, dazed. Penn State's defensive coaches looked at each other in astonishment.

In a major college football practice, the quarterback is not supposed to be touched and he wears a red shirt to remind defenders to stay off. But in football practices that same unwritten rule also applies to star players. After all, what good would it do a team to have a key player injured by a teammate in *practice*? But Shane Conlan came to Penn State to get noticed, not to adhere to some wimpy unwritten rule.

A couple of days after he ripped into McCloskey, Conlan set his sights on Curt Warner, Penn State's star halfback, also not to be hit. Reading the offense executing a screen pass, Conlan first buried a pulling offensive lineman, then straightened himself and knocked the hell out of Warner for a loss. The rest of the offensive line converged on Conlan like angry hornets stirred from a nest and coaches had to break up what nearly turned into a riot.

The day before the varsity's first game, Conlan, who was told that he would most likely sit out his freshman season as a redshirt, dressed for the Nittany Lions' junior varsity game that afternoon. As he emerged from the locker room, Ganter stopped him. "You're not redshirted," Ganter told Conlan. Shane Conlan was too good to waste on the J V.

Fortunately for the 1986 Nittany Lions, Conlan didn't play in a varsity game that year, meaning he preserved a season of eligibility as a redshirt after all. As it was, Conlan still had to make a choice to play his senior season. He had become a starter midway through his sophomore year and had a brilliant junior season, leading the Nittany Lions in tackles. N FL scouts told Conlan he'd be a third- or, at worst, a fourth-round draft pick if he decided to come out after Penn State lost to Oklahoma in the 1986 Orange Bowl. But it really wasn't much of a decision. The Penn State team that would come into the 1986 regular season was loaded. They were close. And to a man, they all thought they could win a national championship.

SHANE CONLAN CAME INTO the 1986 national championship game wearing the wounds of a long season. Penn State's one month of preparation for the game didn't include time to heal. The Lions were going at it full bore in practice. Paterno was not about to let his team get soft.

But Conlan's teammates were conditioned to rely on their defensive captain and expect the same ferocious performance whether Conlan was healthy or had a bone sticking through his skin.

"Shane would come off the field with an injury and we'd think nothing of it," recalled Bauer. "It was like, 'Yeah, Shane's hurt. Right.' We knew he'd be back in a play or two."

And so it was that balmy night in Tempe.

Quiet and unassuming off the field, Conlan turned ferocious once the game began. Early in his career at Penn State, he had gotten a couple of teeth knocked out of his upper set while making a tackle. Like a hockey player, he wore a plate of false teeth that filled in the gap, removing it just before the game began.

During pregame warmups, Penn State spread out over much of the Sun Devil Stadium field since Miami had not yet come out of its locker room. Once the Hurricanes emerged, each team was supposed on stay on its own side of the 50-yard line. A couple of Lions did not quite conform. Jimmy Johnson walked toward them and started yelling.

"All of a sudden I see Shane walk over to Johnson, take out his teeth, and start yelling back," Tom Bradley remembered. "I'm thinking, 'Okay, here we go already.' I grabbed Shane and said, 'Not now, not now.'"

Conlan made Penn State's first tackle in the game, ramming Melvin Bratton out of bounds after a five-yard end sweep. Conlan seemed to be in every play from that moment on, whether it be on a head-on collision with Bratton and Miami's other great back, Alonzo Highsmith, or in coverage in Jerry Sandusky's tricked-up defense—when Testaverde dropped into the pocket, he saw Penn State defensive backs everywhere, covering normally open flanks.

On Miami's second series, a first and 10 at the Hurricane 15, Bratton again swept right. Conlan pursued with Marques Henderson to make the stop, but so did cornerback Duffy Cobbs, who dove at Bratton, whipping the back of his legs upward and inadvertently slashing Conlan. The blow hit Conlan's right knee like an axe to an oak tree and Conlan dropped to the turf in pain. He was helped off the field and plopped onto the Penn State bench, where trainers and doctors worked to stabilize the knee.

Was he done for the game?

It was a Penn State fan's biggest fear. The thought even dawned on Bauer as Miami was putting together a multiplay drive and Conlan was absent from the Nittany Lions' defensive huddle for more than the usual one or two plays.

Was it a just a sting that wore off, or was it will that brought Conlan back into the Penn State lineup? Whatever the case, Penn State's All-American linebacker returned with about thirteen minutes left in the half, survived that final thirteen, and then reenergized for what would be thirty of the most heroic minutes a player could have.

Nearing the five-minute mark of the third quarter, the score still tied at 7–7, Testaverde moved Miami to the Penn State 23. On a third and three, Vinny took the snap but, in the process of dropping back, he slipped on the now-dewy turf. Off balance, Testaverde tried to throw left to Irvin on an out pattern, but Conlan read the quarterback's eyes, moved into position, and picked off the pass. With clear sailing ahead and a possible touchdown staring him down, Conlan started up the field. But his weakened legs gave out and he stumbled and fell.

Twenty years later, watching the video with his two young sons, Conlan offers no excuses. He turns to his son Chris and says, "Your dad's pretty much a dork, huh?"

Minutes later, that "dork" would make the play that would lead to Penn State's winning touchdown.

3

THE QUARTERBACK

JOHN SHAFFER WAS ATTENDING a funeral in Leechburg, Pennsylvania, standing innocuously at the back of the parlor with his grandfather when Penn State's January 2, 1986, Orange Bowl loss to Oklahoma—and Shaffer's part in that loss—hit him hardest. A man walked by with his wife—Shaffer didn't know him—saw the Penn State quarterback and stopped.

"Honey," the man said, turning to his spouse, "I want to introduce you to the guy who lost the Orange Bowl and lost us a thousand bucks."

Et tu?

The date was March 1, two months after the Orange Bowl loss and only a few months before Shaffer's final season as a college quarterback. They were agonizing months—days and nights of self-doubt and fear and loathing that the rest of his days at Penn State would be spent sitting on the bench, defrocked, with his hands no longer on a football but on a sideline clipboard, charting plays for the new starter.

He had known nothing but success. Going into that Oklahoma game in which Penn

On second down at the Miami four, the play clock winding down to the final couple of seconds of the first half, John Shaffer took the snap from center Keith Radecic, turned to his left, faked a handoff to Manoa, and then pivoted to his opposite side on a bootleg. Rolling right in a semicircle that took him beyond the 10-yard line, he looked toward the corner of end zone for his tight end, Brian Siverling. Faking a pass that kept Miami's cornerbacks frozen for just a split second, Shaffer tucked the football and darted forward for the end-zone pylon. Two Miami defenders converged, but they got there too late. Shaffer had scored. Freeing himself from the pile, the Penn State quarterback leaped up and pumped his fist as if to say to all the people who had maligned him all these years and who doubted that he could ever lead his team to a national championship, "Take that!"

State had been undefeated and ranked No. 1 in the nation, Shaffer had not lost a game he'd started at quarterback. *Ever.* Since the seventh grade, he had been an astounding 54–0. But under the hot lights of a New Year's bowl game for the national championship, he melted, completing just 10 of 22 passes for 74 yards with three interceptions.

It was an embarrassing final game for Penn State. The Nittany Lions would suffer five turnovers all told, losing to Barry Switzer and the brash Sooners 25–10. But the burden would fall mostly on Shaffer. Football fans throughout the country, including the most die-hard Penn State fans, had forever doubted his ability. He was a product of a conservative system rather than a quarterback with the talent to actually *win* games, they said. His performance against Oklahoma only justified the critics. Shaffer had even piled on himself by admitting to the press after the game that the loss was *his fault.*

After that Oklahoma game, Shaffer struggled to find allies among his teammates and, especially, his own coaching staff. A couple of days after the game, when the team had returned home to State College, Paterno called Shaffer into his office. Neither Joe nor longtime quarterback coach Bob Phillips was willing to commit to Shaffer as the No. 1 quarterback on the depth chart for next season.

If it was Paterno's way of motivating Shaffer, John wasn't exactly on board with it. He walked away from that meeting feeling as if he'd been shot and the wind was blowing right through the holes in his body.

Shaffer had come to Penn State with a decent enough pedigree. He was the starting quarterback for one of the most powerful high school football programs in the nation—Moeller High in Cincinnati. His dad, John Sr., had moved the family in and out of several places with job transfers working for Procter and Gamble. The Shaffers found a home in Cincy and young John evolved into a stellar athlete there.

Moeller was a football factory of sorts, churning out Division I-A football players as a matter of course. Its longtime coach was Gerry Faust, who before Shaffer's senior season left to take his dream job as head coach at Notre Dame. Moeller High games regularly drew some 20,000 people, and Moeller was a place where players had to earn a starting position through time and attrition because there was always someone better in the class ahead.

Shaffer didn't become the Moeller starting quarterback until his senior year, but, like others before him, he kept the train running. With a green Shaffer taking over the helm, but a star running back, Hiawatha Francisco, as the bellwether, Moeller came into the 1982 season as the No. 1 ranked high school team in the nation. And that's where they finished. Moeller beat state power Massillon High for the Ohio state championship before some 45,000 fans. Also that season, in a highly anticipated nonleague game, Shaffer had outdueled Steve Beuerlein of Anaheim, California's Servite High. When it was all over, Beuerlein and Francisco would become teammates under Faust at N D, while Shaffer, his undefeated record still intact, sorted through his top six final college choices: Notre Dame, Pittsburgh, Michigan State, Boston College, Ohio State, and Penn State.

Shaffer had always wanted to be a Buckeye. But the Ohio State program was in disarray. Earle Bruce, the crusty skipper who had taken over years before for Woody Hayes, was the coach. His top assistant, Dom Capers, had left for pro ball, and the Buckeyes' recruiting in the southern part of Ohio, where Shaffer performed, was suffering. Shaffer had a familiarity with Penn State; he attended several Penn State football camps as an underclassman at Moeller. Meanwhile, the Nittany Lions were also coming off a national championship season having upset Herschel Walker and Georgia in the Sugar Bowl that year.

"Penn State's recruiting was totally different than anyone else," Shaffer said. "They weren't Pitt, and they weren't Notre Dame—schools that would call you fifteen times a day. Penn State offered you a scholarship and left you alone.

"Joe Paterno recruits parents almost as much as kids. He came into our basement and told my mom and dad that whether the kids who come to Penn State play or don't play, he would graduate them. That's what the parents want to hear. And he's not telling fibs, either."

For Shaffer playing time at Penn State manifested almost right away. In an attempt to replace the graduated Todd Blackledge, whom Kansas City had picked in the first round of the NFL draft only months before, Penn State struggled to find an identity at quarterback, going with untested Doug Strang. But in the first game of the 1983 season, the Kickoff Classic at the Meadowlands against Nebraska, Strang struggled. And so did backup Dan Lonergan. From his bench seat on the sidelines, a scared Shaffer heard Paterno scream, "Get Shaffer ready!" Bob Phillips dissuaded the head coach, not wanting to throw Shaffer in the deep end yet. The following week Paterno had Shaffer play in the fourth quarter of a rout against Cincinnati, and it wasn't a stretch for Nittany Lions fans to figure that they were seeing their starting quarterback for the next several years.

Shaffer was nothing fancy; he was just a good leader, which played out in many ways, not necessarily only on the football field.

In the first game of the 1985 regular season, Penn State opened with a 20–18 win at Maryland on a sizzler of a day in early September when the temperatures on the field reached more than one hundred degrees.

The Lions had taken two small commuter airplanes to get to College Station and, now back at the airport, they were in a hurry to get out. Paterno had structured the trip to have the defense ride in one plane and the offense in the other. Penn State's offensive linemen ran to their planes, dug into coolers of sandwiches provided for the team, and plopped their massive bodies in seats in the back. That sudden weight drop lowered the back end of the plane like the bottom end of a seesaw. A taillight on the back smashed down hard on the asphalt and cracked.

Before too much panic settled in, team officials unloaded the plane as several Penn State players walked around the tarmac in a daze.

"No way I'm riding in that plane!" yelped offensive tackle Stephen Davis. "I'm taking a bus home!"

Paterno took charge. Placing his players back on the wounded plane, JoePa embraced a depth-chart mentality. Penn State's *starting* offensive and defensive teams would take the airplane that didn't have the broken taillight. The others, the ones who wore the green, gold, and white jerseys during Penn State's practices, would take the other plane. That's why they had a depth chart in the first place.

Shaffer wasn't about to let that happen without his input. The quarterback went to Paterno and volunteered to ride with the second team on the broken taillight plane. Paterno informed both teams how their quarterback saw the situation. Several first-teamers got off the first plane and went with Shaffer into the second. John Shaffer seemed too good to be true.

Until, that is, Penn State and Shaffer blew a gasket at the end of that season in a horrific loss to Oklahoma in the 1986 Orange Bowl.

After the loss to the Sooners, the choice of the fickle became Knizner, a junior-to-be from Youngwood, Pennsylvania. Knizner was about the same size as Shaffer but more mobile and with a much better arm. Whenever Shaffer struggled as a Penn State starter, whether it was for a game or a series, the crowd yelped for Knizner. They wanted a swashbuckler. Knizner seemed to be more like that. Shaffer was more the bank-president type. And no one wanted a bank president taking snaps against the best college football defenses in America. Besides that, Knizner seemed to be better liked by his teammates. Among his roommates in a new apartment rented on College Avenue that summer was none other than team offensive star D.J. Dozier.

"I couldn't worry about where other people's loyalties may have laid," Shaffer recalled. "I couldn't worry about what people thought of me. I had to motivate myself."

So Shaffer worked. He knew that the Nittany Lions were about to tweak their offense. Wide receivers coach Jim Caldwell, whom Shaffer admired, would be given more influence to pull Penn State away from its classic conservative offensive approach. The Lions, long under Paterno, had shown affection for running plays on first and second downs, leaving the offense in a precarious position to convert third down and long with defense pressure coming hard at the quarterback. Caldwell's vision was to install a pass offense, one that would utilize the short-passing game in the flanks and get the tight end in seams five yards down the field on early downs.

Every night Shaffer ran and threw. On Sunday nights when most of his teammates were resting from a hard week of spring practice, Shaffer was dragging offensive lineman Mark Sickler and tight end Brian Siverling, his roommates, to Penn State's indoor practice facility. The quarterback always crossed his fingers that the door had been left open. If it was, Shaffer would calmly hit the light switch, station Sickler and Siverling 18 yards away, and begin firing lasers at them, about a hundred a session. If the door was locked, Shaffer merely improvised, moving the group to a lighted parking lot. In that dimness, it was not uncommon for Shaffer to bean Sickler and Siverling in the head. They were taking one, or many, for the team.

When the games began, Siverling became one of Shaffer's main targets—the big tight end always seemed to be open when the quarterback needed him. A 6'7", 253-pound product from near Erie, Brian Siverling was close to never becoming a Nittany Lions football player. At Harbor Creek High he was also an all-state basketball player and came from a long line of academics. His mother, father, and older brother were all valedictorians of their high schools. Siverling loved basketball—he averaged 24.5 points and 15.6 rebounds his senior year following Harbor Creek's football season. He seemed to be the perfect Ivy League basketball forward.

At first Paterno didn't realize how good his prospective tight end was on the basketball court. Once he found out, Paterno quickly dispatched Tom Bradley to Harbor Creek with specific instructions.

"Go up there tonight, look him in the eye, and tell him that his future is not in basketball," Paterno said.

Bradley came to a game in which Siverling exploded for 48 points, setting an Erie city record. When the Penn State assistant returned to State College, Paterno summoned Bradley to his office.

"Did you tell him?" Paterno asked.

"Uh, well, Coach, that was kind of difficult," Bradley replied.

Siverling had been offered a full ride to play basketball at William and Mary and was considering taking it. But he also had a Penn State pull. His mom had gone to Penn State, as did two of his aunts and an uncle. In the end, the prospect of playing football before nearly 100,000 fans, as opposed to playing basketball at a mid-major school such as William and Mary, won Siverling over and brought him to Penn State.

Siverling only dabbled with basketball after that. His junior year he lived in West Halls, a dormitory in close proximity to Rec Hall, Penn State basketball's home court. Conlan, who also was a high school basketball star, was Siverling's West Halls neighbor. The two Penn State football players would recruit a couple of other guys on the team who played hoops and challenge the Nittany Lions varsity basketball team in pickup games, games that were often won by Siverling's squad.

"We used to say to them, hey, we don't even do this for a living and we're kicking your ass?" Siverling recalled.

The Blue-White Game, Penn State's annual spring football extravaganza that concludes spring practice, offered no clues as to whether Shaffer or Knizner would start. As it turned out, neither did the first three weeks of autumn workouts. Paterno played a game of psychological warfare as complete as a military exercise, scrambling up both of his quarterbacks' heads until one of them solved the riddle. Shaffer called it "Classic Joe."

Neither quarterback knew which jersey he would wear from practice to practice. Sometimes Shaffer and Knizner got a first-team "green," and sometimes they got a second-team "blue"—the jersey being left in their lockers the day of practice. Neither player knew which jersey would be hanging there when he cracked open the metal doors.

Siverling saw the stress weigh heavy on his roommate. Shaffer had told his roommates about the off-season incident in the funeral home and they were incredulous. And now, days before the season was to begin, it seemed as if Shaffer had the whole world against him. Magazine and newspaper stories and sports radio shows were trashing Shaffer and touting Knizner. It was tough for Shaffer to even walk around campus without some student taking a verbal shot at him. Siverling remembered thinking how fortunate he was *not* being a quarterback, especially a quarterback of a team that was expected to contend for a national championship.

"John never really talked about it, but inside you could see it was killing him," Siverling said. "John, in a lot of our minds, had earned the right to be the starter. I mean we had only lost one game the year before. Yeah, that was a big game, but it was just one loss. And I think that all along Joe was going to start John. He just wanted to make him sweat a little."

Paterno didn't announce that Shaffer would be his starter, though, until three days before the Nittany Lions' opener against Temple. The coach didn't have a grand ceremony for the announcement. He didn't even call Shaffer into his office or contact him by telephone. The starting quarterback for a team that was coming into the season as a contender for the national championship found out just like every other starter—it was posted on an 8½ × 11 sheet of paper and tacked to the locker-room bulletin board.

It was "Classic Joe."

Shaffer, meanwhile, took the assignment in stride, knowing that it was his body of work that would be judged, not an opening-game 45–15 win over the Owls that night in which the senior from Cincinnati threw for 194 yards and a career-high three touchdowns. It was *Temple*, after all, griped the Nittany Lions faithful. In fact, it wasn't until Penn State beat Alabama that year, and then Notre Dame late in the season, that fans finally got behind John Shaffer.

The Lions beat Boston College, East Carolina, Rutgers, Cincinnati, and Syracuse before getting their first real test of the season at Tuscaloosa. Alabama was ranked No. 2 in the nation, just behind Miami, and boasted a prime-cut linebacker combo of its own with Brian Bosworth and Cornelius Bennett.

Ray Perkins, the Alabama coach, compared Bennett to Lawrence Taylor, saying that if he could put together a team, be it college or pro, Bennett would be one of the four linebackers he'd choose. Earlier in the season, in a 'Bama win over Notre Dame, Bennett had made six tackles, four behind the line of scrimmage. One of those tackles had leveled Irish quarterback Beuerlein, knocking him out of the game with a concussion.

Shaffer, the stoic, seemed unfazed by the threat in front of him. Paterno played it smart, harnessing the Nittany Lions offense so as not to play into the hands of Alabama's play-making defense. Penn State kept the ball on the ground and in the hands of Dozier, who gained 63 yards on 15 carries, and Blair Thomas, who had 57 yards on eight carries. That loosened things up enough for Shaffer, who wound up having one of the best days of his career. The Penn State QB completed 13 of 17 passes for 168 yards and threw no interceptions. On one of the Lions' touchdowns, Shaffer threw a key block on a reverse that Thomas took into the end zone.

"We felt all along that we could move the ball against them if we had the proper balance," said Shaffer afterward.

In this game, Paterno had wisely bought stock in his defense. Penn State limited Alabama to just 44 yards rushing, with dangerous Bobby Humphrey (12 carries for 27 yards) having one of the worst days of his career. The Lions won easily, 23–3.

When Penn State arrived in South Bend to play the Irish on November 16, the second-to-last game of the regular season, the Lions were 10–0 and already being mentioned as the opponent for surging Miami in a perfectly written national championship script. The Irish were in a transition year and licking wounds from a mediocre 4–4 season. But they would take Penn State to the wire and would have won the game were it not for some heroics from the Nittany Lions defense as they were backed against their own goal line on the game's final series.

Had the Lions lost, no one would have remembered that Shaffer put forth one of his most clutch performances of the season.

Penn State trailed late in the third quarter, 13–10, when Shaffer hooked up with wide receiver Ray Roundtree on a perfectly executed fly pattern for a 24-yard touchdown after Roundtree beat the Irish coverage by about 15 yards. Paterno, who mostly left the offensive calls to coordinator Fran Ganter, called this play as part of a game-long strategy.

"Joe Paterno works in mysterious ways sometimes," Shaffer said. "We had been throwing short all game long in front of the left corner. I was getting a little frustrated because I thought we could beat him long. But Joe's thing was to take it slow. Lull the kid. Don't burn a big play too early in the game. Use it when we need it and when it will definitely work. The corner bit short and Ray ran right past him."

Penn State won the game, 24–19. Beuerlein, now the Irish's starting quarterback, passed for a career high against the Lions. But he found himself on the losing end again to Shaffer, who four years prior had guided Moeller past Beuerlein's high school team.

A win the following week against Pitt made the Lions 11–0—their second straight undefeated season with only a national championship game left.

LIKE BAUER, Shaffer had also known 'Canes defensive end Dan Stubbs from high school all-star games. And, like Bauer, he thought it was peculiar that Stubbs had joined this band of renegades. He told Stubbs that he would have looked better in plain blue and white. Penn State was here to win a football game. It was as if Miami was here for some other reason and they'd just win the football game as part of the postseason experience.

There had been an orchestrated strategy for Penn State players in dealing with the media, which was to deal with it sparingly. Budd Thalman, a kindly, conservative man dressed most of the time in blue blazer and button-down oxford with striped tie, was the perfect public relations man for a school like Penn State and was on the same page as Paterno with this strategy. Thalman had limited Nittany Lion players to just two media sessions in the week that preceded the Fiesta Bowl, even though the demands called for many more. There would be no one-on-one where those crafty TV people could trap a Penn State player into saying something Miami could use against him. Thalman followed Bauer, in particular, everywhere. If he could have put a muzzle on Bauer, he would have. Thalman survived a week of Bauer without incident until that unguarded moment when Penn State's outspoken linebacker slipped though a proverbial crack and told a reporter to "bet the mortgage on Penn State."

Miami's antics during the week weren't new to the Lions.

The year before, in the Orange Bowl, Shaffer watched his counterpart, Oklahoma quarterback Jamielle Holloway, walk around the grounds with a garish purse. Keith Jackson, the Sooners' tight end, had worn a mink coat in Miami with the temperature at eighty degrees. Brian Bosworth, the crazy linebacker, had carved a thunderbolt design on the side of his crewcut. Back then, Penn State simply didn't have a strong enough team to be able to put the opposition in their place. This time they felt they did.

Paterno thought he had the proper offensive trickery to get the Lions off to a good start by throwing the football. That was all well and good until Stubbs, the kid John Shaffer thought should have been on his side, burst through on the first play of the game and buried the Penn State quarterback before he had even completed his five-step drop. Then on a third and long, Bill Hawkins sacked Shaffer. The Lions began their drive at the 30 and wound up having to punt from the 14. It was the worst possible start they could have imagined.

They knew this was a game they'd have to put together small piece by small piece in order to win.

As it turned out, Shaffer needed only to lead his team on one big offensive drive. Toward the end of the first half, he led the Lions 74 yards down the field. He completed two huge passes in the drive, the best being a 22-yard strike over the middle to wide receiver Eric Hamilton on a third and 12. He then sent Tim Manoa up the gut for 20 yards and a first down. On a third and six at the Miami 17-yard line, Shaffer rolled right and completed a pass in the flat to Manoa for 12 yards. That brought the ball to the five.

Shaffer fumbled the snap on the next play, but Darryl Giles slid in to recover it to keep Penn State's possession going. On the next play, Shaffer rolled right and desperately dove at the pylon. Miami defenders buried him there, but the Penn State quarterback broke the plane of the goal line for a touchdown to tie the game at seven. Shaffer bounced up and pumped his fist in glee. The Lions were in this game to stay.

THERE WERE 14 SECONDS on the game clock when Pete Giftopoulos stepped in front of what would be the final pass of Vinny Testaverde's college career. Gifto thought about kneeling, but the adrenaline rush wouldn't let him. Instead, he started forward with the ball, then stammered around a bit, trying to milk some clock, until he knelt down at the 10-yard line.

John Shaffer thought only about one thing: he had to kill the rest of the clock.

Most of his teammates were ashen-faced by then, their nails bitten to a nub, their thoughts lost in prayers as they watched the Hurricanes methodically march some 70 yards down the field on their final drive. Shaffer knew what was going on. But the Penn State quarterback sat on the bench far away from the madness, calculating in his head what the offense would have to do if Miami scored. If the defense somehow stopped them, he knew he had to kill the clock. The time to celebrate was when the clock finally clicked down to zeroes.

Nine seconds left in the game. Frantically, security personnel tried to clear the field of revelers. Penn State was penalized for excessive celebration and the Lions got the ball back on their own five-yard line. Shaffer was thinking only one thing: *hold onto the football*. He did. Taking the snap, he knelt. Miami had no timeouts left. The clock faded like a shooting star. Five, four, three, two. . . .

For the first time in his Penn State career, John Shaffer was carried off the field on his teammates' shoulders. Clutching the football to his pads, he looked weary and exhausted but happy. Penn State had slain the mighty. Shaffer managed to get down from the human pyramid that saluted him and sought out Testaverde.

"Great game," Shaffer said.

Other words never came. There was nothing he could tell Testaverde that would make him feel any better. Shaffer could see tremendous disappointment on his adversary's face. A lengthy NFL career and millions of dollars later, losing to Penn State would continue to gore Vinny Testaverde like a flaming arrow to the heart.

John Shaffer had been the anti-Testaverde. He was the guy with a fingernail's worth of Vinny's talent who had to expend all his energy on *not* making a mistake. That's how he played quarterback all his life. Execute the fundamentals. Football was not a game where you could afford to be careless. That's how he managed to win all those games as a starter. His teammates trusted that John Shaffer would not make a mistake, so they followed him. That's the way he wound up winning the biggest game of his life.

Unbeknownst to the Lions' coaching and training staffs, Shaffer had played the game with a mangled left hand. Three days before the Fiesta Bowl, starting offensive guard Dan Morgan had closed a car door on it.

Paterno had allowed his senior players to have rental cars for their bowl week. One night Shaffer piled into Morgan's car with Siverling and Sickler and the foursome headed to downtown Phoenix for dinner. Morgan parked the car, got out, and closed the driver's side door, thinking that Shaffer, who was seated in the back seat behind him, would exit from the passenger's side of the two-door vehicle. Shaffer, however, had started to come out the driver's side door, grabbing into the door seam for leverage. The door closed, trapping the quarterback's hand completely in that seam.

"My hand! My hand!" Shaffer screamed.

Morgan frantically tried to open the locked door, inserting his keys in the lock. Remote controls had not yet been invented. The door was stuck.

"Holy shit, we broke his hand!" Siverling screeched.

Siverling dove into the car from the other side as if he was recovering a fumble, trying to open the door with the handle, but it was still stuck. With Shaffer screaming in pain, Siverling lifted the handle and lowered his shoulder into the door, which jarred it open.

The freed Shaffer slumped to the ground. Morgan, Siverling, and Sickler were beside themselves. Should they call the coaches? Should they call the trainers? Shaffer urged them not to. He didn't want Paterno to even *consider* sitting him out of the biggest game of his life. Shaffer's left hand swelled up and there was an indentation between the first and second knuckles. But the quarterback would say later that what saved him was that his hand was perfectly flat at the impact and had almost form-fit the door seam. At the quarterback's urging, the foursome continued on with their dinner plans, with Siverling sheepishly asking the waitress, "Can you please bring us a bag of ice?"

Back at the hotel, Siverling, Morgan, and Sickler checked on their quarterback hourly, bringing him a steady supply of ice from the hallway machine. Shaffer's hand was sore for the next few days. At kickoff, Shaffer told Siverling that his hand was fine but the tight end would always wonder whether Shaffer's fumbled snap later in the contest had been influenced at all by the car door incident.

"The thing about John Shaffer was that he never showed any panic in any situation," Brian Siverling remembered. "He was just very calm in the huddle, always, and that made guys believe in him. He was an emotional guy, but he never screamed at players or anything like that. He just got in there and said, 'Okay, here's what we're going to do.' It was the way he carried himself. He was very self-confident. He was able to handle any situation that came about."

Miami cornerback Bennie Blades told a newspaper reporter that John Shaffer would not complete a pass to his side and that the Penn State offense would be incapable of moving the football against the Hurricanes. Miami drenched themselves in a hype that Penn State, especially Shaffer, saw as surreal. Besides wearing those combat fatigues, all week long they gave one bombastic interview after another. They took braggadocio to a whole new level.

David Hartman, the host of ABC's *Good Morning America*, was floating around the team's locker room as if he were a coach. Melvin Bratton worked on Hartman, imploring the TV man to give him a cohosting gig. Ex-Miami players such as Jim Kelly threw footballs around with Jerome Brown and Michael Irvin, jousting with the two players as if it were a family barbeque. Miami players posed poolside, lathered up with suntan lotion, for photographers at their posh hotel.

Years later John Shaffer would feel that the downfall of the Miami Hurricanes on January 2, 1987, came because they had spent too much energy trying to win the game before it even started.

4

A CASE FOR THE DEFENSE

JERRY SANDUSKY IS STILL DOING his best to work out a game plan.

It's summer camp season for The Second Mile, the charity for underprivileged children Sandusky started in 1977 when he was still Penn State's highly respected defensive coordinator and the man many credit for engineering a defensive game plan that smote the mighty Miami Hurricanes in the 1987 Fiesta Bowl.

From his spartan office off Business Route 322, in the shadows of the stadium he once patrolled, Sandusky organizes a schedule that keeps him busier than in any football season. Sandusky is on the road at least three days a week. When he's not organizing and administering Second Mile activities, he's stumping for contributions. Sandusky has to raise about $2 million a year to keep The Second Mile viable. And he's not about failure. In a few hours, Sandusky will be off to Lock Haven, Pennsylvania, to spend time with kids for whom roughing it in log cabins for six weeks is Xanadu since many of them come from broken homes or no homes at all. Years later, if one of his camp kids rises from these ashes to become somebody and

The lump in Jerry Sandusky's throat grew to the size of a bowling ball.

Sandusky thought Penn State had the game won. The Lions, leading 14–10, had Miami pinned way back at its own 27-yard line on a fourth down and six with just two minutes left in the game. But Vinny Testaverde completed a pass on the left sidelines to Brian Blades, and Blades whirled away from Penn State cornerback Eddie Johnson and nearly broke the play for a big gain.

And now the 'Canes had the ball, first down at the Penn State five-yard line.

Penn State's defense was confused. They looked to the sidelines for Sandusky's call. But suddenly the defensive coordinator couldn't think. He turned to defensive assistant Jim Williams and muttered, "Uh . . . same . . . uh . . . defense."

But the call came in too late. By then the players had turned away and were making their own call in the huddle. The call was wrong—Testaverde had some open receivers. But Tim Johnson broke through and sacked the Miami quarterback.

calls to tell him about it, especially if it's Father's Day, Sandusky feels as good—maybe better—than watching his defense win a national championship.

Jerry Sandusky looks terrific. He's still tall, sinewy, and vascular, even if the hair is a little grayer and thinner—a man in full in the glowing twilight of his life. At one time ambition burned at him inside to become a head football coach somewhere, instead of simply being a defensive coordinator overwhelmed by the very large aura of Joe Paterno. Now he's content to follow the coaching careers of his sons, satisfied that he's found his true calling.

In 1998 Sandusky traded in his hundred yards for The Second Mile permanently. He resigned as PSU's defensive coordinator that spring, stunning Nittany Lions fans who had come to rely on his impenetrable defenses and his notable contribution to Penn State's becoming nationally known as Linebacker U. At the time, there were whispers that Sandusky and Paterno, two strong-willed men who clashed often over the years, could no longer coexist. Stories were rampant that Paterno had given a vacuous promise to Sandusky that he'd be the next Penn State coach. As far back as 1987, pregame stories of the Fiesta Bowl had broached the subject. By 1998 speculation was that Sandusky was simply tired of waiting for the old man to go.

Jerry Sandusky smiles. It is a toothy smile, where the corners of his mouth nearly touch his earlobes and his eyes squint to nearly half their size. It is either a smile of resignation that people are going to believe what they want to believe about his relationship with Paterno and that they're probably going to want to believe the juicier story, or that there is some truth to the speculation—that by 1998 his edges with Paterno were finally frayed beyond repair and he *had* to go.

Sandusky tells it this way:

Running a charitable foundation could no longer be compromised. It needed his full-time attention. In the spring of 1998 state employees, including teachers and coaches at Penn State University, were given a retirement window during which severance and retirement packages were enhanced in order to reduce the school's overall payroll. Sandusky was torn. He spent the better part of the next couple of months thinking and consulting with friends and family. He was in the middle of teaching at Penn State's football camp when the final decision day arrived. Cold sweat poured out of Sandusky as he watched a group of youngsters hit a tackling sled. He was a thought away from abandoning a profession he had followed for some thirty years. That night he leaped. He gave up football and has never looked back.

Sandusky says that today he doesn't socialize with Paterno, but that's no big deal, he says, since the two men aren't the socializing type anyway. The last time he saw Joe, he happened to be driving on campus, looking for a parking space near the football offices en route to a workout. As he made a turn, he nearly bumped into a man walking through the lot. It was Paterno. He rolled down the window. They had a conversation. They vowed to get together soon. A vapid promise men often make to other men they have no plans to visit any time soon. That's just the way things work sometimes.

IN THE LAND OF PENN STATE FOOTBALL, there is only one king. Offensive and defensive coordinators may design the game plan. They are given total solidarity—as long as those game plans work. Joseph Vincent Paterno, who came to the school in the 1950s, is the man who has final say. If Paterno doesn't like what he sees, if something his coaches have designed isn't working, the head coach reserves the right to change things. And he does that often. Sometimes Paterno will eat up countless hours during the week working on something *he* wants to see included. Sometimes coordinators roll their eyes in displeasure because it's not something they want to see or something they feel won't work. That circumstance often frustrated Jerry Sandusky.

But in December 1986 Paterno sat kindred to Sandusky and his defensive game plan to throttle the mighty Miami Hurricanes. After viewing hours of tape on Vinny Testaverde and the Miami offense, the defensive coordinator came to a simple conclusion: Miami's skill-set was so bright, so brilliant, it would devour any conventional attempts at pass coverage.

The Lions had a major problem. Their defensive backs—corners Duffy Cobbs and Eddie Johnson—and safeties Ray Isom and Marques Henderson were tiny. They weren't that fast either. Sandusky knew that any attempts to play man-to-man coverage against the likes of All-American receivers Michael Irvin, Brian Blades, and Brett Perriman, all of whom had NFL-level talent, would be futile against Testaverde's rocket right arm. Sandusky watched his Miami game film and shook his head. He used up an entire evening watching the Hurricanes' bowl game the year before against Tennessee. He saw the Vols attempt to blitz Testaverde. And he saw that it hardly had any effect at all on the Miami quarterback.

But also on film, Sandusky saw that during the past regular season Testaverde rarely had to face adversity. His line protected. He merely sat his lanky, 6′5″ body in the pocket and waited for one of his lightning-bolt receivers to find an open space before he delivered a completion. The speed of Miami's receivers and their ability to get open seemed to widen the field for Testaverde. At times it was as if the Miami quarterback was playing Frisbee with an entire student body in a meadow. Somebody was going to catch it. What could Sandusky do to stop it? Blitz and run the risk that Testaverde would gash the Lions with a big pass play down the field with the Lions in man-to-man coverage in which they were overmatched? Sit back in a deep zone and watch Vinny wait for his receivers to clear into a seam of that zone before he unloaded the dart?

"The nights I watched a lot of Miami film were the nights I didn't get a lot of sleep," Sandusky said.

It was time for something different, something innovative. Sandusky knew it. The Penn State defensive coordinator was about to throw caution to a Hurricane wind.

What Penn State had was a group of linebackers who were tough, smart, and quick. Led by the irrepressible Conlan, it was a four-man group—along with Bauer, Giftopoulos, and Don Graham—quick enough to close on a ball carrier but also capable of dropping back in pass coverage. And so the formula was born. Sandusky's defense against Miami would have six, sometimes seven, Nittany Lions in pass coverage—the four defensive backs and up to three linebackers. When Testaverde looked downfield, he would find suddenly that white and orange jerseys were just specs amidst a sea of blue.

Sandusky had only a month to install a whole new highly complicated defensive game plan. But he counted on the experience and guile of this upperclassmen-laden team to catch on quickly. The defensive coordinator became a mathematician and created a new numbers system. Penn State's base defensive calls became attached with elaborate prefixes and suffixes, but they were all based on this simple premise: If Miami lined up one way, Penn State would station itself accordingly. If Testaverde lined up two or even three receivers on a certain side, Penn State defenders would also flood that side. The Lions would have a base defense. But there would be a series of prefixes and suffixes attached to the base defensive call, called by safety Ray Isom, all designed to make the Penn State defense adjust on the fly. Sometimes, Sandusky figured, Conlan would play his own little game of hide-and-seek. He'd line up *behind* Bauer. When Vinny surveyed the defense before the snap, he'd only see three linebackers. Then, at the snap, Conlan would flare out as stealthy as a panther to the side of the field he sensed Testaverde wanted to throw and either disrupt the play or make the interception. That was Conlan utilizing the prefix that Isom had just called.

The Lions would show Miami this new defense only a little at a time. They'd start the game with base defense. In the second quarter, they'd add a few wrinkles. In the third and fourth, they'd show a little more.

Would the new math work? Sandusky didn't know. What he did know was that the master plan wouldn't even get off the ground unless two things happened. First his defensive backs—Isom, Henderson, Cobbs, and Johnson—had to blast the Miami receivers when they were attempting to make catches. Second, his defensive front, rushing only three players—Tim Johnson, Mike Russo, and Bob White—needed to get *some* pressure on the passer. It was a gamble. But because his players were so smart and so experienced, it was a gamble Sandusky was comfortable taking.

BOB WHITE HAD THE MOST CIRCUITOUS ROUTE to Penn State of anybody on the Nittany Lions' eighty-man roster.

White was one of eight children in the migrant workers' town of Haines City, Florida, about a half-hour southwest of Orlando. Before the Walt Disney Company purchased much of the middle part of the state, Haines City was an underdeveloped area that lured masses to low-paying farming jobs like picking oranges or tobacco leaves. White lived in a melting pot among poor blacks, Native Americans, Hispanics, and the Caucasians who were carelessly labeled "white trash." Raised by his mother and grandmother, Bob White carried his father's last name but never met him.

He was on his way to becoming just another statistic until a guardian angel happened upon his life, a white man whom White considers just as much a part of his family as any of his siblings. Like many easterners who tired of the cold winters, Bob Eisenberg, a Pittsburgher, had come to Florida looking for the sun and a good teaching job. He got a job teaching fifth grade in a school where Bob White was a student and quickly took a special liking to the boy. White was a good kid in a bad socioeconomic situation. Eisenberg wanted better for him.

After a few years in Florida, Bob Eisenberg received an offer to return to the Pittsburgh area and teach at Freeport High, his alma mater. Eisenberg accepted the job, but as he relocated north he made sure he stayed in contact with White.

By his freshman year in high school, Bob White had become another one of Florida's pedigreed athletes. He was growing big and swift and pretty much conquered any sport he tried. Eisenberg had an idea: He was willing to become White's guardian if the kid was willing to move to Pennsylvania, where his educational and athletic opportunities might be better.

At Freeport High, Bob White would become a football star. By the end of his senior year, White had offers from Ohio State, Georgia, Florida State, South Carolina, and Pittsburgh, but he wanted desperately to come to Happy Valley. Paterno was slightly leery of whether White could cut it academically at Penn State, but he cut him a deal. If he could make progress through a summer of tutoring with the coach's wife, Sue Paterno, reading and understanding literary classics the head coach had loved—*Moby Dick* and *Lord Jim,* Chaucer and Hemingway and Faulkner—Bob White could have a Penn State scholarship. White buried himself in those books that summer. By the fall he earned a spot on the Nittany Lions varsity.

LIKE MANY OF HIS TEAMMATES AND COACHES, Bob White marveled at how gifted the 1986 Hurricanes looked on film. Though they came into the 1987 Fiesta Bowl undefeated, White and the Lions knew they hadn't played against anybody with Testaverde's ability. During that month of preparation, it was hammered into the defensive linemen's heads that they could not let Testaverde get outside their rush. *Take the rush up field, not inside. Don't let Miami's offensive tackles push you inward.* If Testaverde was going to break out of the pocket, Lions defensive coaches wanted him do it up the middle, where Bauer and Graham waited to pounce.

But White saw something else on tape. He saw that Miami hadn't been in nearly as many tense battles as the Nittany Lions. Like a prizefighter who gives up the early rounds while finding his stride, Penn State was conditioned to go the distance no matter how long the defense had to be on the field. They had just been though that kind of a war with Notre Dame. They weren't going to go away no matter how much Miami tried to break them with its silly pregame shenanigans or its early game success.

White, trained as a highly skilled football player but also an academic, thought it peculiar that the Hurricanes would expend so much energy on nonsense. When the teams arrived in Tempe, the Fiesta Bowl committee sent welcoming committees to the tarmac. As the players walked down the stairs of the plane, they were given packs of oranges. Miami players boarded their bus on the tarmac, immediately pulled down the windows, and started throwing oranges at committee members, immediately introducing themselves as incorrigibles who, as if in the Old West, had come to take over the town. In retrospect, White thinks the Hurricanes were trying to overcome an insecurity complex as if they knew deep inside they didn't have the heart to win a street fight and tried to get by instead executing a bullying facade.

"I think they were used to talking a lot of their opposition out of the game before it even started," White says. "It didn't dawn on them that it wasn't going to work on us until it was too late."

FROM THE SIDELINES OF SUN DEVIL STADIUM, Ray Isom, Penn State's feisty strong safety, watched the Penn State offense try to execute simple plays against Miami's defense in the early moments of the national championship game and in his head formed a rather succinct suggestion: *Punt the ball on first down; at least that way we won't lose any yards!*

Isom's thoughts were symbolic of the division between Penn State's offense and defense. The derision between the two units was akin to a civil war, a battle between castes. The defense, composed of stalwarts such as Isom and Conlan and Bauer, and Johnson and White collectively felt that they were the superior entity of this nationally ranked team and that most of the time the offense didn't pull its share of the load. Because the offense had trouble all year consistently moving the football, because it didn't possess any quick-strike ability and most scoring drives had to be the grind-it-out kind, the defense felt that it was its responsibility to, well, constantly save the team's ass.

In practice, Isom and his mates tried often to punish the first-team offense. In the defensive huddle, Isom would instruct his mates sternly, "Don't even let them get a first down!"

It was an insult to the defense if it gave up a first down to Shaffer's offense. They would go as hard at the quarterback and his teammates in practice as they would against an opponent on a Saturday afternoon. It was as if the defense was screaming in desperation to the offense to pick up their pace. A few defensive players had become increasingly frustrated by Dozier's nagging injuries, ones that often kept him out of practice. They'd see Dozier run like a locomotive in games and wondered why these nagging injuries would constantly bog him down. It was wrong to question their star running back's heart, they knew, but they wanted him *out there*. Isom sometimes would say, loud enough for the coaches on the sidelines to hear, "Man, let Blair Thomas carry more; every time he's in there, the offense does something!" Prohibited from hitting Shaffer because of the hands-off red jersey he and all the quarterbacks wore, they'd go hard after Dozier to make a point. Only after a little of this would Paterno call off the dogs, instead making the first-team offense go against the *second*-team defense. That left the unlucky Knizner and his second-team offense to face the hungry wolves led by Isom and Conlan.

Ray Isom was Penn State football's incorrigible. Fiercely independent, with a chip on his shoulder the size of a football and a pig-headedness that bordered on belligerence, he battled constantly. In practice. In games. With teammates. And, perhaps most often, against the Penn State coaching governance. He'd test them constantly.

Isom did not enjoy lifting weights. He thought it was too boring. At the team's mandatory weekday weight sessions, the strong safety would mostly goof around and laugh at the offensive lineman grunts who strained under the heft of a bench press or squat. When assistant coaches approached Isom, telling him that weight-lifting was indeed part of the necessary process that would help him better develop as a football player, Isom battered them back over the head with logic: *Well, I never even lifted one weight in high school and you guys thought I was good enough to play here then.*

During Isom's junior year in 1985, perhaps because of the rebel reputation he helped cultivate, he was tagged as the leader of a defensive team practice walkout. It was late in the season. The Nittany Lions were headed to a major bowl, perhaps one that would determine a national championship. But many of the players, especially those on defense, were banged up and looking forward to a light Thursday practice of no hitting, as was their routine. But on this day, Paterno had thrown his team a curve ball, having them in full pads for a full-contact practice. One by one, defensive players came to Isom, pleading their case for relief.

Duffy Cobbs was hobbling on a bum ankle. "Ray, I'm not going to be able to make it." Cobbs pleaded.

"Do the best you can, Duff," Isom told him.

"But why are we practicing?" Cobbs wondered.

A few minutes later it was Conlan who came to Isom. "I'm done, Ray. I'm hurting."

Isom was done, too. He was hurting worse than Cobbs or Conlan.

Cobbs suggested that the defense just take it into the locker room. Fatigue had started to win out over responsibility. The entire defense up and walked off the field! The Penn State coaches just watched. The offensive coaches assumed that the defensive coaches were giving their guys a break. The defensive coaches assumed that Paterno had given the order himself. When the Nittany Lion coaches finally figured out the truth of the matter, the coaches ascended on the showers, berating the players with bile Isom had never heard before.

The next day Paterno called Isom into his office. "Did you lead the walkout?" Paterno asked.

Isom told him no.

"Who did?"

Isom told his coach that *who* didn't matter. What mattered was that the team was tired and hurt and as a group decided that it was something they had to do in order to be healthy enough to play the game on Saturday.

"But, Ray, why didn't you go to the trainers?" Paterno asked.

"That wouldn't have done any good," Isom replied.

"Why?"

"Because I knew what the trainers would have told me; they only tell us what you want them to tell us," Isom said.

"And what's that?"

"To tough it out."

Paterno shook his head and smiled.

RAY ISOM ARRIVED ON the Penn State campus in August 1983 from just down the road in Harrisburg. It was a place he had never expected to be.

Isom had always desired to enlist in the Air Force. He was fascinated by airplanes and saw himself in the cockpit of a jet, darting through clouds and looking through the acres and down at the trees and mountains he hadn't seen growing up in urban Harrisburg. *This is your captain, Ray Isom. If you look down below, you will see the mean streets where I grew up.* But Ray Isom was too good in sports and was also good in the classroom. Like his brothers before him, he would go to college. A father who had grown up dirt-poor, who as a youngster had to go to work to support his family and had never gotten the chance for college, was determined to give that gift to his children.

Ray was the middle child, the youngest of three Isom boys who grew up amidst a clan of Isoms on and around Walnut Street, a typical inner-city street of row-homes directly across the street from a gas station that had become infamous for perishing in a fierce and fiery explosion during a racial riot in the late 1960s involving the Black Panthers. Ray and his family lived at 1412 Walnut. His grandmother was at 1425. His aunt stayed at 1522. Around the corner from Ray Isom's house lived several more aunts. The Isom sandlot games could almost go eleven on eleven with cousins.

Isom's dad, Marion Isom, had grown up in Brooklyn, but each summer he would migrate south to work the tobacco farms of North Carolina and send money back north to help support his family. Years later Marion would meet his wife, Winnie, in Carolina. They married and a couple of years later headed back up north with Winnie's extended family to Harrisburg, where there was work for Marion Isom in the Hershey chocolate factories.

Ray's oldest brother, Marion Jr., 6′1″ and 190 pounds, was the first of the boys to roll off the Isom athletic assembly line, getting a full ride to Purdue as a running back. Ricky, 6′, 225, was a bruising fullback who got a scholarship to North Carolina State and would wind up playing briefly in the NFL. Ray was shorter, lighter, and more squat and, like his brothers before him, became a star football player at Harrisburg High. But the comparisons to his brothers covered him like a Harrisburg frost. He wasn't as fast as Marion. He wasn't as powerful as Ricky. Isom coated his insecurities with a hard-shell finish. He needed to protect *his* turf. He became obstinate, reclusive. "All I wanted to do was play the game," Isom said. "I tried the best I could. I wasn't any of my brothers. I was just me."

Still, Ray Isom became a star. On offense at Harrisburg High, he was an option quarterback. Harrisburg coach John Johnson had converted him from running back because Isom was simply the smartest guy on the field. But it was on defense that the major colleges had noticed him. Isom made up for a lack of size—he was 5′8″, 170 pounds—by being a shutdown cornerback and a killer tackler. More than that he had an innate ability to know what the offense was going to do; he seemed to be in the right place all the time.

Years later, Jerry Sandusky would lament the fact that he had not realized how good of a football player Ray Isom was until later in Isom's Penn State career. As soon as Sandusky gave the kid from Harrisburg an increased role, the Nittany Lions defense took off.

Isom had been ambivalent about attending Penn State. The school recruited him, but Isom didn't think they recruited him hard enough. To Isom, it seemed as if Penn State's chief recruiter at the time, defensive assistant Tom Bradley, saw him as an afterthought—only when he was passing through Harrisburg's airport en route to recruiting a bigger-name player. Most high school stars growing up in the shadows of Penn State *dreamed* of playing in Happy Valley. But Ray Isom, who had been fighting all his athletic life for identity, wanted Penn State to find *him* special, not the other way around.

In addition to his general ambivalence about State, there was pressure on Isom from many Harrisburg townies *not* to go there. People in Harrisburg held a long-standing grudge against Penn State. The last black star the city had sent there, a quarterback from the late 1960s named Michael Cooper, had never gotten a fair shot to play. Cooper was a starter briefly, but he wound up being replaced by a white quarterback with half Cooper's talent, Bob Parsons, and then later by a sophomore named John Hufnagel. The Isoms routinely got lectured on the streets or received letters at their home—mostly from people they didn't know—suggesting that Penn State discriminated racially in its athletic programs. Marion and Winnie Isom didn't pay much attention to that, but the circumstance certainly didn't make Ray Isom long for Happy Valley any more than for any other school that recruited him.

Meanwhile, Boston College, whose coach, Jack Bicknell, was in the early stages of rebuilding the Eagles into an eastern power, was making a strong play for Isom. BC recruiters came to Isom's home. They came to his school. They made Isom feel *wanted*. The night before the national letter of intent signing date in February, Bradley, assuming he had Isom locked up, called to say he was faxing Isom's letter of intent to the school the next day for him to sign. Bicknell had already told Isom that he would *bring* the letter to Harrisburg High. Isom told Bradley not to bother. The other school wanted him more. He was going to Boston College. And that's what he told Bicknell that night.

The next day at school Isom was called out of class to the principal's office. Waiting for him there were Paterno, Bradley, and Isom's parents. Ray couldn't ever remember his dad taking off even one day of work in deference to his football career. But here he was, wearing a suit and sitting in the school office with Joe Paterno.

Bradley called Ray Isom over to the side. "See how serious we are, Ray?" the assistant coach said. "When Joe comes down, it ain't no joke."

Within ten minutes, Isom was convinced. He told Paterno that he'd sign a letter of intent to go to Penn State, but that right this minute he had to get back to sociology class since he had already missed a lot of that class because of football and the teacher was determined to sanction Isom for any more absences.

"Don't worry about it, Ray," the principal told him. But Isom didn't even trust his own principal and ran back to class.

Several minutes later there was a knock on the classroom door. Through the glass of the door, Isom and his classmates could see Joe Paterno with the Harrisburg High principal. *Excuse me, sir, but your student Ray Isom has to leave for a few moments to sign a letter of intent to play football at Penn State University.* Floored by Paterno's presence, the teacher excused Isom for the rest of the class.

That's how Ray Isom became a Nittany Lion. But he was about to be judged guilty of neglect. In the confusion, he had forgotten to inform Bicknell, who was on his way down to Harrisburg from Chestnut Hill, Massachusetts, to get Isom's name on a BC letter of intent. Coach Johnson tracked down Isom in the gymnasium after Bicknell arrived at the school.

"Coach, tell him I'm not here," Isom said.

"You've got to face up to this and tell him yourself," Johnson told Isom sternly.

A couple of minutes later Isom found Bicknell, walked up to him sheepishly and delivered the bad news. The Boston College coach was aghast.

"What? Ray, this is not what we talked about. You gave me your word. People have to stand up to their word," Bicknell told Isom.

Then the Boston College coach tried to salvage things. "All right, don't worry about it," he said to Isom. "We can get that letter annulled. We can go to the NCAA and explain the letter was something you really didn't want to sign and you got pressured."

"No, Coach, I'm sorry, I want to go to Penn State," Isom said.

Bicknell exploded. "That's just disrespectful, Ray! I'll tell you what—when we play you guys, you'd better strap it up. Because we're going to knock your head off!"

Isom felt horrible and not because he feared getting his head knocked off when Penn State played Boston College; Jack Bicknell was a good man and didn't deserve the treatment he had just gotten. A few minutes later Bicknell was gone. While Isom could breathe a little easier, he remembered not being able to sleep very well that night.

RAY ISOM COULD NEVER REMEMBER himself crying after any athletic contest, but he cried the night Penn State got pasted by Oklahoma in the 1986 Orange Bowl. It wasn't the loss that hurt him, but the devastation he had felt for senior teammates. He had wanted it badly, especially for Mike Zordich, Penn State's tough-as-nails strong safety, who had been Isom's mentor. Penn State had been so close to winning a national championship. Isom knew the Nittany Lions would be a contender again the following year. But Zordich would no longer be with them. That's the way it goes in college football. Guys come and go. But Isom cursed the cruel twist of fate.

Still, the Nittany Lions came into the 1986 regular season determined to erase the Oklahoma mistake. They used the loss as fuel for their preparation. Spring workouts were intense. Players solidified their bonds as teammates. Many of them stayed through the summer term to work out.

While there was little question that the Lions' best defensive player was Shane Conlan, there was also no doubt that Isom was that unit's leader. He may have been an incorrigible, but Ray Isom was also a guy with whom you went to war.

When preseason workouts started in August, Isom was laid up in Centre Community Hospital in State College with a severe case of bronchitis. He spent two days there, just enough time to miss the Lions' vaunted time trials, which measured the players' physical condition through a series of timed runs. When Isom *did* return, coaches told him he was not exempt from the running exercises.

Isom flat-out told the coaches he wasn't running. It wasn't his fault he had been in the hospital with bronchitis. Ron Dickerson, the Lions' defensive backfield coach, told Isom he *had* to run or he wouldn't play in the Lions' first game of the season against Temple. It was an idle threat, Isom reasoned. He knew the coaches *had* to play him. He was the best D-back they had. To make him run, in Isom's mind, would be unfair. He wasn't about to give in—a circumstance that was noticed by Isom's teammates.

Conlan stepped in. He grabbed Bob White. "Come on, Ray, we'll run with you," Conlan said.

What could have been an issue dissolved in seconds. Isom ran with Conlan and White in tow. It was an example of a togetherness that would serve the Nittany Lions well.

Jerry Sandusky trusted Ray Isom to be his coach on the field. The defensive coordinator appreciated the fact that his tiny free safety was like a kamikaze pilot. He had learned the requisite amount of craziness from Bauer. Sandusky recalled one particular practice when Isom eased up on a backup receiver named Herb Bellamy, who just happened to be Isom's best friend on the team. Bellamy had come over the middle and turned back toward the quarterback to locate the ball coming his way. Rather than crack him, Isom yelled, "You'd better not catch that, Herb!" Bellamy wound up dropping the ball, but that wasn't good enough for Bauer.

"What the fuck are you doing?" Bauer yelled at Isom. "You have no friends out here on this football field, do you hear me? No friends! Hit him next time!"

But Sandusky also knew that Isom was smarter than he was crazy.

The way Penn State called its defense was this: Sandusky would signal something to Bauer, who would make that call in the Lions' defensive huddle. Then, depending on what set the opposing offense was in, Isom had license to call an audible. Part of what went into the safety's final decision was the physical condition of his teammates at that particular part of the game. Conlan had been banged up all year. Isom knew it. And Conlan wasn't foolishly proud enough to withhold his weakness from Isom. Sandusky's call had sophisticated terminology that would cover both a pass and a run. Isom would see the formation and pare down the terminology to focus on what he read as *either* a pass or run. Then, if Conlan told him he was hurting, Isom would compensate even more to make sure the Lions had adequate manpower to Conlan's side. Mostly it was Isom, the strong safety, who would cover up for *everybody*.

But who would cover up for Isom if *he* was hurting? Nobody on the Lions defense really thought much about that. The Penn State defensive players relied on Ray Isom as near invincible, much like children rely on their fathers. He was *always* there for them. He was indestructible.

Against Cincinnati that year, Isom went low to make a tackle on a Bearcat ball carrier. The running back's cleat ripped open a gash near Isom's left eye, which caused the skin to distort in such a way that the Penn State safety's eyelid curled up into its socket like a released window shade. Lying prone, Isom heard a Cincinnati offensive lineman yelp, "Oh, my God, his eye's out!"

That triggered a panic in Isom. "My eye's out, my eye's out!" he screamed in terror. A trainer rushed to the field and pulled his eyelid back down.

"Oh God, thank you! I can see!" Isom yelled.

They took Isom out of the game after that play. It was the third quarter, and Cincinnati, a double-digit underdog, scored a touchdown to tie the game at 14–14. A subsequent field goal gave the Bearcats a 17–14 lead, and suddenly the Nittany Lions were in danger of blowing their undefeated season and a chance to win a national championship in just their fifth game of the season. The gash on Isom's eye was nasty. It would require at least ten stitches. He appeared to be done for the game, but his Penn State teammates kept beseeching him on the sidelines to play.

Isom went to the team doctor. "Can I play with this?" he asked.

"Let me send the surgeon over," the doctor said.

Minutes later, Isom was getting stitched up, right there on the sidelines. The surgeon reattached Isom's eyelid with two butterfly bandages so it wouldn't roll up again. He came back into the game and immediately announced to his defensive mates, "Look, we have to score. The offense isn't doing anything. Cincinnati is going to be smart. They're going to hold the ball. We have to get a fumble, an interception. We can't give them a first down!"

The issue was settled when, with five minutes left, Blair Thomas, in the game because either Dozier had aggravated a groin strain or Paterno had lost faith in his star running back, came out of the backfield and converted a swing pass for 32 yards on a third down and 10, getting the ball to the Cincinnati 11. Two plays later, David Clark punched in a touchdown. The defense, with Isom back in tow, then solidified the win when Conlan blocked a punt for a safety with just 1:15 remaining.

An example of Isom's autonomy would come later in the season. Against Alabama, Cobbs, who as Isom's roommate had the most clout with the free safety, had responsibility to cover 'Bama's tight end. But he noticed the tight end was being primarily used as a blocker and had rarely gone out in pattern. Cobbs wanted a shot at Tide quarterback David Shula on a cornerback blitz.

"Ray, the tight end's not releasing," Cobbs said excitedly. "I'm blitzing."

What Isom saw, though, was the inexperience of Lions strong safety Marques Henderson, the player who had replaced Zordich. Henderson was the second youngest of Penn State's defensive backs. Perhaps because he judged him as not being worthy of Zordich's standards, and perhaps because, frankly, Isom didn't like Henderson that much, Isom didn't trust him. Henderson, Isom thought, was too cocky and hadn't yet earned his stripes to be so cocky. There was also a social reason. The year before, a Penn State defensive player had had a couple of dates with a Penn State coed. The relationship didn't work out. Isom found out that Henderson, weeks later, had moved in to date the same girl. That was a no-no in Isom's book. It was a classic "man" rule. You just didn't date a girl who had previously dated a friend. You shouldn't do that to *anybody*, much less a teammate. That showed no character, Isom reasoned. You couldn't really trust a guy who would do that.

Isom turned to Cobbs. "Duff, you can't blitz! I've got to help Marques on that side."

"But, Ice, I can get to this guy!" Cobbs insisted.

Isom compromised. "All right, let's do this: if the tight end lines up on this side, signal to me and I'll give you the okay to go," Isom said.

As Alabama broke the huddle, its tight end lined up on the side that made the Tide vulnerable to a Cobbs blitz. Isom gave his buddy the signal to go. But on second glance, Isom noticed that 'Bama had also placed two wide receivers also on that side of the field. Penn State would be shorthanded in a pass pattern without a corner on that side of the field! But it was too late to change the call. Conlan came to the rescue by flattening the flanker, taking one receiver completely out of the play. The Lions wound up with double coverage on just one wide receiver. With nowhere to throw, Shula succumbed to Cobbs's sack.

"Duffy comes up to me after the play and yells, 'See, Ray, I told you I could get him!'" Isom recalled. "I said, 'Man, shut up and get back in the huddle. And go over and give Shane a kiss on your way there.'"

There was never any doubt about Isom being in charge.

Against Notre Dame, the epic that Penn State survived in South Bend late in the season, Isom even won out over Sandusky. Penn State's defensive coordinator had long been an admirer of Irish coach Lou Holtz and his clever and oft-unexpected offensive twists. In turn, Sandusky had studied Notre Dame tapes diligently to round out his knowledge of how to defend against his opponent. One constant of Holtz's sets, however, was that when Notre Dame set up with two wide receivers on one side of the field, the ND coach invariably placed the tight end on the opposite side. Sandusky game-planned a corner blitz for this formation, with linebacker Giftopoulos sliding up to cover the tight end.

But as Notre Dame broke into this formation, Holtz unexpectedly shifted a wide receiver to the tight-end side. That receiver was dangerous speedster Tim Brown, who was having a brilliant junior season—he would win the Heisman Trophy the following year. Suddenly, panic gripped Giftopoulos, who knew he'd be considerably overmatched in covering Brown.

"Isom!" Gifto yelled, asking for help.

But Isom had already made a call for the other side of the field.

"No!" Isom said back to Giftopoulos.

"No? Ice!" Gifto screamed in terror.

Isom ignored him.

Giftopoulos looked over to the sidelines to Sandusky for help. Sandusky took off his headsets and walked away, knowing there was nothing he could do to alter Isom's insolence. The ball was snapped and Brown took off, Giftopoulos trailing like a rhino trying to catch a cheetah. It would have been a touchdown, except that Bob White sacked Steve Beuerlein. Gifto hasn't forgiven Sandusky or Isom yet.

With Sandusky putting in about one hundred different varieties of defense for the upcoming national championship game against Miami, Isom knew he'd be in study hall for a straight month. He had to know Miami's formations up and down, which meant hours in the film room. Those film sessions with Sandusky usually lasted well into the night. The defensive coordinator, once he felt Isom had learned the new defenses he was putting in, as well as Miami's formations, tested him constantly.

"All right, Ray," Sandusky would begin, "Miami is coming out three wide, with one back, and they're at their own 40-yard line. What are you calling?"

It went on like that.

While these sessions fueled Isom's knowledge, they also tweaked his competitiveness. He and Cobbs were watching film one night and they both saw Irvin go into the stands to celebrate after he had caught a touchdown pass.

"Man, lemme tell you something: if Michael Irvin goes up into the stands on me, I'm going right after him," Cobbs sniffed.

"You can't go after him, Duff," Isom replied. "That's a penalty. Joe will have a fit."

"All right, then we just can't let them have any touchdown passes," Cobbs said.

This defensive backfield may have been up against their most daunting task of the year, facing the Heisman Trophy quarterback and his band of soon-to-be-NFL receivers, but they sure as hell weren't going to be embarrassed.

Isom became so obsessed with Penn State's defensive game plan that when the team finally got to Tempe, he never took part in any of the activities Fiesta Bowl organizers had staged for the teams. That would only have taken away some of his study time. He heard about all of Miami's pregame antics and it only made him want to study harder, to leave no stone unturned. If Isom had any say in the matter, the Miami Hurricanes were going to be in for the fight of their lives.

The way Penn State's defensive backs saw it, Sandusky had designed the simple yet perfect game plan. The idea was to confuse Testaverde and, if he completed a pass, they would make the receiver pay. It wasn't as if Isom and his mates thought Testaverde was dumb, but they knew he hadn't had to make many involved decisions all year. Teams didn't make him think. They allowed him to just sit back there and wait for one of his wunderkinder to break open. In this game Isom and his mates were determined to make Vinny make adjustments on his adjustments. With a play clock blinking in his face down to single digits and then to five, four, three, two, one, that was going to be difficult even for a Heisman Trophy winner.

In the Fiesta Bowl's early moments, Isom and Testaverde played an interesting game of chess. Vinny brought Miami to the line and looked over the Penn State defense. He called an audible. Isom countered with an audible of his own, putting four Penn State defensive backs across in a straight line. Vinny called an audible on his audible. Isom countered with an audible that put Penn State into a two-deep set. In frustration, Testaverde called time-out. Isom started jumping up and down.

"Yeah! Yeah!" he yelped. "I got him! He's stupid!"

Often, Testaverde would read a Penn State corner and think he had an open receiving area. But just before the snap, Isom would change the defense. *What's that linebacker doing there now? He wasn't there before. Where did he come from?* Testaverde's brain must have been in a mad scramble. That was the whole idea. Isom was still studying the beefed-up defensive playbook on the sidelines *during* the game because Sandusky was putting in new stuff each quarter. Miami was good at making adjustments from the booth. The idea was that once the Hurricanes caught on to what Penn State was doing defensively, the Lions wouldn't be doing that anymore and would instead be on to something else.

Go right through them. That was the DB's mantra—even on plays where they weren't directly involved. If Miami ran a screen pass and a receiver tried to run interference, just come up and blast them. Make them know that every play for them was going to be physical. Early in the game, Testaverde tried to connect with Irvin on a short pass to the right sideline. Cobbs latched onto Irvin and drilled him into the sidelines. Eddie Johnson, the sophomore who was the defensive backfield's youngest player, saw what Cobbs had just done and said to himself, *Oh, this is the way it's going to be. Okay. I see.*

A little later, in the middle of the field, Isom gathered a head of steam and cracked into Irvin, breaking up the pass. It was the same Irvin who before the game had looked down at Isom and snickered at his size. Isom looked down at the prone Irvin and said, "How'd that feel, superstar?!"

Oh, there was trash-talking galore despite Paterno imploring his team *not* to get involved in that with Miami. The Lions just made sure that their old-school head coach didn't hear any of it. Brett Perriman came across the middle on one play and Isom nailed him, knocking the wind out of the Hurricanes wide receiver. He stayed down on the ground for a few moments. Isom knew that Perriman had a brother who played defense for the 'Canes. He came close to the Miami sideline and yelled loud enough for Perriman's brother to hear, "Yo, other Perriman, you better come and git yo' brother! He ain't gettin' up!"

Finally, when Pete Giftopoulos had intercepted Testaverde's final pass and the game was over, Isom went berserk. Though emotionally and physically spent, Isom summoned one more charge, ran up and down the Miami sideline, faced the Hurricane fans, and screamed, "Take that!"

Sportsmanship? After witnessing a week of fatigue clothes, barbeque walkouts, and an opponent that clearly looked down on them, Isom wasn't about to consider that premise.

The way Ray Isom saw it, Miami got what it deserved.

THE MAN WHO MADE the most famous interception in Penn State football history lives in relative obscurity these days caught up, as most of us are, in a transition of life that searches for what is next. Pete Giftopoulos wanders from Pennsylvania to his native Canada through various jobs and college classes, recovering from a divorce and dealing with a family separated.

He played for several years in the Canadian Football League with his hometown Hamilton Tiger Cats. A food and hotel management major at Penn State, he ran his own eatery (Gifto's Family Restaurant in Hamilton) for a while. He spent a few years back at Penn State, living in a tiny apartment and deferring his expenses as the apartment complex's maintenance man while he took some classes to pursue a career in kinesiology.

He has tried to put "The Game" and "The Interception" in his past because he knows glory moments like that can weigh one down. But he does get a kick out of the moments when his two young children in school in Pittsburgh are asked by their teachers on the first day of class, "Giftopoulos? Are you any relation to Pete Giftopoulos from Penn State?"

"My kids only know me as the fat guy who's their dad," Giftopoulos says. "When someone brings up the fact that I played football at Penn State, they get a little shocked. But all of a sudden, I become a bigger deal in their eyes."

It's self-deprecating humor. It's what Giftopoulos has always done—now and when he made up one-fourth of perhaps the best linebacking corps Penn State ever had. He was the Canuck from Hamilton, Ontario, Canada, where people talked funny and played a funny brand of football. Giftopoulos was the insult sponge of the 1986 Penn State Nittany Lions, the one who kept everybody loose because he could take the jabs and bounce back a smile at them.

They mocked his accent, putting "eh?" on the end of every sentence they said to him. They even called him "Gifto Eh?" Whenever any teammate, especially that wiseacre Bauer, spotted Giftopoulos on campus they would serenade him with a bad version of "Illegal Alien," a popular song at the time by Phil Collins. They would kid him about his long, moppy hair, which he'd have trimmed only when he went back to Canada because his dad was a barber and he could get a cut for free. Gifto couldn't understand how barbers in the States could charge eight bucks for a clip. Those eight bucks could buy a couple of six-packs of a good Canadian beer.

They kidded Gifto because they loved him.

So how did a kid from Hamilton, Ontario, come to be a starting linebacker who made the game-saving play on a national championship team at Penn State? Pete Giftopoulos likes to think he orchestrated it all along.

American college football recruiters have a tendency to look skeptically at Canadian footballers. The rules are different. There are more players on the field. The field is wider. It's just a little too odd for the pigskin purist. But all of the above seemed to work in Giftopoulos's favor.

First of all, he had visibility. Because his hometown was also home to one of the country's most popular football teams, people with American football pedigrees surrounded him. Back then a Canadian football roster was filled with players from the States, especially the skill positions. Those players and many of the teams' coaches had friends who coached at major college programs.

Giftopoulos had already stood out for his ability. He was a 6′3″, 240-pound defensive lineman who flew all over the vast Canadian football field tracking down ball carriers and receivers. If he could do that up there, where the field was wider and longer, he could surely do that down here. Besides that, he was just a great athlete. Giftopoulos also starred in basketball. His high school team from Hamilton competed in tournaments throughout the States. In a tournament in Cumberland, Maryland, Hamilton lost by just a basket to highly ranked DeMatha High from Washington, D.C., the same school that would produce his future teammate Steve Smith.

Recruiting in big-time college football is a phenomenon not unlike a spreading wildfire. Once a player gets on the radar of a big-time football school, others soon come running. Because Hamilton was not that far from Buffalo, New York, where Penn State had recruited Conlan, Giftopoulos was on recruiting lists of many schools in the Northeast corridor. But for Pete Giftopoulos, recruiters also came from Georgia, Arizona, and Washington State. He had decided he would stay as close to home as possible and narrowed his final recruiting list to three: Penn State, Michigan, and Syracuse. Then Giftopoulos studied hard to figure which of those three programs had the best chance to win a national championship in the next few years.

Giftopoulos loved Syracuse, but the Orangemen were not yet at a top level. Michigan was one of the best football programs in the country, but the Wolverines were locked into the Rose Bowl, where each year they played against a team from the Pac-10. That, Gifto felt, restricted their ability to win a national title. Penn State, meanwhile, had just won a national championship in 1983. The program was hearty. And they were also known as Linebacker U. That was *his* position. So, Penn State would be his school.

It turned out to be harder for Giftopoulos to find a home at linebacker at Penn State than to survive a Canadian winter. Paterno played him on the defensive line at first then moved him to tight end later in his freshman season to fill a spot vacated by an injured player. Gifto had heard from someone inside the football department that tight end was where the Penn State coaches had decided to keep him. He went to see Paterno.

"Coach, if I would have wanted to be a receiver, I would have gone to BYU," Giftopoulos told Paterno, intending the remark to be a joke.

But Paterno was a bit put off. Who was Pete Giftopoulos, this green kid from Canada who hadn't yet earned his place on the Penn State team, to snipe at one of the greatest college football coaches in history? Even if the comment was just meant to be a quip. If Gifto wanted to be a linebacker, then he was going to have to earn it.

One of Penn State's practice drills involved a linebacker standing some four yards away from an offensive lineman. When a coach blew the whistle, the two players engaged in a mano a mano head-banging. When it was Giftopoulos's turn, Paterno perched his offensive lineman—usually Todd Moules or Mitch Ferrotte, the two most intense bulls the Penn State coach had at that position—seven to eight yards apart so they could get a better head of steam.

"C'mon, Giftopoulos!" said Paterno, the coach's raspy voice filling the serene mountain air. "Lower your shoulder and take him on! Let's go!"

He was testing Gifto for toughness. Gifto passed.

Moved to linebacker for good the next season, Giftopoulos played behind star linebacker Rogers Alexander. By the start of his junior year, after Alexander graduated, Gifto beat out Mike Beckish to become the starter at what Penn State coaches call the "Fritz" linebacker position. Conlan always lined up as an outside linebacker, Don Graham was an outside linebacker who often lined up as a rush end, Bauer was always lined up as an inside linebacker, and Giftopoulos, the "Fritz," was lined up all over the place as both an inside *and* an outside backer. Penn State's defense often switched back and forth during the same game from a 3–4 to a 4–3 defensive alignment. The "Fritz" had to be versatile enough to make that adjustment.

The defensive coaches had come to rely on Alexander's steadiness, which caused them to judge Gifto a little harsher. Through the first five games of the 1986 season, Sandusky was on Gifto unmercifully, until the day Penn State played at Alabama and the Canadian kid staked his own turf. After one unsuccessful defensive series Sandusky got in Gifto's face. Giftopoulos, who had had enough, fired back, hailing Sandusky with a few choice curse words right there on the sideline. Stunned, Sandusky backed off his Fritz linebacker. For the rest of the season, perhaps satisfied that Giftopoulos had summoned the requisite fire, Penn State's defensive coordinator left Gifto alone.

Giftopoulos idolized Shane Conlan. He tried to be like him on and off the field. He followed him everywhere. Togetherness was one of the things that marked the 1986 Penn State Nittany Lions. Everybody was a friend to everyone else. Everybody stepped up for everyone else. If Conlan was hurting and had to come out, Keith Karpinski came in, made plays, and never bitched about his role. Same with guys as obscure as Aoatoa Polamalu, who had come to Penn State all the way from Orange, California, and was a backup for two seasons to Mike Russo.

"And look at Gary Wilkerson," Gifto recalls. "Sits on the bench all game long, then comes in and breaks up a pass in the end zone that saves the game for us at Notre Dame. Everybody was on the same page. That's what makes a championship team."

Was there a war between the offense and the defense? Yes, Giftopoulos says. But it was a pseudo war, one based on competition and not dislike.

"You look back on it now and you realize that Joe ran the style of offense for what those guys were," Giftopoulos says. "We were a team whose best asset was to run the ball and take time off the clock."

In Tempe, Giftopoulos and his defensive teammates were made to believe that they *would* be able to stop the mercurial Miami attack. Sandusky had emphasized this for a month: they want the big play, so we're not going to give them the big play. Not many defenses had gotten to Testaverde all year, even by blitzing. Sandusky figured if Penn State couldn't get to the quarterback with eight people boxed up in some kind of sophisticated blitzing scheme, it was the same as just trying to get to him with three down linemen. So, instead of putting eight players near the line of scrimmage, the defensive coordinator dropped eight defenders in the area where Testaverde wanted to throw the ball. The strategy was designed to force the Hurricanes to make the mistakes.

It had already been determined that Penn State would stand up to these bullies from Miami.

Had reporters had the wherewithal to follow the party, they may have had a few more juicy stories to report the week of the Fiesta Bowl. The drinking age in Arizona in December 1986 was eighteen years old, which meant that legally nearly every player on both rosters could hit the nightclubs on off-football hours. Naturally, players from both Miami and Penn State had gathered the intelligence that identified the Phoenix area's best party spots. Often, Hurricane players sparred verbally with the Nittany Lions they ran into at those "It" clubs.

"We were close to a couple of off-the-field fights that week," Giftopoulos said. "But our better sense took over. And in the end all that stuff did was get us pumped."

In the game after Duffy Cobbs picked off Testaverde in the first quarter, Giftopoulos, blocking for Cobbs's return, got into a small altercation with a Miami offensive lineman. A frustrated Testaverde stuck his nose into the altercation. Gifto, still jacked, called him a "dago bastard." Gifto said, "I can't believe I said that. But it was just so unbelievably intense out there. F-bombs were flying everywhere out there that night. We were just sick of all of their shit.

"I remember during the week hearing Brian Blades talk about how good he and the Miami receivers were, and him saying that we were a good team, but not a championship team. We had just come off a game where we shut down Tim Brown. And we were going to be worried about Brian Blades?

"During the game there was a shoving match between Melvin Bratton and Donnie Graham on the Miami sidelines. The next week I played with Bratton in a college all-star game. He's telling me the story and he says, 'Man, I got in his face and flipped the ball at him and he threw it right back at me! You guys weren't intimidated at all, were you?'

"Now how in the hell did Melvin Bratton expect that a kid like Donnie Graham, a kid from Pittsburgh who had worked in the steel mills during summers, whose parents and brothers and uncles had worked in the steel mills, was going to be intimidated in a football game?"

Like most members of the Penn State defensive unit after the team that had been on the field for one hundred-plus plays and what seemed like hours, Pete Giftopoulos never thought Penn State would lose—even as Miami inched closer to the Nittany Lions goal line in the final minute. People ask him all the time about "The Play." He wishes he had some sophisticated answer for the interception that preserved Penn State's national championship.

"He just threw it right to me, what can I say?" Gifto says, who after the game had a stream of blood running from the bridge of his nose down his face. "There were five of us there. We were in drop-back coverage. I just think he felt pressure and wanted to get rid of it before he got sacked. If I had dropped it, we still would have won the game. But it was a lot nicer that I held on to it. And after I caught it, I heard everybody screaming at me to get down. Hey, I wasn't stupid. I knew what I was doing. I was just trying to run down some clock."

Since the game was technically still alive, Giftopoulos never got a chance to keep the football that made Penn State history. After he knelt down and the whistle blew, Gifto flipped it back to the official. He said it never crossed his mind to walk off the field with the football after he made the play and keep it as a trophy.

"Why should I keep it?" he asked at the time. "If you keep it, you've got to give the NCAA $50. That's $75 Canadian."

In his mind that football, that game, will live forever. "As a Canadian kid, I don't think at the time I appreciated a college football national championship as much as the kids from the States. But what I realize now is how much that year lives on. Over the years, if I had friends visit me when I was living in State College and we went near Beaver Stadium, they were always in awe. They'd turn to me and say, 'You played here?' It's a pretty neat feeling."

THE DAY AFTER PENN STATE WON the national championship, Ray Isom figured he'd catch up on all the activities he had missed during the week when he stayed in his hotel room to study defense. Too tired from the game to party afterward, he went right to bed and had planned to rise early to go horseback riding.

The next morning Isom was loping around on a thick-legged palomino when he saw one of the Penn State trainers rushing on to the field after him.

Isom had been listed as an alternate for the Japan Bowl, a college all-star game that was to be played the following weekend in Tokyo. But he was so brilliant against Miami that the game organizers now wanted him on the playing roster. Isom was literally pulled off the horse and rushed to his hotel room so he could pack and catch his flight to Japan via San Francisco. All members of the team would stay the night in a Bay Area hotel and then depart on the same airplane the next day for Tokyo. While he was resting in his room that night, Isom's phone rang. He answered.

"Yo, this Ray Isom?"

"Yeah, who's this?"

"This Alonzo Highsmith. Yo man, you guys played a great game. Come on down to the hotel bar and have a drink with us. Me and Jerome Brown are down here."

"Is this a joke?"

"Naw, man. We're down here. Come down and hang with us."

"I don't think so," Isom said.

"Why not?"

"Because I don't know you guys." Isom, streetwise from Harrisburg, figured a posse in the bar was waiting to jack him up. He went to sleep.

The next day, Brown, the leader of Miami's combat fatigues Rat Pack, sought out Isom on the plane.

"Yo man, what, you too good to have a drink with us?" Brown said, laughing. "We weren't gonna do anything to you. We just wanted to congratulate you."

After Japan, Ray Isom figured his football career was over. He had one semester to get his degree at Penn State. If college football wasn't much of a thought in Isom's mind when he was in high school, pro football was a thousand miles away in his head. Isom hadn't even filled out the NFL form every prospective draftee was required to sign. Come draft time in May, Isom started getting calls from pro scouts. Several teams had been interested in him, but they didn't have any information on him; they couldn't find his draft form.

"I didn't sign that form," he told one scout.

"You don't want to play pro football?"

"I never gave it much thought," Isom said.

A scout contacted his brother Ricky. Ricky called Ray. "Are you out of your mind?" Ricky asked incredulously. "This is your chance to make some money in this game. You've been playin' it for free all your life!"

So Isom went to Paterno, who went to the NFL, who rushed a form to Isom to fill out and sign. But the form required that Isom have an agent. He didn't know any agents and it was too late to do the research. He had a business professor who had played football at Penn State and was now teaching there. Isom remembered doing pretty well in that class, so he asked the business professor to be his agent. Seven rounds of the NFL draft passed with Isom not being picked. Now, he figured, his football life was over. Except then, about five teams contacted his brand-new agent about signing Isom as a free agent. Isom found out that the teams would pay him $500 a day and, in addition, $100 per day in meal money for every day he lasted in camp. To Isom, it was like being recruited for college all over again. Instead of thinking about making some pro team's roster, Ray Isom thought he had just landed a good summer job. Five hundred a day? He started to do some calculations in his head. If he managed to survive three days of practice in each city, that's three times five, plus $100 for meals; that's $1,600 a city! Multiply that by five and he could take eight grand back to Penn State for his final semester. His first stop was with the Tampa Bay Buccaneers.

"There was no way I thought I could play in the NFL," Isom said. "I figured those guys were way too good. And then I started playing and I'm saying to myself, 'Hey, I'm just as good as these guys.'"

Tampa Bay thought so, too. So they put a full-court press on Ray Isom to sign a contract. Isom told them no, that he had a few other stops and a few more $500 days to make. Bucs officials were aghast. They told him they had spoken with his agent and that his agent had told them it was a good deal and Isom would sign. Isom called his agent. The agent hadn't spoken to the Tampa officials. The Bucs had tried to pull a fast one. This pro football thing was different. He was only in it for one day and already people were lying to him. You didn't do those kinds of things to Ray Isom. He was too streetwise. He told them he still wasn't signing. Finally, Tampa Bay officials arranged for a conference call with Isom in the office and his agent on the line. The agent told Ray through a speakerphone that was a good deal and advised him to sign, so he did.

The next day, after a morning practice, Isom told another free-agent defensive back he had befriended that he had just signed. The friend told him that he too had just signed.

"How much did you get?" Isom asked him. The kid told him. It was more than what Isom had just signed for. He went ballistic and ran after his defensive backfield coach.

"Hey, you guys tricked me; you paid the other guy more!" Isom screamed. "I'm not playing. Just release me. I'm going to those other camps." The act was childish and unprofessional, but he wound up getting the same amount as his buddy. Later that day after lunch, Isom ran into that teammate. He had tears in his eyes. The Bucs had just cut the player. Discussing his salary with another teammate was a contract violation. Isom felt like crawling under a rock.

As a pro player, Ray Isom was an in-betweener—too slow to be a corner and too light to be a safety. The Bucs wanted Isom to play at 195 pounds, which was 12 pounds heavier than his Penn State weight. Isom ate everything in sight. He was being fined $100 a day per pound that he was under the limit. He stepped on the scale. It said 190. Isom didn't know how he could gain any more weight.

One of the Bucs' veteran cornerbacks gave him a veteran trick. "Take 50 dollars to the bank and get rolls of quarters," the player said. "Put those rolls in your pockets next weigh-in. They will never know."

At Isom's next weigh-in the scales read 195.

He never felt that comfortable as a pro player. The weight problems annoyed him. And because he couldn't gain weight, he kept getting hurt. Football stopped being fun. In his two years in Tampa Bay, though, he made ironic friendships. The Bucs had drafted Winston Moss, who played on that 1986 Miami team that lost to Penn State. Moss was good friends with Highsmith, who had been drafted by the Oilers, and Brown, who had been taken by the Eagles. Highsmith and Brown would come to Tampa to hang with Moss, and Isom became a regular in that group.

"They turned out to be pretty good guys after all," Isom said.

Ray Isom stands on the deck of his house in the Harrisburg suburbs, content. He's got a nice, big backyard where his kids can play and the family cat can chase field mice. It's a far cry from the house on Walnut across the street from the gas station that was landmark to a race riot. He works as an insurance agent and has turned down a few job promotions because he likes the pace of his employment situation—it allows him to work from his home and spend more time with his children and help out with the chores while his wife, Tracey, employed by the state government in Harrisburg, works nine to five. Isom has filled a lot of his afternoon hours coaching various sports at different Harrisburg-area schools. He has had most of his success as a coach of girls' high school basketball teams, blending his fierce competitiveness with such a gregarious personality. The kids love Ray Isom.

Ray and Tracey were high school sweethearts and have been together ever since. Their only biological child, daughter Shaquita, recently made them grandparents. After Shaquita, the Isoms tried to have other children, but they never came. So, a few years ago the couple adopted. They were looking to adopt a young boy and girl. An adoption agency from Ohio found that for them. When they got out there, the Isoms saw that if they adopted the two children, a third member of the family, another boy, would have to be split from his siblings. So they adopted all three when they were seven, six, and four years old. As a tribute to their African roots, the new Isom boys are named Zaire and Jelani, and the girl Xaria. Isom takes delight in the fact that they will have a big suburban home and a good school district in which to grow up. He hopes his children will create their own identity.

Ray Isom is not the kind of guy who washes himself with memories. On his dining-room wall is a photo of him making a tackle in a game his senior year against East Carolina. The tackle is technically perfect. Isom dives his shoulder into the ball carrier's legs. The ball carrier is falling back. Someone he met in the insurance business played on that East Carolina team. It was his buddy whom Isom was tackling. The buddy had the photo. The guy thought Isom might like it so he sent it to him. There's another picture of him in a Tampa Bay Bucs uniform. Tracey hung them over Ray's protests.

Life moves on. There are too many things that need attention when you're an adult. You can't afford to think about how great it was back then.

But even a classic cynic like Ray Isom knows that in 1986 he was part of something that was pretty special. "We beat Miami," Isom says. "And the whole world was watching."

JERRY SANDUSKY CHOKED. Some twenty-five years later, he isn't embarrassed to admit it. The game against Miami, which raced toward its heart-palpitating conclusion with the Penn State defense coming apart thread by thread as Testaverde methodically took the Hurricanes from his own 23-yard line deep into Penn State territory, was so emotional, so exhausting, that the cooler-than-cool defensive coordinator couldn't muster enough energy to make a defensive call to his team in the final seconds.

Sandusky thought Penn State had the game won. The Lions had Miami at fourth down and six at the Hurricanes' 27 with two minutes left in the game when Testaverde dropped back, looked to the right sideline, and threw to Brian Blades. Penn State was in a "contain" defense with seven defenders placed in the secondary to better defend a possible Miami pass, each one itching for the chance to break up the final pass that would give them the national championship. Blades caught it and pirouetted up field. Eddie Johnson, a sophomore and the youngest member of the Penn State secondary, had gotten there late and then missed the tackle. The Miami wideout nearly broke the play for a game-winning touchdown before Conlan and Isom, both flying across from the other side of the field, got him at the Penn State 43-yard line.

For Miami it was a second life.

On first and ten from the 43, Testaverde hit Blades again for eight. On second down, Vinny hit Perriman for nine more to give Miami a first down at the Penn State 26 as 1:42 showed on the clock. Irvin, who had been quiet for most of the game, came alive, catching a Testaverde pass over the middle for four yards and then on the next play finding a seam in the Penn State defense before snaring a Vinny spiral for 12 more. On the play, Conlan was injured, again, and limped off the field.

Bauer came to the Penn State sidelines looking for a defensive call that would stop the bleeding.

Sandusky, trying to ease the tension, said with a smile, "What are you doing over here, Trey? I can't help you. It's pretty rough out there, isn't it?"

He sent Bauer back on to the field with a defensive set and told his linebacker that if Testaverde dropped back or ran a play with no huddle, to call for a 5-King, the Lions' basic defense, and then to add a prefix that would put the secondary in the right set for a pass. But in the huddle, Bauer, spent, his Adam's apple the size of a grapefruit, couldn't get the call out of his mouth. Somebody in the huddle yelled, "Stay with 5-King!" They broke.

On first and 10 at the Penn State 10, Testaverde hit Irvin again, to the five, with 52 seconds left. The sellout crowd, most of them Penn State fans, offered an eerie wail that hovered over the stadium. To Penn State fans, a medieval torture was taking place.

The Lions defense looked again to the sidelines. Sandusky, who had always prided himself on being in the moment, suddenly couldn't think. He turned to defensive assistant Jim Williams and muttered, "Uh . . . same . . . uh . . . defense." By the time Williams could signal, the players had turned inward to the huddle and nobody saw it. The Lions would stay in their 5-King without the prefix. If Testaverde had two more seconds, he likely would have completed a pass in the end zone against Penn State's suddenly disorganized secondary. Instead, Tim Johnson broke through, grabbed Testaverde by the helmet, and sacked the Miami quarterback.

"Purely divine intervention," Sandusky remembered.

DIVINE INTERVENTION? Tim Johnson thinks about that a lot. It wasn't as if God was a Penn State football fan, or even a football fan at all, who had a stake in the outcome of the 1987 Fiesta Bowl. Even Johnson, now a pastor in Nashville, Tennessee, won't go that way. But there was something, some calming force, some metaphysical circumstance, that engulfed Tim Johnson that night and that week.

Johnson had become a born-again Christian two years before the night Penn State beat Miami. He was just a wet-behind-the-ears sophomore then, dealing with the failures and injuries of being a major college football player. Johnson had come from a poor area of Sarasota, Florida, a star athlete—the Florida defensive lineman of the year at Sarasota High—wooed by most every major football power, including a few from his own home state, most of whom had offered the massive defensive lineman financial incentives to play ball for their school. Johnson chose Penn State, a program that had offered him nothing—a program that on his recruiting visit had packed him in a dorm room with four other beefy recruits on a cold, wintry day—because a voice in his head told him this Penn State thing would be an experience that would help him grow into an adult.

The state of Florida produced athletes, especially football players, as bountiful as orange crops. Johnson had seen many of them spawn from his own hometown. They'd go to the U (Miami), Florida State, or Florida. When their careers were over, it seemed as if the only thing left for them if the NFL didn't call was to come back to the same place and have nothing left but glory-day tales and time for trouble. Johnson thought that he had needed to put himself in an environment to survive on his own, a place where he'd need to communicate with a cross-section of people different from the folks in Florida. He wanted broader horizons.

Johnson's recruiting weekend visit to Penn State was marked by two feet of freshly fallen snow and fifteen-degree temperatures. He didn't bring a winter jacket—he didn't *have* a winter jacket—so a Penn State assistant coach scurried up a sweatshirt for Johnson from the equipment room. The assistant had first made it a point to phone the athletic department's NCAA compliance officer to find out for certain that lending a recruit a sweatshirt was not a violation of NCAA rules. Penn State was so square; it was just perfect for him, Johnson remembered thinking.

Where does an eighteen-year-old come up with a game plan that is so worldly?

For Tim Johnson, it didn't come from a father figure. Johnson's father left the family when Tim was just two years old. He'd never even seen a photo of his dad. His mother, Emma, worked two jobs while raising Tim and his three brothers and one sister. Emma was captivated by Paterno's recruiting pitch in which the Penn State coach emphasized education. What sold Emma and Tim even more was the fact that Paterno had come to Sarasota to visit the Johnsons personally only two days after Penn State beat Georgia in the Sugar Bowl for the 1983 national championship. Joe Paterno was coming to recruit her son two days after winning maybe the most important game of his life? How selfless was that? Emma figured Penn State would be a great place for her son Tim.

But when he got to State, things didn't work out as smoothly as Tim Johnson had figured. Other schools had all but guaranteed him a starting job, but at Penn State he could hardly get on the field. And Johnson was repeatedly getting injured. One minute it was his leg, the next his shoulder. He was a backup who played only sparingly behind Bob White. Then after his sophomore season, he was hit hard with a mysterious illness. Late that summer before his junior year, Johnson found himself on his back in Centre Community Hospital unable to move, going through tests for spinal meningitis. Doctors tapped his spine with a needle as long as his arm without anesthesia. He was a football player. He was supposed to be tough. He didn't want the anesthesia. When the needle went into his spine, Johnson screamed a scream that curdled the blood of patients on the floor *below* him, cursing his agony and asking for help from a God he believed in but had never thought that much about.

Nobody could find anything wrong with Tim Johnson, but he was still ill. He was still on his back. He looked upward, muttering to no one in particular. *God, if you're up there, why is this happening to me? Tell me what's going on.* Then he made a specific deal: *God, if you help me out here, I promise you I will start reading my Bible.*

Now, the story doesn't connect the dots in a straight line. Johnson recovered from this mysterious illness—they still never figured out what it was—and became the co-MVP in Penn State's Blue-White game that spring. He started at defensive tackle for the Lions that fall as a junior, launching into a season that would earn him a third-team All-America selection. But it wasn't until the following spring when he attended a fellowship meeting headed by former Lions quarterback Todd Blackledge that he truly cemented his relationship with God. Johnson says, "I was cheating. You make these promises and then you start recovering and getting success and then you forget all about who was responsible for all of it. I started to think I was invincible again. Those are the times you get knocked down again. Fortunately, I caught it in time. And at that prayer meeting with Todd, I felt some kind of power that took me over. I was reading the Bible, but it may as well have been in Greek, or the words upside down. I started reading it again and the words started making sense."

That's when Johnson says he truly felt born again.

At Penn State, and especially under Sandusky, the defensive linemen are the grunts, guinea pigs that take on the double-teaming and the stunts and schemes to allow the linebackers to make tackles. After all, it's Linebacker U. Johnson's style was dervishlike; he was a motor always running, always getting nicked up, and always coming back for more. During the 1986 regular season, he finished with only 16 solo tackles to go with 17 assisted tackles, but those 33 tackles were the highest total of any Penn State down lineman that year. Johnson added five sacks. But he brought more than just numbers to the Penn State defense. Tim Johnson brought a sense of calm.

And so it was in the final seconds of the Fiesta Bowl.

Johnson never thought the Lions would lose. The possibility had never entered his mind even as Miami, behind the unstoppable Testaverde, kept rolling down the field against the beleaguered Penn State defense. This was a team that just couldn't get flustered. Nothing that Miami had done in the days preceding the big game put a dent in the Lions' armor. Johnson had played alongside Jerome Brown and with Alonzo Highsmith in some Florida high school all-star games. Those guys had yapped at him all game long and Johnson, playing with a quiet confidence, said nothing. The famed barbeque walkout? Johnson remembered thinking at the time that that was really going to come back to haunt Miami. Paterno had taught this group how to be champions. Before the season started, the coach told his team to remember what it felt like to prepare for this moment. To come off the deck after an embarrassing loss to Oklahoma the year before and work their butts off to get ready for the upcoming season—that was really the hard part. This was gravy. All they had to do was finish this game.

"That's why Joe Paterno is such a brilliant football coach," Tim Johnson says. "He goes beyond the realm of just being a football coach. He gets you to play the game in your heart. The Bible says that as a man thinks in his heart, so is he. Joe played the game in our heads and made it come out of our hearts. That year, we *thought* as champions."

The play that should have made Miami a winner because Penn State's defensive backfield was in the wrong set made Johnson forever a hero. The 'Canes, Johnson noticed, were also a little discombobulated. They were working without a huddle. Testaverde was calling plays on the fly. On that second down no receiver lined up on Johnson's side to chip him. He would cleanly beat Miami offensive tackle Maurice Maddox with a quick move to the outside. As Testaverde looked to the end zone, Johnson grasped for him. Vinny wriggled away. Johnson stayed in the path and reached for Testaverde's helmet. He got it and twisted the Miami QB down. It was third down at the 13-yard line now with just 25 seconds left. Testaverde, forced out of the pocket to the right, threw incomplete. Fourth down, Gifto intercepted Vinny's hurried toss to the goal line. It was finally over.

AS JOHN SHAFFER KNELT ON THE BALL and the clock reached zeroes, Jerry Sandusky retreated to the Penn State bench, put his head in his hands, and cried. He has no recollection of the team carrying Paterno on their collective shoulders, the bespectacled coach pumping a weary fist in the air. Sandusky had been through some harrowing finishes in his lengthy Penn State coaching career, but nothing like this. It was as if he and the team had been thrown into a pit of fire and rose unscathed. The locker-room celebration was like nothing he'd ever seen. Players and coaches and parents and fans were hugging and bawling like schoolchildren. Joe Sarra, a Lions assistant coach, ran over to Sandusky, hugged him with a vise grip, and hoisted him into the air. The Lions had won a national championship in 1983, beating Georgia in the Sugar Bowl. But it wasn't as intense as this. The magnitude of this game was much larger. This Penn State team had been together for five years and had been beaten up pretty badly in their early years at State. The Lions had beaten a team that many football observers felt couldn't be beaten. The Penn State party went into the wee hours of the night. Jerry Sandusky was exhausted; he barely had enough energy to lift himself to his bed. And once there, he was just too tired to go to sleep.

FOOTBALL NEVER GOT BETTER for Bob White than it was that night in Tempe, Arizona.

The 6′2″, 255-pound defensive lineman was drafted in the sixth round of the NFL draft that spring by the San Francisco 49ers. He projected in the pros as a linebacker. But, embroiled in a contract dispute, White got to camp late. By then he was behind the rest of the players, and the Niners released him just before the regular season started—too late for White to hook on with anyone else.

In the off-season that year, he worked out hard to get another shot and wound up signing as a free agent with Marty Schottenheimer's Cleveland Browns, who promised him playing time. But pro football is an often hard and deceitful business. The Browns had spent two of their first three picks in the 1988 draft on linebackers. White stood around a lot that camp. Football wasn't much fun anymore. One day he just packed up and walked away to get on with his life.

For Bob White, the road wound right back to State College. He went to work for the university in the winter of 1989 as an admissions counselor. He finished his master's degree at Penn State in counselor education and then served as a Penn State lobbyist for several years in Washington, D.C., and later on as the director of marketing and operations for Beaver Stadium's spiffy new club boxes, where he organized the stadium's special events.

White has never met up with his father, Solomon. An effort was made when Bob White was just thirteen years old. An older brother found out that Solomon White was living in Atlanta. Bob was a member of a summer Florida all-star track-and-field team that had been invited to participate in a national competition at Marshall University in West Virginia. The team's airplane was to make a stopover in Atlanta. The older brother had made contact with Solomon White to meet his younger son for the first time at the airport. Solomon never showed.

Tim Johnson is the pastor of Bethel World Outreach, a multicultural, multi-denominational church in Nashville. He was ordained in 2000, after playing seven seasons in the NFL with the Pittsburgh Steelers, Washington Redskins, and Cincinnati Bengals. He moved to Nashville specifically to start this church and has others planned for up the road, including one on the radar for Orlando. He is married to his high school sweetheart, Le'Chelle. The couple has three girls—Kayla, Carrah, Christa—and a boy, Shaun.

Tim Johnson thinks about the 1987 national championship game often. He has no doubt that his faith in God helped him and perhaps the whole Penn State team that night in Tempe.

"I was at a college all-star game later that year in Japan with Alonzo Highsmith," Johnson recalls. "We were talking one day and he said to me, 'Ya know, there was something with y'all that night.' I didn't have enough time to give him a sermon."

JERRY SANDUSKY GREW UP literally in a recreation center in the Pittsburgh suburb of Washington. His parents ran the center—the family lived upstairs—which opened its doors to everyone, rich or poor, black or white. Sandusky played some sport or did some craft every day of his life and in him grew a soft spot for those who didn't have that access or any access at all. Years later this experience would fuel an ambition to create The Second Mile.

When Jerry and his wife, Dottie, found they couldn't have biological children, they adopted six and welcomed in many more as foster children. Two of the couple's children, E.J. and John, both of whom were walk-on players at Penn State, followed the old man into coaching. John became assistant at Western Carolina, and E.J. the head coach at Albright in Reading, Pennsylvania.

In 1977, as Penn State football was finishing up on a decade that would bring them a mythical national championship (only Richard Nixon thought Texas was better than State in 1970) and a Heisman Trophy winner (halfback John Cappelletti), Sandusky had the brainchild for a regional charity that would fund summer camps for the underprivileged. Today, The Second Mile is a statewide, nonprofit organization serving some one hundred thousand children in Pennsylvania's sixty-seven counties. Some of The Second Mile's staff is paid. Sandusky's salary comes from small stipends based on expenses and consulting fees and from the Jerry Sandusky Football Camp, which he conducts each summer in State College and Reading. His current salary is considerably smaller than what he made as Penn State defensive coordinator.

Sandusky hadn't sat down to watch a replay of the historic 1987 national championship game until recently. As he does, certain things come back to him vividly. Miami players, he remembered, were walking around all week with cigars sticking out of their mouths. "Victory cigars," they said they were. The Hurricanes tried to tantalize the Lions, screaming derogatory remarks at the Penn State players whenever they saw them. One day a group of Miami offensive players started yelling at Sandusky just because he was the defensive coach and just because he was there.

Faux anger. Was it a product of bravado? Or insecurity.

Sileo, the flare-mouthed defensive lineman, told reporters, "As far as I'm concerned, Friday's game is just the end of the season."

Irvin, the boisterous wide receiver, relished the mismatches he would see in the Nittany Lions secondary. "Conlan covering me will be good for us. I'm sure I can run right past him. We're looking to put them away early." During the week the 6'2" Irvin had sidled up to the 5'8" Isom and laughed in his face. "You're Isom?" Irvin chortled. "Oh, mannnnnn." Later, Highsmith walked up to cornerback Duffy Cobbs and said, "You shouldn't have come, you know. But it's too late to turn back. You've chosen your own death now."

Jerome Brown, the captain of the fatigues brigade, had not-so-flattering remarks for the Penn State offense. "You know what I think of John Shaffer and D.J. Dozier?" Brown mused. "I think they're nothing. Shaffer thought he had a bad bowl game last year. That was nothing. After this game he'll wish he'd graduated. The dude's about to star in a nightmare."

Sandusky remembered being on the Sun Devil Stadium field in pregame warmups, watching his defensive backs practicing their back-peddling drops. He looked to his left and saw Miami coach Jimmy Johnson and Testaverde also eyeballing the drill. He noticed a smirk on Testaverde's face, a smirk suggesting Vinny would have an easy time with these tiny men whom his teammates earlier in the week nicknamed "Smurfs." It made Sandusky a little angry, but the sensible side of his brain said, "Geez, maybe they're right; we don't *look* very impressive."

But above anything else, they competed. The week before the Syracuse game, coming off a Saturday in which they had survived lowly regarded Cincinnati, Syracuse-area newspapers focused on how the Lions would cover against the Orangemen's vaunted passing attack. Bearcats coach Dave Currey didn't mince words.

"[The Syracuse] receivers better tie their shoes on pretty tight," Currey said, "or they're going to get knocked out of them.

In truth, Sandusky and Paterno knew that with the 1986 Penn State Nittany Lions they were presiding over a team that had an abundance of heart, guile, and experience. The majority of this Lions team had been together for five years. They had been through some bad times and had been humiliated in a bowl game only the year before. Also, the regular season had been a taffy pull with the Lions surviving several games that season in the end by just outlasting the opposition. They had been tanned and were leather-tough. In this game-within-a-game against the incorrigible Miami, they had enough savvy not to get sucked into, and in fact, laugh at, the circus the Hurricanes were trying to create.

WHY DIDN'T JERRY SANDUSKY ever become a head coach? Sometimes he asks himself that very question. Then he smiles that toothy smile. It just never worked out.

As an assistant at Penn State, he didn't really look for any head-coaching jobs. When he was thirty years old, he took the head-coaching job at Marshall for one hour. Joe McMullen, an ex-Penn State player, was the athletic director at the West Virginia school. After Sandusky accepted the job on the telephone, he walked down his stairs to be met by Christopher, one of the Sanduskys' foster children. Christopher wanted to play ball. Sandusky walked out to his backyard. One of his other children was sledding in his neighbor's yard. Sandusky came back into the house and called McMullen to tell him he wasn't coming to Marshall.

He was hooked on the charm of living in State College. Sandusky was comfortable. Somewhere in the back of his mind was the notion that if he stayed there, eventually—his dream job, the head football coach at Penn State University— would fall down to him. Paterno had never officially promised him anything, but the two men had talked about it. Joe kept motoring along. By 1998 Sandusky was tired of waiting.

Two years after he retired from coaching football, Sandusky was approached by the University of Virginia to become their head man. He waffled. The Second Mile had become too important to him to leave it. Virginia hired Al Groh.

But Sandusky is still a Nittany Lion at heart.

He watches Penn State games these days from his Beaver Stadium seats. He still pays close attention to the game's strategy, watching what his former assistant, Tom Bradley, who succeeded Sandusky as defensive coordinator, comes up with on, say, a third down and long. In his Second Mile office his cell phone rings. The ringtone is "Fight on State," the Penn State fans' rally cry.

His relationship with Paterno remains entangled in a web of speculation. Did Paterno renege on a promise to step down and hand the Penn State head coaching reins to Sandusky years ago?

"Joe Paterno is entitled to do whatever he wants to do, so far as coaching Penn State football is concerned," Sandusky said flatly.

This is what Sandusky says of Paterno: He's very competitive. He's demanding of himself and others but by no means unreasonable. He puts his fist down often, but he's also intelligent enough to know when to back off. He has that Brooklyn background, a mixture of pride and arrogance.

Most of the great coaches are like that. The great assistants are the ones who can put up with that kind of attitude and get things done from their own blueprint while making the head man think he was the one who came up with the idea in the first place. The people who know Sandusky say he never reached that kind of nirvana with Joe Paterno. The two men sparred often over strategy. Sandusky was fired a few times in the heat of Paterno's anger. Sandusky quit a few other times in the heat of his own anger. The relationship sustained but, as the years went on, by only arm's length. It got under the defensive coordinator's skin when Paterno, overreacting to a mistake made in a game, would suggest and then implement a new way of doing things.

"I bore rather easily," Sandusky says. "Joe's ideas were often good ideas. But then we'd spend all the time in practice on that—even though it became clear that it didn't fit."

Sandusky ponders. He seems willing to expound. Then he smiles that toothy smile and stops.

Is it odd that two people who coached together for so long, and who still live in the same town, barely think of each other anymore? Maybe. It's like anything else, really. Work with somebody for more than a quarter of a decade, like in an old rock band, or a law partnership, or a football coaching staff; the good memories will always rise up, but maybe the years' worth of battle, the consternation, creates some kind of a gashing wound that perhaps can never fully heal.

5

THE SEASON, DAY BY DAY

FOR THE 1986 NITTANY LIONS, the quest to return to the national championship game began immediately after the Lions were spanked by Oklahoma in the Orange Bowl on January 1. But it officially began on August 15 with the opening of fall practice.

Strangely enough, not much fanfare accompanied the start of practice for a team that most experts predicted would contend again for a national championship. The *Centre Daily Times*, State College's hometown newspaper, devoted only one story—in the sports section—to the event. And for the first few weeks of practice, that newspaper only ran a story on Penn State football every other day.

The 1986 season began with a minor snag. Penn State's new indoor practice facility, which had been hyped for much of the preceding year as a key program improvement, would not be ready for at least another month. Paterno carped about his team having to practice outdoors in State College's unpredictable upcoming autumn weather and running the risk of ruining their outdoor practice fields if those fields got wet.

Penn State was leading the Tide 17–3. But Alabama got the ball in scoring position when All-American linebacker Cornelius Bennett chased down Thomas, stripped him of the football, and recovered the fumble at the Lions' 29. 'Bama had a fourth and one at the 20 and, trailing by two touchdowns with time running down, was forced to try to convert the first down instead of attempting a field goal. Quarterback David Shula called an off-tackle rush to his best running back, Bobby Humphrey. But from his inside linebacker spot, Bauer read the play and crashed into Humphrey, causing a fumble. Pete Curkendall scooped up the football at the Penn State 37. And the game was over.

"Ah, I've been through this so many times with the project people," Paterno said in resignation. "I don't know what's going on anymore."

In the papers, Paterno promised a more difficult preseason than what the Lions had the year before, which caused Bob White, through clenched teeth, to say, "Having gone through last year, it's hard to see how he could make it any harder." Paterno was starting his twenty-first season as the Nittany Lions' head coach. Normally ultra-cautious in assessing his team, JoePa allowed this time for some praise:

We should be better than last year. I don't think we have what you call a weakness. But the problem is the schedule. The teams we play away [Boston College, Alabama, West Virginia, and Notre Dame] play much tougher at home. And the teams we play early all felt we were lucky against them last year, so now they think they can beat us.

Penn State had beaten Temple (27–25), East Carolina (17–10), Syracuse (24–20), and Maryland (20–18) the year before by a collective 15 points.

Most of the important Nittany Lions reported to August practice healthy, save for fullback Tim Manoa, who was gimping around a bit on an injured knee suffered in a summer racquetball class. White, the starting defensive end in PSU's 3–4 alignment, reported to camp having gained twenty-four pounds—from 228 to 252—to better prepare himself for whenever the Lions shifted into a 4–3 defense and he would have to move inside to tackle. White had been a terrific story. After his tutoring by Sue Paterno before his freshman year, White volunteered to red-shirt in the fall so he could concentrate on his progress in the classroom. By fall 1986, White's academic progress had been so great that he only needed three more credits to graduate.

The quarterback controversy fueled by John Shaffer's impotent showing against Oklahoma was still in full bloom. Matt Knizner was placed on the cover of a State College magazine and dubbed "The People's Choice." Inside, Shaffer, still sporting a pretty good résumé of having only one loss ever as a starting quarterback at any level, seethed. But he went along. "I think you're doing somebody an injustice if you tell them they have the No. 1 position, regardless of what the position is and how you perform," Shaffer said. "That lack of competition and lack of desire only makes you go a little bit backwards."

On August 29, a little more than a week before the Lions would play host to Temple in the season opener, Paterno sounded a note of panic when he suggested that the Lions were *behind* in their progress. Offensive-line starters Dan Morgan and Mike Wolfe had been missing time with hamstring pulls, as were running back Dave Clark and highly touted wide receiver Michael Timpson. Offensive tackle Stan Clayton, the team's most experienced offensive lineman, had a dislocated shoulder. Ray Roundtree, a starting wide receiver, was missing practice time due to a pulled groin muscle.

Paterno still had not told the world who would be his starting quarterback. Shaffer and Knizner, Paterno said, were still "even." He said he would have to find playing time for both quarterbacks in the first few games of the season, "though I'm not sure there I'm going to find an easy way to do that." On Wednesday, September 2, just three days before the opener, Paterno *still* hadn't named his starter. The next morning a banner headline across page 1 of the *Centre Daily Times* blared "Paterno Picks Shaffer." The starter who ended last season would stay as the starter.

PENN STATE CAME INTO the first night game in Beaver Stadium history bent on stopping Temple running back Paul Palmer. Palmer had scorched the Beaver Stadium turf the year before for 206 yards rushing and two touchdowns as the Owls nearly pulled off a major upset. In the second quarter Isom slashed into Palmer as he tried to turn the corner, giving the Temple back a hip pointer. Still, Palmer played. He finished with 96 yards on twenty-nine difficult carries, caught three more passes for 33 yards, and returned four kicks, including a 74-yard return, for a total of 139 yards. But it wasn't nearly enough as Penn State won easily, 45–15.

The Saturday of the Temple game also happened to be Shaffer's birthday. The Penn State quarterback celebrated in fine style, completing twelve of eighteen passes for 194 yards and three touchdowns.

"It's amazing the amount of friends I've made in the past three days," Shaffer said during the week after the Temple game.

Paterno still managed to send a small dig into the player he had only reluctantly named as starter by replacing him with Knizner in the first quarter—even though Shaffer had led the Lions to a quick 21–0 lead. After the game, asked whether his confidence in Shaffer had increased, Paterno snapped.

"I never had any trouble with confidence in John Shaffer," the Penn State coach said. "You can take all the polls you want. You can act like jackasses all you want. But you're not around these guys in practice and you don't know how they do in different situations."

A couple of days later, Paterno would apologize for the "jackasses" remark in his Tuesday night conference call with reporters.

But as the Lions moved up to No. 5 in the AP college football poll after the Temple game, Owls coach Bruce Arians wasn't exactly effusive in his praise for Penn State. "I think their secondary could be a weakness for them," Arians said. Isom filed the comments somewhere in his competitive soul.

Meanwhile, the "jackasses" comment turned out to be the lightest of Paterno's controversies for the week. Political and editorial writers locally and nationally were blasting the Penn State coach for appearing in a thirty-second campaign spot for Republican U.S. Rep. William Clinger, whose political district included central Pennsylvania. In the advertisement, Paterno says to Clinger, "You have always been there when we needed you." When questioned about it, Paterno said that his appearance was not meant to be an endorsement of a candidate and that he was only lauding Clinger for his commitment to education in general and for Penn State in particular. It would not be the last time in his career that Joe Paterno would tip off his Republican political loyalties.

As Penn State rested in a bye week, Miami blasted Texas Tech to go to 3–0 for the season and take firm hold of the No. 2 ranking in college football behind Oklahoma. Michigan was third, followed by Alabama and then Penn State. Penn State would have little trouble at Boston College on September 20, beating the Eagles, 26–14, behind a great effort from Dozier.

But there was some trouble brewing in the ranks. In the first two games, Paterno made wholesale substitutions, replacing much of his first-team offenses and defenses with second-team guys. Knizner in the BC game was sent in to replace Shaffer, who thought he had solidified the job with his performance against Temple.

In the days following Boston College, Penn State's starting quarterback expressed his frustration. "It was tough. I can't say that it wasn't," he said about being replaced with Knizner in intervals. "It's tough to sit out and then have to go back in and get things going right away for fear you're going to be pulled out."

Confronted with Shaffer's remarks, Paterno fired back. "I don't care what John Shaffer thinks," the coach said. "My job is to do what I think is best for this team now and in the future."

The next week, Penn State crushed East Carolina, 42–17, but not even home-town columnists were impressed, especially after witnessing Miami's impressive, nationally televised 28–16 win at home over Oklahoma in a rare, early season clash of No. 1 versus No. 2.

"The Hurricanes and Sooners are in a class by themselves and a rematch on the same turf [for the Orange Bowl] New Year's night could decide the national championship," wrote the *Centre Daily Times*' Ron Bracken.

The following week Penn State beat Rutgers, coached by former Nittany Lions assistant Dick Anderson, 31–6. One of the game's best plays was a 34-yard end-around run for a touchdown by wide receiver Ray Roundtree. The play, which Penn State would use many times during the season, would come to be known as the "End-Around Tree."

The Scarlet Knights had come into Beaver Stadium undefeated (3–0). Base-ball great Joe DiMaggio, as part of an Orange Bowl committee traveling team, attended the game and was presented a Nittany Lion statue on the field. After the game, DiMaggio was unavailable for further comment on the Nittany Lions. He had been whisked out of the stadium immediately afterward to catch a flight from State College airport because of his brother Vince's sudden death.

The Nittany Lions' win, meanwhile, did nothing to impress the pollsters. Penn State stayed fifth in the poll behind Miami, Alabama (which had defeated Notre Dame, 28–10), Nebraska, and Michigan. Paterno didn't even seem impressed with his team's victory—all he could talk about after the game was the 102 yards in penalties assessed against the Lions and a couple penalties the coach found especially galling.

Tim Johnson had gotten a 15-yard penalty for running on the field and jawing with a Rutgers player. Immediately, right there on the field, Paterno rushed into his defensive end's face and berated him before some 84,000 fans at Beaver Stadium.

"Stupid clips!" Paterno squawked after the game. "They're very aggressive, which is what you want. You can't be aggressive and not have penalties, but some are just nonsense, just plain old nonsense.

"And then we have a guy who goes brain dead on the field. Just uncalled for," the coach said, referring to Johnson.

In the locker room afterward, Johnson gave *his* side of the story. "A guy hit D.J. and then knocked him down when he tried to get up and that moved me," Johnson said. "I told Joe, 'Hey, that's my teammate out there!' Joe tried to beat me up, but he couldn't."

After the game, when asked by reporters to clarify his comments about his team needing to be more "disciplined," Paterno got into another jousting match with the media. "Are you telling me how to coach the team?" Paterno said to one reporter. "I tell you I got a problem. You want to tell me I don't have a problem?"

"No, I don't," said the reporter.

"Okay. I tell you I got a problem and that's it! Somebody asked me if I was concerned [about the lack of discipline] and I answered that question. Period. I'm not going to get into specifics."

The semi-tense mood surrounding the Penn State football team was lightened somewhat that Monday when comedian Robin Williams performed at Rec Hall on campus. Williams wore a Penn State football jersey on stage.

His fire from the previous week still smoldering, Paterno went off again on the media at his weekly teleconference. The Lions that week were preparing to play Cincinnati. A national reporter doing a story on the college football ranking system suggested to JoePa that his team wasn't necessarily getting the proper respect because it was playing "turkeys."

"I resent that attitude, calling them turkeys," Paterno replied. "We're going to play Temple and BC and Rutgers because those are traditional games for us and they are all working hard in building their programs. I don't think they're 'turkeys' and we're going to play them for a long time."

Which was all well and good, except that after Penn State barely survived the Bearcats that Saturday—needing a big play by freshman Blair Thomas and a blocked punt at the end of the game to seal the deal, 23–17—the Nittany Lions *dropped* in the AP poll to sixth overall. Miami, now No. 1, beat West Virginia, 58–14; No. 2 Alabama took care of Memphis State, 37–0; No. 3 Nebraska beat Oklahoma State, 30–10; and No. 4 Michigan beat Michigan State, 27–7. Meanwhile, Oklahoma won big and the voters pushed the Sooners back into the picture and *above* Penn State into the fifth spot.

Paterno beat himself up after the Cincinnati game. "I had a bad day," he said. "I could have helped the assistant coaches with some things. I'm not so sure that in the back of my mind, I thought we could have scored more points. When you do that, I'm not so sure the kids then don't know it."

To make matters worse, his star running back was now angry with the coach. Dozier, who was nursing a strained groin and hadn't practiced until Thursday of the week prior to the game, had been pulled out of the lineup with the game on the line, replaced by Blair Thomas. At the beginning of the second half, Dozier told one of the assistant coaches that he needed more time to stretch, suggesting that he might not be ready to go on Penn State's first series of that half. Paterno apparently took that to mean that Dozier was not at a competitive razor's edge. In the game's most crucial moments, the Penn State coach yanked his star player.

The Cincinnati game was a major downer. The Lions felt the sting of the nation's sporting pundits, many of whom suggested that if Penn State struggled against a lowly team like Cincinnati, they couldn't possibly be one of the best teams in the nation. Going into the following week's game against Syracuse, the Penn State players were determined to make up for such a slipup.

The next week the running game finally blasted off. Thomas gained 132 yards on three carries, including a 93-yard touchdown, the longest run from scrimmage in school history. Tim Manoa added 96 yards on 12 carries. Dozier amassed 84 yards on 19 carries as the Lions buried Syracuse, 42–3. The defense, questioned all week whether it could harness Syracuse's mobile-option quarterback Don McPherson, made McPherson a nonfactor. The Lions had prepared for McPherson by pressing freshman quarterback Tom Bill into impersonating McPherson on the scout team. Conlan had tried to ease Bill's nerves in practice by going up to the frosh and saying, "Don't worry, we're not gonna kill you or anything."

If there was any cause for concern after the Syracuse game—other than that Penn State remained No. 6 in the polls—it was with kicker Massimo Manca, who had missed a 46-yard field-goal attempt in the game. That miss had made Manca, who had been nearly automatic the year before, a cumulative three for nine on field goals in the young season. Lions special teams coaches worried, figuring they'd need the old Manca in their upcoming game against defensive-minded Alabama at Bryant-Denny Stadium.

The Lions and Paterno stayed low-key during their practice week. 'Bama went into the game as a solid favorite. Pollsters who had disrespected Penn State for their "turkey" schedule and waited on a southern *whupping* of PSU were stunned when the Nittany Lions dominated the Tide, 23–3. The Penn State defense had its finest hour, making the play of the game in the fourth quarter to seal the victory.

Trailing by two touchdowns with time running down, 'Bama had to try to convert a first down. Shula called an off-tackle rush to Bobby Humphrey. But Trey Bauer read the play and crashed into Humphrey, causing a fumble. "That was the greatest moment of my Penn State career!" said the effusive Bauer afterward. "To make a hit like that and cause a fumble in a game like that on national television—that's why you come to a school like Penn State."

Even the conservative Paterno was moved by his team's effort. "Someone has to play awfully well to beat us the way we're playing right now," he said after the game. "I think we're an awfully good football team."

Manca had responded. The Italian-born kicker who hadn't made a three-point kick since the Rutgers game booted field goals of 37, 29, and 42 yards. Finally, the pollsters gave in. With the win, Penn State rose to No. 3 behind Miami, still No. 1, and Michigan. For the first time, bowl executives not tied into conference affiliations could see a dream matchup pitting independent Miami against independent

Penn State. Immediately after the Penn State–Alabama game, Sunkist, corporate sponsor of the Fiesta Bowl, announced that it would add money—a reported $2 million—to its payout pot for teams playing there.

But after Penn State shut out West Virginia the following week to go to 8–0 (and climbed to No. 2 in the polls), the Gator Bowl, centered in Jacksonville, Florida, climbed into the fray.

In a national story, Gator Bowl officials said that they also were in the process of accumulating an additional $2 million in an attempt to lure Miami and Penn State. In that story, Gator officials hinted that the Gator Bowl would be more cost effective for both teams and their fans since Jacksonville was closer geographically to both schools. Now officially embroiled in a recruiting war with a competitor, Bruce Skinner, the Fiesta Bowl committee head, fired back. Skinner said that *his* bowl would include stipends for travel expenses for both teams. Skinner then took a shot at the Gator Bowl organizers by sniffing, "Our money is in the bank."

Meanwhile, the Lions didn't respond well to their newfound poll prosperity.

At home against Maryland, a team that had taken them to the limit the previous year, Penn State survived, 17–15, only when the Terrapins failed to make a two-point conversation in the game's final seconds. The Lions had a 17–9 lead after Manca hit a 36-yard field goal with just 1:10 left. But the Penn State defense allowed Maryland QB Dan Henning to swiftly move the ball 75 yards down the field and complete a touchdown pass with just 14 seconds left. The Lions needed a great defensive play by linebacker Keith Karpinski, who hurried Henning into an errant throw for the two-point try, to nail down the victory.

Fiesta Bowl officials who had come to the game hoping to curry more favor with the Penn State athletic hierarchy saw their dream game nearly disappear before their eyes. Still, they weren't feeling that good even with the Penn State win because they feared the Lions would drop in the polls. And that's exactly what happened. Penn State woke up Monday morning now No. 3 in the rankings, behind Miami and Michigan, which moved back into the No. 2 slot by defeating Purdue, 31–7.

With Notre Dame, at South Bend, on deck, Paterno began lamenting that his team was "tired." He announced that he would ease up on his troops during the upcoming week of practice, giving them a light workout with no pads on Tuesday. Tuesday was usually Penn State's *toughest* day of practice. That set pundits into motion, with commentators and columnists sending out this word of caution: the last time JoePa eased up on his team like this late in the season was in 1980. The Lions proceeded to lose their last two games—to Notre Dame and Pitt, ironically, the last two opponents on *this* schedule—to finish 6–5 and miss out on a bowl game entirely.

As if sensing a Penn State fall, odds makers installed the Lions as just a five-point favorite at Notre Dame. That set off the irrepressible Bauer, who said, "We're 9–0 and No. 3, and they're 4–4. I would think [the point spread] should be a lot more. It's time for people to start respecting us."

The respect would come after Penn State eked out a 24–19 win at South Bend, while Minnesota upset Michigan. On Monday the polls showed 10–0 Miami (which beat Tulsa, 23–10) and 10–0 Penn State ranked No. 1 and 2, respectively. The win over the Irish was less convincing as it was indicative of what Penn State had been all year: survivalist. The Lions needed Gary Wilkerson, a backup defensive back, to break up what would have been a game-winning touchdown from ND quarterback Steve Beuerlein to tight end Joel Williams. That play was part of a major defensive stand that stopped the Irish after they had gotten the ball to the Penn State six-yard line with a 1:14 remaining.

Said Shaffer after the game: "There were a lot of guys saying a lot of prayers who never said prayers before on the sidelines."

The game had been a feisty one, with extracurricular battles all over the field all game long. One major clash involved Beuerlein, who was magnificent in completing 24 of 39 passes against Penn State's vaunted defense for a career-high 311 yards and two touchdowns. After his second touchdown toss, Beuerlein taunted Conlan. The Penn State linebacker briefly looked as though he was about to take Beuerlein's head off, but used better judgment and instead walked away. After the game Conlan refused to comment on the confrontation.

Even Bauer, who had witnessed the Beuerlein–Conlan byplay and had been ready to jump right into it with his teammate, held back his comments after the game. "My mother told me not to say anything if I don't have anything nice to say about someone," he said. "I don't have anything nice to say about [Beuerlein]."

Only two things—thought to be of minor detail—needed to occur for Miami and Penn State to meet for a national championship. Penn State had to beat 5–4–1 Pittsburgh at home, while Miami had to defeat East Carolina a few days later on a special Thanksgiving night game.

Meanwhile, the Fiesta Bowl had become a target of criticism from the NCAA. First, the NCAA made a fuss that the Fiesta Bowl officials, in order to reap the maximum marketing benefit and be the only game on tap that day, late in the season had changed the date of the Fiesta from January 1 to January 2. Walter Byers, the NCAA's executive director, threatened to deny the Fiesta Bowl its needed NCAA certification. "It's on their application, time and date," Byers said sternly. "They cannot arbitrarily change that. They're approaching that subject with a degree of arrogance as if what they put on the application is irrelevant, and that disturbs me."

The truth was that Byers was getting besieged with complaints from schools with certain conference bowl affiliations that the Fiesta Bowl was running amok with this national championship hype, hence reducing the importance of their own bowls, such as the Rose, Cotton, and Orange. Fiesta Bowl officials were also publicly discussing the notion of adding overtime to their game to prevent a tie and determine a true national champion. Overtime had not yet been introduced in Division I college football.

But those issues were reciprocal to the conclusion of the regular season for Penn State and Miami, both of which needed to win their last game. The Lions did their part, handling Pitt, 34–14. And five days later, Miami, playing without Testaverde, who had gotten scuffed up in a motorscooter accident, beat East Carolina, 36–10, with backup QB Geoff Torretta.

The Penn State–Pitt game, the traditional state rivalry, turned out to be a war, with three separate brawls between the teams. Penn State took a 17–7 lead in the first half on a 26-yard run by Dozier. After Dozier scored, Pitt defensive back Quintin Jones grabbed the tailback's jersey and swung him around in the end zone. Keith Radecic went after Jones. Shaffer followed in an attempt to rescue his center from any further trouble, wound up in the middle of a cluster of players, and got clocked in the head. Later the Penn State quarterback found out the culprit had been Pitt's Steve Apke, a friend and teammate of Shaffer's at Moeller High School.

Later in the game, Panthers punt returner Teryl Austin took exception to the way Penn State's Brian Chizmar had shoved him out of bounds and fired the football at Chizmar's chest. A Penn State player was then flagged for a late hit, and three players—two from Pitt and Don Graham—wound up being ejected. Paterno, meanwhile, had rushed all the way across the field to separate battling players and read the riot act to several of them, including a few from Pitt, right there on the field.

After the game, reporters outside the Pitt locker room heard Panther coach Mike Gottfried's angry voice coming through the walls. "I'm not going to let an hour go by next year without forgetting what [Penn State] did, and I'm not going to forget what their coach did to me on that sideline and how their fans embarrassed us," Gottfried screamed.

The Pitt coach apparently had been alluding to a game-long chant from Penn State fans, which sounded like, "If you can't go to college, go to Pitt."

Asked about his explosion in the locker room afterward, Gottfried denied that it had ever happened. But Pitt's outspoken defensive end Burt Grossman was more than willing to share his views with reporters. "Joe Paterno yelled at us that we have no class," said Grossman. "They tackled our punt returner almost against the [stadium] wall. They called the penalty on them and somehow he thought we were the ones with no class."

A couple of days later, Paterno attempted to explain his role in the melee.

Before I ran across the field, I first made my team stay back along the sideline. I looked over and saw two Pitt kids on top of the tarpaulin [against the stadium wall]. They were very close to the fans and I was afraid the fans would get into it.

But at no time did I say that the Pitt kids had no class. I was as upset with our kids as I was with theirs. I told both sides that they were a disgrace to the game of football. And I told my kids after the game that it that's the way the game of college football is going to be played, I don't want to coach it. That stuff does not belong in the game. I just don't like it. But there is that syndrome—it's a style, a fad—where people talk to each other, trying to intimidate each other.

My intention in going over there was to prevent something serious from happening. If Mike Gottfried takes exception to that, that's his problem.

Meanwhile, after Miami had taken care of their business by beating East Carolina, and a Penn State–Miami game for the Fiesta Bowl was all but set, Hurricanes coach Jimmy Johnson couldn't help himself from poking Penn State and Paterno with a sword coated in irony. Asked for his opinion about the subplot of a national championship game that would pit the "good guys" of Penn State against the "bad guys" of Miami, Johnson used the Pitt game as his backdrop. "I've been reading the last couple of days headlines about 'Big, Bad Penn State,'" Johnson said. "Paterno said they had four or five guys who would fight at the drop of a hat. You mean the 'good guys' of Miami against the 'bad guys' of Penn State?"

And just like that, the dream game was on.

On Friday, November 28, the matchup became official: No. 1 Miami would meet No. 2 Penn State in the Fiesta Bowl on January 2 for the national championship. Miami, with so many prospective pros on its roster, would be a solid favorite. East Carolina quarterback Charlie Libretto, who had played against both Penn State and Miami during the season, added his confirmation. "I don't think Miami would have any problems with Penn State," Libretto said in an Associated Press story.

Penn State started working out for the January 2 game on December 1, a full thirty-three days before kickoff.

Meanwhile in Miami, Hurricanes receiver Michael Irvin got his team's postseason off to a rollicking start. Irvin was cited in a police report for an incident on campus where he allegedly ran over the toes of two Miami students with his car. A University of Miami law student named Steven Naturman said that he and two fellow students were standing in the road talking when Irvin drove toward them and honked his car horn angrily. When the students yelled back, Irvin allegedly said, "I'll just run you over, then." Naturman said that Irvin then backed up his car and ran over the toes of his two friends. He then, allegedly, defiantly said to the trio out of the window of his car, "You've got my license number. My name's Michael Irvin." And then he drove away.

Awards presentations took place in the brief interlude to the college football season. Both Penn State and Miami had managed to collect a few nice postseason gifts.

Testaverde first won Philadelphia's prestigious Maxwell Award, given to college football's best player. Days later, the Miami quarterback was a runaway winner of the Heisman Trophy. Testaverde arrived in New York City wearing a Penn State sweatshirt. He explained to reporters that he was warned to bring a sweatshirt to chilly Manhattan, and the Penn State issue was the only such one he had back in Miami. But Miami football insiders saw it as an example of the soft-spoken Testaverde's cryptic humor. It was Vinny just trying to tweak the Nittany Lions.

Meanwhile, Testaverde found an unlikely buddy in Shane Conlan. Conlan was on the same Los Angeles–bound flight as Testaverde as the two headed to a taping of the Bob Hope Christmas special, which featured the 1986 All-American football team. Conlan had been named first-team defense (offensive lineman Chris Conlin, Tim Johnson, and Ray Isom were named to the second team). The two football enemies hit it off immediately and wound up hanging out together in L.A. Upon returning to State College, Conlan revealed that Testaverde had told him his first college choice was Penn State, but that the Nittany Lions hadn't shown him any interest.

During the days of Penn State's practice sessions for Miami, Paterno made the cover of *Sports Illustrated* as *SI*'s Sportsman of the Year. A few days later, he was named the AP's national Coach of the Year. And so on Sunday, December 21, 1986, Paterno's birthday, the venerable football coach had many things to celebrate. Paterno, reflecting on his age, said in an interview:

I'm not the man I used to be. I think it's stupid if you think you can do at 60 what you did at 45. This is a young man's game. When I was 45, I had all kinds of energy. Four or five hours was nothing to me to sleep. I had the projector going from 6 A.M. to 12 at night. There wasn't a thing that went into the offense, defense, or kicking game that I didn't have a great bearing on.

But you can only do that so long. This job is ten times harder for me than it was when I started.

AT 10 A.M. FRIDAY MORNING, the day after Christmas, 125 Penn State players flew to Arizona from Harrisburg after a send-off by Governor Dick Thornburgh. The pilot was a man named Lou Zimmer. A Penn State graduate, Zimmer led a few cheers for the Lions over the airplane's intercom system before setting the jet airborne.

Immediately after the announcement that Oklahoma's Brian Bosworth had tested positive for steroids and was banned by the NCAA from the Sooners' upcoming bowl game, Penn State players went through their mandatory drug tests. Two days later, the NCAA announced that no Penn State player had tested positive.

Miami came to Arizona on Saturday night, December 27. As the Hurricanes made the long walk down the departure stairs to the tarmac, the world saw that many of them were dressed in full military fatigue uniforms. Said Testaverde: "It's going to be a war out there and we came dressed for a war."

Added Jerome Brown on Penn State: "They're overrated with all that nice guy stuff. Joe Paterno saying all the stuff is a bunch of jive. I know a couple of their players and they're just as crazy as I am. Penn State's not all that clean."

During the week of practice, Jimmy Johnson was asked about possibly recommending to the NCAA that they add overtime to decide college games. "I could do it, but I think that it would have more clout if 'St. Joe' proposed it," Johnson said cynically, referring to Paterno.

Among the loot the players received was $533 in cash, as well as commemorative watches and sweatshirts.

And then there were the parties.

The infamous barbeque took place on a ranch in Rawhide, a western-themed Arizona town near Scottsdale. Caterers served some 1,200 steaks to about 250 people. Part of the night's agenda included skits performed by selected members of the Penn State and Miami teams. John Bruno, the punter and perhaps the team's most effusive personality, was selected as the Nittany Lions' emcee. Bruno, reflecting the lack of pretension of this Penn State team, unwittingly made a racial remark when he said that the one difference between the Lions and Miami was that "we even let the black players eat with us at the training table once a week." Bruno also mocked Jimmy Johnson's stiffly coifed hair.

Bruno then introduced an act called "Irving B and the Boys," in which backup nose tackle Irv Bellamy and a few other Nittany Lions sang a made-up song to the tune of the "Super Bowl Shuffle," which the world champion Chicago Bears had made famous the year before. Those Lions then did a skit aimed at Testaverde, in which team manager Brad Caldwell dressed in a baggy white uniform and struck the Heisman pose.

Then it was Miami's turn. Jerome Brown and a group he called "Miami Vice" came up on stage and started a song that sounded also like the "Super Bowl Shuffle." Then suddenly they stopped. Brown peeled off his outer layer of clothes to reveal the combat fatigues he had worn on the plane and uttered the famous words, "We're here to play football. Did the Japanese go and have dinner with Pearl Harbor before they bombed them? Well, fellas, let's go!"

As the Hurricanes walked out of the barbeque and into their team bus to depart Rawhide, Bruno climbed back on stage and said, "You'll have to excuse them. They had to run off for the filming of *Rambo III*. But besides that, I think the Japanese lost, didn't they?"

Asked about the walkout the next day, Paterno said, "Ah, let them have fun if they want to; let them jive a little bit."

Johnson, meanwhile, seemed to justify the walkout based on Bruno's racial remark, and then added a few concerns:

I don't want to make more of this than it already is; skits are skits. But it's just an explanation of why our guys were offended. Our players are tired of it; we're just tired of hearing about this bad boy image. They were ready to leave anyway. They're not really big on country-western music.

I would be very disappointed if our players poked fun at coach Paterno. Paterno preaching about Penn State's nice guy image is a bunch of jive.

Some nine hundred press credentials were issued for the Miami–Penn State matchup, including three hundred alone for NBC, the network televising the game. Outside Sun Devil Stadium, scalpers were getting as much as $325 for a ticket, an outrageous sum for the time. Ray Scott, the venerable voice of the Green Bay Packers in the heyday of Vince Lombardi and Bart Starr, who in 1986 had been broadcasting Penn State games, predicted that the Lions would win the game. But he was one of the few football fans in America who thought so. A national poll conducted by the *Miami Herald* revealed that the overwhelming majority of sports fans picked Miami. And the betting line in Las Vegas installed the Hurricanes as a 6½-point favorite.

The night before the game, some three thousand Penn State fans showed up at the team hotel in Scottsdale to stage an impromptu pep rally. Curt Warner, Todd Blackledge, and Kenny Jackson, three key members of the Lions' 1983 national championship team, were staying with the Penn State contingent at the hotel and all three spoke at the rally. Shaffer thanked the fans for their support. Paterno had ended the team's practice sessions two days before the big night, saying his team was "ready to play."

Meanwhile, the day before the game, Jimmy Johnson took his team from its Phoenix hotel to a small place called the Carefree Inn in tiny Carefree, Arizona, forty miles away from Phoenix so they could get away from such distractions. The day of the game, Johnson had his team attend a movie. Penn State players, meanwhile, stayed around their hotel, visiting with family and attending short game meetings.

AFTER PETE GIFTOPOULOS MADE "The Play" and John Shaffer ran out the clock, bedlam reigned in Sun Devil Stadium. Isom went running around like a madman. The team hoisted Paterno on its shoulders and carried him off the field, the Penn State coach pumping his fist into the air. Sandusky hid on the bench and cried.

In the Penn State locker room afterward, Paterno, though exhausted, glowed with a happiness few had ever seen before:

It's kind of an unbelievable situation. I had a little trouble sleeping last night because I was so consumed. I'm a great believer in the self-fulfilled destiny kind of thing. These guys literally made up their minds they were going to win a national championship. I don't know how you *will* it, but enough people got together and said they were going to do it. The kind of commitment they made . . .

I said to the team, "Be patient, be patient. They're going to make their yardage. They're too good. But be patient. You're out there to win the football game, not to see how many stats you can get."

ON JANUARY 17, a chilly, five-degree day in State College, the town, after waiting for students to return from holiday break, threw a party for the national champion Penn State Nittany Lions. Some thirty thousand people lined College Avenue and its surrounding arteries for a colossal parade. There were eleven bands in the parade, about a dozen fire companies and their blaring trucks, floats, and decorated trucks and vans. The caravan moved through the streets for about an hour and a half. The party then culminated on the lawn of Old Main on campus, where players whooped it up with fellow students.

John Shaffer grabbed a microphone. Leading his team to a national championship had vindicated the quarterback who a year ago wasn't sure he still had a starting job at Penn State. He smiled at the large crowd. "I'm kind of nostalgic, so if you'll all scoot together, I'd like to take a picture of you all," he said as the crowd roared and some teammates in the background yelled, "Senator Shaffer! Senator Shaffer!"

"In the paper, all we saw was Penn State good, Miami better. Miami did all their talking in the newspapers. Penn State did theirs on the field. Penn State good, Miami, better. Penn State 14, Miami 10!"

The senator had spoken.

Shane Conlan, playing with his typical ferocity, stops Alabama star Bobby Humphrey in one of the Lions' most significant wins of '86. (Photo courtesy of Joe Bodkin)

Penn State linebacker Don Graham stands triumphantly over a fallen Vinny Testaverde. Graham had seven tackles in the Lions' Fiesta Bowl win over Miami and nailed Testaverde for a nine-yard loss. (Photo courtesy of Joe Bodkin)

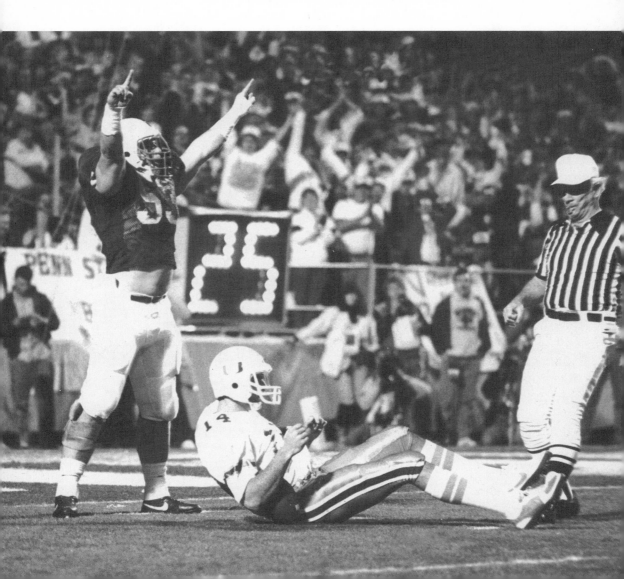

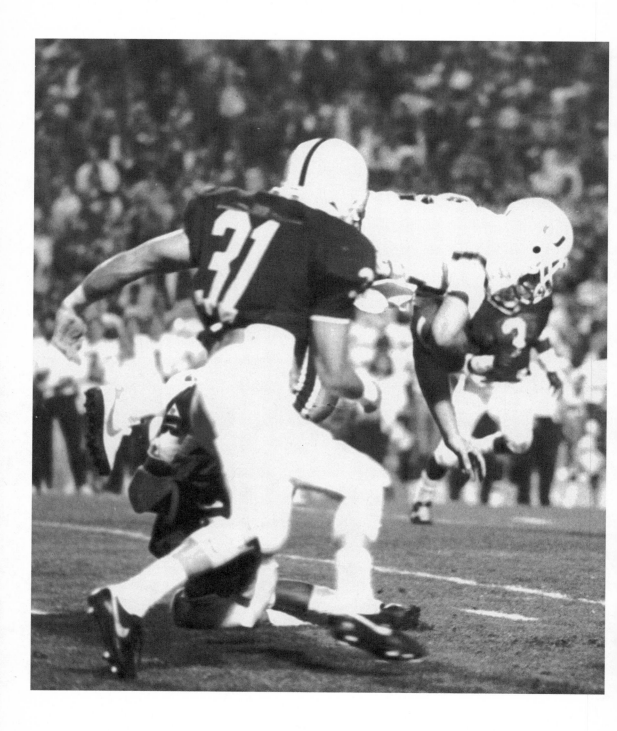

The hits on Miami's Vinny Testaverde the night of the 1987 Fiesta Bowl came high and low. Here, cornerback Duffy Cobbs makes the ankle tackle with linebacker Shane Conlan poised for the kill. (Photo courtesy of Joe Bodkin)

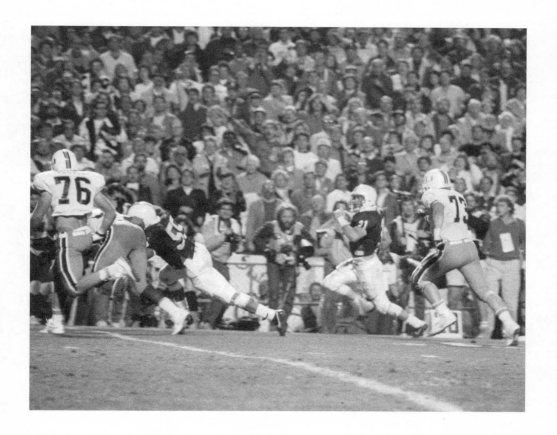

Looking to take it to the house, Shane Conlan rumbles with a key fourth-quarter interception of Testaverde. The play set up D.J. Dozier's Fiesta Bowl game-winning touchdown. (Photo courtesy of Joe Bodkin)

Linebacker Don Graham fells Miami quarterback Vinny Testaverde—typical of the heat Penn State placed on the Miami quarterback in the 1987 Fiesta Bowl. (Photo courtesy of Joe Bodkin)

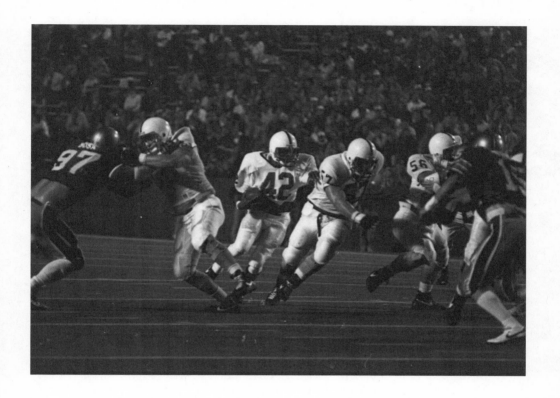

Brian Siverling (left) and Keith Radecic (right) open a gaping hole for halfback D.J. Dozier to follow Chris Conlin in a 26–14 win at Boston College, Penn State's third straight win of the 1986 season.

Much-maligned Penn State quarterback John Shaffer rolls right, looking for a receiver against Rutgers. Shaffer passed for 154 yards that day as the Nittany Lions spoiled Dick Anderson's Beaver Stadium homecoming by beating Anderson's Scarlet Knights, 31–6.

Alabama star Bobby Humphrey is buried by an avalanche of Penn State defenders led by linebacker Don Graham as the Nittany Lions opened the nation's eyes with a 23–3 thrashing of 'Bama in Tuscaloosa.

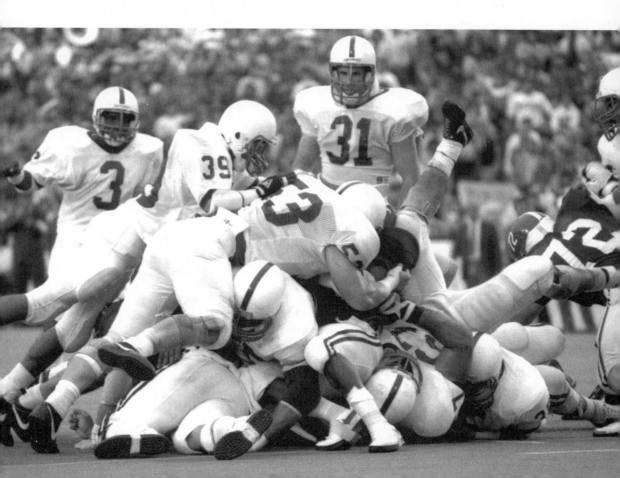

Sure-fingered Brian Siverling snared this key pass from John Shaffer to help Penn State follow up its emotional win at Alabama with a 19–0 shutout at West Virginia.

Defensive tackle Pete Curkendall rambles 82 yards after intercepting a Dan Henning pass to ensure a too-close-for-comfort 17–15 win at Maryland.

D.J. Dozier high-steps his way to another big gain against Maryland. Dozier rushed 25 times for 111 yards and two touchdowns as the Nittany Lions survived, 17–15.

Penn State's undefeated regular season was saved by the Nittany Lions' desperate defensive stand at Notre Dame. Here, Bob White, Pete Giftopolous, and Trey Bauer chase ND quarterback Steve Beuerlein into a mistake on the Fighting Irish's final, unsuccessful scoring drive as the Lions win, 24–19.

Vice President George H.W. Bush, shown here with Notre Dame president Theodore Hesburgh, was part of the pregame flag-raising ceremonies prior to the Penn State–Notre Dame game on November 15, 1986.

Speaking to the Penn State student body on campus following a post–Fiesta Bowl parade, Nittany Lion co-captains: from left, John Shaffer, Steve Smith, Shane Conlan, and Bob White. (Photo courtesy of Joe Bodkin)

Steve Smith in a rare carry for the Los Angeles Raiders. Hard-nosed and leather tough, the former Penn State fullback delighted in blocking for Raiders stars such as Marcus Allen and Bo Jackson.

Steve Smith and his wife, Chie. The Raider and the Raiderette had a true Hollywood romance. (Photo courtesy of Chie Smith)

Steve Smith, his Adonis football body ravaged by ALS, surrounded by his at-home support system: from left, daughter Jazmin, son Dante, and wife Chie.

Steve Smith and some heavy-hitter Raider buddies at a memorabilia show for his benefit. From left: Howie Long, Willie Gault, Marcus Allen, Bo Jackson, and Tim Brown. (Photo courtesy of Chie Smith)

Pete Giftopolous (as he looks now).

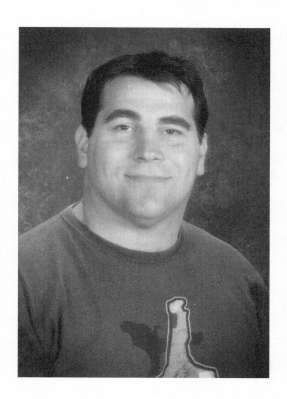

Ray Isom, the man who rocked Miami's receivers in the Fiesta Bowl, with his family. Clockwise from the top: wife Tracey, daughter Shaquita, and adopted children, Xaria, Zaire, and Jelani. (Photo courtesy of the Isom family)

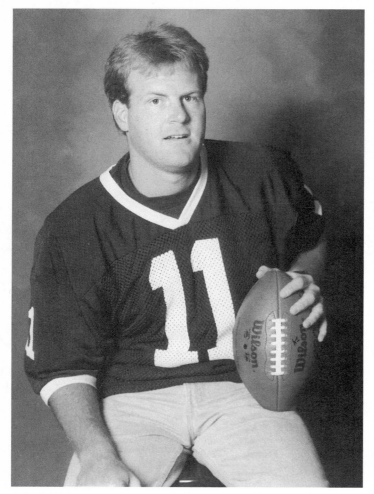

(above left)
Bruno making the infamous comments that preceded a Hurricanes walkout at a barbeque for both teams. The Penn Stater died of melanoma in 1992. (Photo courtesy of the Bruno family)

(above right)
The surviving Bruno family. From left, mom Alfrieda, sister Cheryl, and dad John Sr.

(left)
Penn State's John Bruno may have been the Nittany Lions' most valuable player the night the Lions beat Miami. (Photo courtesy of the Bruno family)

(above)   The Dozier family. From left: Mindy, Abriah, Nadja, Gabriella, D.J., William-Elisha

(below)   The Conlan family. From left: Shane, Danny, Caroline, Christopher, Patrick, Mary Katherine.

(above)   The Shaffer family. From left: Reed, Marta, John, John Jr., Kohl, Hayley.

(below left)   Jerry Sandusky. (Photo courtesy of Greg Grieco)

(below right)   Bob White. (Photo courtesy of Greg Grieco)

6

PENN STATE VS. MIAMI, PLAY BY PLAY

PENN STATE AND MIAMI played for what seemed like an eternity the night of January 2 in Tempe, Arizona. The teams rattled off 182 plays in the game—the telecast of which, on NBC, ran well more than three hours. Of those 182 plays, Miami's offense ran 106. And the Hurricanes' time of possession almost doubled Penn State's.

The following is a play-by-play account of the 1987 Fiesta Bowl:

First Quarter
PENN STATE POSSESSION

1. Miami's Mark Seelig kicks off to Penn State. Blair Thomas receives the ball at the 13-yard line and runs 17 yards to the 30.
2. 1st down at the 30: John Shaffer, sacked by Daniel Stubbs and Dan Sileo for −14 yards.
3. 2nd down at the 16: Tim Manoa gains 4.
4. 3rd down at the 20: Shaffer sacked by Bill Hawkins for −6. 4th and 26 for Penn State.
5. 4th down at the 14: John Bruno punts (44 yards). Miami's David Kintigh receives at Miami 42-yard line, four-yard return to 46 (Miami penalized 10 yards for holding).

MIAMI POSSESSION

6. Miami, 1st down at UM 36: Melvin Bratton around right end for five yards.
7. 2nd down at 41: Vinny Testaverde passes to Michael Irvin on quick out for 13 yards for first down.
8. 1st down at PSU 48: Alonzo Highsmith carries for two yards.
9. 2nd down at 46: Testaverde, chased by Bob White, throws incomplete to Highsmith.

10. 3rd down at 46: Testaverde complete over the middle to tight end Charles Henry for 10 yards and a first down.

11. 1st down at PSU 36: Miami penalty, −5 (delay of game).

12. 1st down at 41: Highsmith runs for three yards.

13. 2nd down at 38: Testaverde beats Penn State blitz and completes pass to Highsmith for 10 yards.

14. 3rd down at 28: Testaverde rolls right, throws incomplete in end zone to Brett Perriman.

15. 4th down at 28: Miami goes for the first down instead of attempting a 45-yard field goal. Testaverde incomplete to Henry, who drops pass over the middle.

PENN STATE POSSESSION

16. 1st down at PSU 28: D.J. Dozier around left end for five yards.

17. 2nd down at 33: Steve Smith sweeps right for 10 yards and a first down.

18. 1st down at 43: Shaffer incomplete, intended for Smith.

19. 2nd down at 43: Penalty, Penn State, −5 (illegal procedure).

20. 2nd down at 38: Dozier on counter for 10 yards, setting up third and five.

21. 3rd down at 48: Shaffer incomplete, intended for tight end Brian Siverling.

22. 4th down at 48: Bruno punt (50 yards), downed at Miami two-yard line by Keith Karpinski.

MIAMI POSSESSION

23. 1st down at UM 2: Highsmith carries for 1 yard.

24. 2nd down at 3: Testaverde incomplete, intended for Irvin, who dropped the ball when hit hard by Duffy Cobbs.

25. 3rd down at 3: Testaverde complete to Bratton for 12 yards and a first down.

26. 1st down at 15: Bratton sweeps right for five yards, stopped by Marques Henderson and Shane Conlan (Conlan hurts knee on play when hit low by his own man, Duffy Cobbs, in Cobbs's pursuit of the tackle, and is taken out of game briefly).

27. 2nd down at 20: Highsmith off tackle, hit by Karpinski (Conlan's replacement) and fumbles. Miami's Henry recovers. Play results in a plus-one gain.

28. 3rd down at 21: Testaverde complete over the middle to Irvin to UM 44, hit by Ray Isom and fumbles; ball bounces around and is recovered by Cobbs.

PENN STATE POSSESSION

29. 1st down at UM 44: Dozier carries off left-tackle for four yards.

30. 2nd down at 40: Blair Thomas carries for −3, tackled by Rod Carter.

31. 3rd down at 43: Shaffer complete to Dozier in left flat for three yards.

32. 4th down at 40: Bruno pooch punt goes out of bounds at UM 9.

MIAMI POSSESSION

33. 1st down at 9: Highsmith carries for three yards.

34. 2nd down at 12: Testaverde sacked by Don Graham for −9.

35. Miami 3 and 16: Testaverde breaks out on a scramble from his own end zone (Bob White just misses a sack) for 21 yards and a first down.
36. 1st down at 24: Miami penalty, −5 (illegal procedure).
37. 1st down at 19: Highsmith carries off tackle for eight yards.
38. 2nd down at 27: Testaverde, beating blitz, complete in flat to Highsmith for 13 and a first down.
39. 1st down at 40: Bratton carries for four yards.
40. 2nd down at 44: Bratton carries for two yards.
41. 3rd down at 46: Testaverde complete to Perriman for 11 yards and a first down at the Penn State 43.

Second Quarter
MIAMI POSSESSION

42. 1st down at PSU 43: Testaverde incomplete.
43. 2nd down at 43: Draw play to Highsmith for two yards.
44. 3rd down at 41: Testaverde attempts long pass, intercepted by Cobbs at PSU 15, returns to PSU 30.

PENN STATE POSSESSION

45. 1st down at 30: Shaffer attempts deep pass to Ray Roundtree, incomplete.
46. 2nd down at 30: Manoa carries off tackle for five yards.
47. 3rd down at 35: Shaffer rushed, throws incomplete out of bounds to avoid sack.
48. 4th down at 45: Bruno punts (51 yards) to Kintigh at UM 14, returns to 21, but penalty, −10 (holding) Miami, brings ball to UM 11.

MIAMI POSSESSION

49. 1st down at 11: Warren Williams carries for six yards.
50. 2nd down at 17: Testaverde scrambles for three yards, stopped by Pete Giftopoulos.
51. 3rd down at 20: Highsmith dives for one yard and a first down.
52. 1st down at 21: (Conlan back in game for Penn State), Williams sweeps left for one yard.
53. 2nd down at 22: Testaverde complete to Brian Blades for 10 yards and first down.
54. 1st down at 32: Highsmith carries for two yards.
55. 2nd down at 34: Testaverde complete on quick out to Blades for 13 yards and first down.
56. 1st down at 47: Miami penalty, −5 (illegal procedure).
57. 1st down at 42: Testaverde incomplete, intended for Blades over middle.
58. 2nd down at 42: Testaverde incomplete, intended for Williams, who drops it.
59. 3rd down at 42: Testaverde complete to Williams in right flat for 13 yards.
60. 4th down at PSU 47: Jeff Feagles punt (33 yards); fair catch by Jim Coates at PSU 14.

PENN STATE POSSESSION

61. 1st down at 14: Dozier off right tackle for 19 yards and a first down.

62. 1st down at 33: Dozier, stripped by Jerome Brown, recovers his own fumble; results in a −2.

63. 2nd down at 31: Shaffer loses ball after trying to pull back a pass with Brown at his feet; winds up in hands of UM lineman Bill Hawkins for interception.

MIAMI POSSESSION

64. 1st down at PSU 23: Highsmith right end sweep for eight yards.

65. 2nd down at 15: Highsmith left end sweep for seven yards and a first down.

66. 1st down at PSU 8: Testaverde complete to Henry for seven yards.

67. 2nd down at 1: Bratton leaps over the line for one-yard touchdown (only second TD all year given up by Penn State in the first half). Greg Cox PAT. Miami 7, Penn State 0.

PENN STATE POSSESSION

68. Seelig kicks to Penn State, Coates returns to PSU 26.

69. 1st down at 26: Dozier carries for 8 yards.

70. 2nd down at 33: Smith carries for 2 yards.

71. 3rd down at 35: Dozier carries for 4 yards and a first down.

72. 1st down at 39: Shaffer incomplete on attempted screen pass.

73. 2nd down at 39: Dozier on counter for −2.

74. 3rd down at 37: Shaffer complete over middle to Eric Hamilton for 22 yards and a first down.

75. 1st down at UM 41: Manoa up middle for 20 yards and a first down.

76. 1st down at 21: Manoa carries for four yards.

77. 2nd down at 17: Shaffer incomplete, intended for Hamilton at goal line.

78. 3rd down at 17: Shaffer rolls right, complete to Manoa in flat for 12 yards and a first down.

79. 1st down at 5: Manoa up middle, fumbles, recovered by Penn State's Darryl Giles, one-yard gain.

80. 2nd down at 4: Shaffer rolls right, fakes a pass, and dives into right pylon for four-yard touchdown (completing 11-play, 74-yard drive). Massimo Manca PAT. Miami 7, Penn State 7. 1:22 left in half.

MIAMI POSSESSION

81. Manca kicks to Miami's J.C. Penny at one-yard line, return of 24 yards to 25.

82. 1st down at 25: Testaverde incomplete, intended for Bratton.

83. 2nd down at 25: Testaverde avoids Marques Henderson blitz, complete to Perriman for 10 yards and a first down.

84. 1st down at 35: Testaverde incomplete, intended for Irvin.

85. 2nd down at 35: Testaverde complete to Blades for 20 yards and a first down.

86. 1st down at PSU 45: Testaverde chased by White and Giftopoulos, loses ball from his hand; recovered by Miami offensive lineman Matt Patchan for loss of 22 yards.

87. 2nd down at UM 43: Testaverde incomplete, intended for Blades, broken up by Eddie Johnson.

88. 3rd down at 43: Testaverde complete to Irvin for 23 yards and first down, but ruled beyond line of scrimmage, resulting in five-yard penalty and loss of down.

89. 4th down at UM 38: Highsmith carries for 18 yards as the clock runs out, ending first half (Miami 7, Penn State 7)

Third Quarter
MIAMI POSSESSION

90. Manca kicks to Miami.

91. 1st down at UM 15: Bratton carries for two yards.

92. 2nd down at 17: Testaverde incomplete, dropped by Highsmith.

93. 3rd down at 17: Testaverde incomplete, dropped by Irvin.

94. 4th down at 17: Feagles punts (51 yards) to Coates at PSU 31, returns 7 yards to 38. Isom flagged for running into the kicker. Miami coach Jimmy Johnson refuses the five-yard penalty, which would not have given Miami a first down, instead taking Feagles's punt.

PENN STATE POSSESSION

95. 1st down at PSU 38: Dozier off right tackle for four yards.

96. 2nd down at 42: Shaffer fumbles snap; Penn State recovers for no gain.

97. 3rd down at 42: Shaffer incomplete, intended for Siverling.

98. Bruno punts (38 yards) to Kintigh at UM 20, five-yard return to 25.

MIAMI POSSESSION

99. 1st down at UM 25: Testaverde rolls left, throws deep incomplete, intended for Irvin.

100. 2nd down at 25: Testaverde avoids two Penn State sack attempts before tackled by Conlan for −1.

101. 3rd down at 24: Testaverde complete to Perriman for six yards.

102. 4th down at 24: Feagles punts (48 yards) to Coates at PSU 22, returns five yards before Penn State clipping penalty on the return sets up first down at 13.

PENN STATE POSSESSION

103. 1st down at PSU 13: Dozier carries for three yards.

104. 2nd down at 16: Dozier carries, spinning for 16 yards and a first down.

105. 1st down at 32: Shaffer complete over middle to Dozier for nine yards.

106. 2nd down at 41: Miami penalty, −5 (offsides, Sileo), and PSU first down.

107. 1st down at 46: Dozier counter for two yards.

108. 2nd down at 48: Smith carries for no gain.

109. 3rd down at 48: Shaffer intercepted by Miami's Selwyn Brown after pass bounces off Roundtree's hands.

MIAMI POSSESSION

110. 1st down at PSU 40: Highsmith on right end sweep for six yards.
111. 2nd down at 34: Testaverde complete in left flat to Williams for nine yards and a first down.
112. 1st down at 25: Miami penalty, −5 (illegal procedure).
113. 1st down at 30: Testaverde chased, tackled by Conlan for no gain.
114. 2nd down at 30: Testaverde complete to Henry over middle for seven yards.
115. 3rd down at 23: Testaverde slips, tries to throw to left side, intercepted by Conlan, who stumbles and falls in his attempt to return it.

PENN STATE POSSESSION

116. 1st down at PSU 25: Manoa carries for six yards.
117. 2nd down at PSU 31: Manoa fumbles, Winston Moss recovers for Miami.

MIAMI POSSESSION

118. 1st down at PSU 31: Williams carries for six yards.
119. 2nd down at 25: Testaverde play-action, rolls, sacked by Giftopoulos for −7.
120. 3rd down at 32: Testaverde incomplete, intended for Irvin, but Isom called for pass interference. Miami first down.
121. 1st down at 17: Williams carries for three yards.
122. 2nd down at 14: Williams carries for two yards.
123. 3rd down at 12: Testaverde incomplete.
124. 4th down at 12: Seelig attempts 28-yard field goal, misses wide right. Penn State takes over possession.

PENN STATE POSSESSION

125. 1st down at PSU 20: Dozier carries for two yards.
126. 2nd down at 22: Shaffer sacked by Dan Stubbs for −2.
127. 3rd down at 20: Shaffer incomplete on shovel pass.
128. 4th down at 20: Bruno punts (45 yards) to Kintigh at 35, loses two yards on return.

MIAMI POSSESSION

129. 1st down at UM 33: Bratton carries for two yards.
130. 2nd down at 35: Testaverde complete over middle to Highsmith for 11 yards and a first down. End of third quarter. Miami 7, Penn State 7.

Fourth Quarter

MIAMI POSSESSION

131. 1st down at 46: Testaverde intercepted by Giftopoulos at PSU 43, returns it 21 yards to Miami 36.

PENN STATE POSSESSION

132. 1st down at UM 36: Dozier sweeps right end for three yards, colliding with NBC sideline commentator Ahmad Rashad.
133. 2nd down at 33: Smith carries for one yard.

134. 3rd down at 32: Shaffer's pass knocked down incomplete at the line of scrimmage.
135. 4th down at 32: Manca attempts 50-yard field goal, no good.

MIAMI POSSESSION

136. 1st down at UM 32: Bratton sweeps right for three yards.
137. 2nd down at 31: Testaverde over middle to Bratton for 13 yards and a first down.
138. 1st down at 44: Highsmith toss left for eight yards.
139. 2nd down at PSU 48: Highsmith carries for 22 yards (giving him 92 yards rushing at that point of the game) and a first down.
140. 1st down at 28: Bratton sweeps right for one yard.
141. 2nd down at 27: Testaverde incomplete, intended for Blades.
142. 3rd down at 27: Testaverde complete to Bratton for six yards.
143. 4th down at 21: Seelig successful on a 38-yard field goal.
     Miami 10, Penn State 7.

PENN STATE POSSESSION

144. Seelig kicks off to Thomas at 8, returns to PSU 28.
145. 1st down at 28: Dozier carries for three yards.
146. 2nd down at 31: Shaffer sacked by Jerome Brown for −11.
147. 3rd down at 20: Dozier carries for 14 yards.
148. 4th down at 34: Bruno punts (48 yards) to Kintigh at UM 16, five-yard return to 21.

MIAMI POSSESSION

149. 1st down at UM 21: Bratton carries for 13 yards and a first down.
150. 1st down at 34: Bratton carries for no gain, stuffed by Bauer.
151. 2nd down at 34: Testaverde intercepted by Conlan at UM 43, returns 38 yards to UM five-yard line.

PENN STATE POSSESSION

152. 1st down at 5: Shaffer fumbles snap; PSU's Keith Radecic recovers for −1.
153. 2nd down at 6: Dozier carries up the middle for six-yard touchdown. Manca PAT is good. Penn State 14, Miami 10 (8:13 remaining).

MIAMI POSSESSION

154. Manca's kickoff goes through end zone. Miami takes over at UM 20.
155. 1st down at 20: Highsmith carries for 21 yards and a first down; Cobbs makes TD-saving tackle.
156. 1st down at 41: Highsmith carries for five yards.
157. 2nd down at 46: Testaverde complete over middle to Alfredo Roberts, who is stripped of ball by Bauer. Penn State recovers at UM 49.

PENN STATE POSSESSION

158. 1st down at UM 49: Dozier carries for no gain.

159. 2nd down at 49: Shaffer complete to Siverling for six yards.

160. 3rd down at 43: Shaffer incomplete, intended for Roundtree.

161. 4th down at 43: Bruno punts (43 yards) into end zone; Miami takes over at UM 20.

MIAMI POSSESSION

162. 1st down at UM 20: Testaverde complete to Alfredo Roberts for eight yards, but offensive interference penalty on Miami, −10 yards and loss of down.

163. 2nd down at 10: Highsmith carries on draw play for no gain.

164. 3rd down at 10: Testaverde throws deep down the middle intended for Irvin, incomplete.

165. 4th down at 10: Feagles punts (47 yards), fair catch Coates at PSU 43.

PENN STATE POSSESSION

166. 1st down at PSU 43: Roundtree carries on reverse for two yards.

167. 2nd down at 45: Dozier carries for three yards.

168. 3rd down at 48: Manoa carries for −2 yards.

169. 4th down at 46: Bruno punts (39 yards) to Kintigh at UM 15, eight-yard return to 23.

MIAMI POSSESSION

170. 1st down at 23: Testaverde scrambles for four yards.

171. 2nd down at 27: Testaverde incomplete over the middle; nearly intercepted by Bauer.

172. 3rd down at 27: Testaverde incomplete, intended for Bratton.

173. 4th down and six at 27: Testaverde complete on out to Blades, who breaks loose for a 30-yard gain and a first down before being stopped at PSU 43.

174. 1st down at PSU 43: Testaverde complete to Blades for eight yards.

175. 2nd down at 35: Testaverde complete to Perriman for nine yards and a first down.

176. 1st down at 26 (1:43 remaining): Testaverde complete over middle to Irvin for four yards.

177. 2nd down at 22: Testaverde complete to Irvin for 12 yards and a first down.

178. 1st down at 10 (1:01 remaining): Testaverde complete to Irvin for five yards.

179. 2nd down at 5: Testaverde sacked by Tim Johnson for −8.

180. 3rd down at 13 (25 seconds remaining): Testaverde flushed out of pocket, incomplete.

181. 4th down at 13 ("The Play"): Testaverde intercepted by Giftopoulos at goal line, returns 10 yards to 10.

PENN STATE POSSESSION

182. 1st down at 10: Shaffer kneels on ball.

7

FALLEN HEROES

STEVE SMITH LIES IN A RECLINER, powerless. The life he once knew is long gone.

The hearty fullback, who rushed for more than a thousand yards for Penn State, then plowed holes as the lead back for Marcus Allen and Bo Jackson with the vaunted Los Angeles Raiders, is now just a shell of the physical marvel he used to be, his body ravished by amyotrophic lateral sclerosis (Lou Gehrig's disease) and Lyme disease.

He hears but cannot speak. He sees but cannot act. He thinks but cannot process. ALS has made Smith a prisoner of his own body, as if he is in a full-length straitjacket. It is a horrible existence for any human being. For a former professional football player, for whom athletics was once a staple, who in retirement worked in a weekly game of tennis with his wife and tutored his son and daughter on the driveway basketball court, it is beyond cruel.

There is no cure for ALS. Steve Smith is dying. To stave that off for as long as he can, Smith requires twenty-four-hour care. He can breathe only through the pulsing of a machine and a tracheal tube. Every ten minutes or so, mucous must be vacuumed out of the tube protruding from his neck,

John Bruno was watching the drill from the sidelines. The fourth-team defense was on the field against the first-team offense, practicing goal-line plays.

Joe Johns, the Lions' fourth-team safety, anticipated the next offensive play would be a pass since the first-team O had just tried two straight-up-the-middle running plays, and he perched himself some seven yards behind the line of scrimmage.

The play was a run.

Trying to fill the gap quickly, Johns saw fullback Steve Smith, all 235 pounds of him, blasting up the middle, the football tucked in the pit of his massive arm cavity. What Johns knew about Smith was that he took it easy on no one. Whether it was a game with 90,000 people in the stands or a minute drill in a meaningless practice, Smith would make the tackler pay. And sure enough, on this play the fullback crashed into Johns with the furor of a meteor strike. Johns lay flat on the ground. He looked up to see Smith—actually to see two Smiths—staring down at him with concern.

Several minutes later, Johns came to his senses on the sidelines. Bruno, the team's punter and prankster, came over to check on his pal. "JJ," Bruno quipped, "for a moment there, the earth stood still."

then inside the gums of his mouth, or he could choke to death. His body stopped being able to chew or swallow and so he must be fed liquids only—liquids mixed with heavy medication and fed through a tube that cuts directly into his stomach.

His only connection to the outside world is a talking computer screen, which he attempts to operate with the tiniest bit of strength impulse he has left in his once-massive legs. The computer screen has a cursor that jumps around among blocks of words, phrases, names, and letters. He tries to stop it on the word or phrase or name or letters he wants to use by squeezing a red pouch attached to his knees by Velcro, which serves as a mouse.

A visitor has come to his home on this day not knowing what to expect and not knowing, certainly, what to say. Steve Smith attempts to put him at ease.

"H-e-l-l-o," he writes out on his screen. It is a painstakingly slow process. Smith is working so hard to perform this small task; his forehead starts to form beads of sweat.

"How . . . are . . . you?"

IN ANOTHER PLACE AND ANOTHER TIME, the parents of John Bruno, the Penn State punter who had helped the Nittany Lions win the 1986 Fiesta Bowl, stand at the tombstone of their only son.

John Bruno passed away many years ago, his life cut short by a disease that hit him suddenly and without remorse. John Bruno's parents visit his gravesite often. When they do, they talk to their son about the life he may have had. The Penn State punter had a degree in finance and a love for the game of golf. The Brunos kneel at the tombstone and think out loud, loud enough for the spirit of their son to hear, about that golf facility they talked about owning as a family. It would have a driving range and a miniature golf course with windmills and clown's mouth, and the balls would be half blue and half white and maybe the Nittany Lion fight song would play when one of those blue and white golf balls dropped into the slot on the nineteenth hole for a free game. But the life he may have had is just a passing thought that dissipates, a dream that ends at the behest of reality.

John Bruno passed away on April 13, 1992, just a little more than five years after his last football game. Bruno was one of Penn State's brightest stars in that 1987 Fiesta Bowl. He punted nine times and averaged 45 yards per punt. And most of his punts had saved the Nittany Lions, reversing bad field position from a stumbling offense into great field position for their potent defense.

It was skin cancer. It was sudden. One day he felt sick. He thought he had the flu. He started losing blood and thought it might be a bleeding ulcer. His parents took him to the hospital. Doctors there put him through a battery of tests. Hours later, they told him he only had a few more months to live.

"We think about him every day," John Bruno Sr. says. "His mother and I would trade positions with him any chance we got. Sometimes I tell him how much we're looking forward to being together with him again some day."

THE CIRCUMSTANCES OF STEVE SMITH and John Bruno bring us to grips with an inexorable truth: a game is only a game. Smith and Bruno are the fallen comrades of the 1986 Nittany Lions who now exist only in our consciousness, but as something much more meaningful than a final score. In death, Bruno is the inspiration for a foundation started by his friends to raise money for the research, treatment, and obliteration of this type of cancer. Smith's condition has spawned the Steve Smith Foundation, dedicated to the cure and prevention of motor neuron disease, a progressive degeneration of the body's motor system—the cells and nerves in the brain and spinal cord that control the muscles.

That Steve Smith lies helpless and at the mercy of a body that just won't work anymore is surreal. Smitty was an iron horse. At Penn State, he was as dependable a player as Joe Paterno ever had. Highly recruited out of the Washington, D.C., area, where he played for powerful DeMatha High, Smith was never any more than a solid complementary player at Happy Valley. But he helped the team win. He ran the football, he blocked, and he caught passes out of the backfield, and he never complained about sharing the fullback load with Tim Manoa, though Smith had come to State with the better pedigree.

The L.A. Raiders, seeing the need for a versatile, selfless fullback, drafted him in the third round, one pick after Manoa, who went to the Cleveland Browns. Smith was thrilled to be going to the same team as Marcus Allen. He had met Allen once when they were both guests at a dinner presented by Washington, D.C.'s Touchdown Club; Smith was a metro high school star then and Allen had been named college football Player of the Year at USC. The slick, handsome Allen was an idol of Smith's. And now he'd be blocking for him.

Steve Smith's pro career took on a model of consistency. After a rookie year in which he played in seven games for the Raiders, Smith became a starter. That would start a string of seven straight years in which he would play all sixteen games of the season—a near-unheard-of feat for a player whose main role was to smash his muscular 245-pound frame into any oncoming tackler to spring either Allen or, later, Bo Jackson for big yardage.

"I really believe that Steve had this sick satisfaction of getting into that hole and knocking out a linebacker, and I mean knocking him cold, so that Marcus and I could run," Jackson said once in a television interview.

In seven years as a Raider, Steve Smith gained just a little more than 1,500 yards. In his best year, 1989, he carried the ball 117 times for 471 yards. He scored six TDs one year. He had 28 catches in another season. They were modest statistics. But it was Smith's work ethic that endeared him to teammates and fans. He was a pickup truck that just plowed along and never needed any maintenance.

And then there was that fairytale romance.

In 1988 at a Raiders charity function, the Cedar-Sinai Sports Spectacular, he locked eyes on a Raiderette cheerleader named Chie Ohara. She was drop-dead gorgeous, a blend of Japanese, Spanish, and Native American. Unlike other pro football organizations, the Raiders of renegade owner Al Davis had no silly rule that players couldn't associate with cheerleaders. Steve Smith started asking the charity organizers about the beautiful cheerleader and found out that her first name was pronounced "Chee-A."

He approached her. "Hello, Chee-A," he said.

She was impressed that he knew how to pronounce her name. But Chie Ohara had also already noticed Steve Smith. On this night, the Raiderettes' job was to escort the Raiders players into the ballroom. Chie had switched with a cheer-leader friend so she could escort Steve Smith. The guy she gave up to her friend in this beefcake trade was the famed Dr. J, basketball star Julius Erving. Steve and Chie were married not long after that.

When his football career finally ended after the 1995 season (his second year with the Seahawks), Steve Smith moved his family, which now included two children, son Dante and daughter Jazmin, to Jonesboro, Georgia, just south of Atlanta. In the brief stops he had made there as a player, Steve had grown to like the Atlanta area, and it was where he decided to start his full-service carwash, a business venture that had long been a dream.

The carwash business got off the ground, but it also required full-service care. Steve was working fourteen-hour days, which left him very little time for his family. He was ready for a change. A carwash customer told him about a business called "Philly Connection," a shop serving Philadelphia-style sandwiches that was being franchised throughout the Southeast. They were expanding to the Dallas area. So, in June 2002, Steve bought into a franchise and the Smiths packed up and moved to Plano, Texas.

The Smiths were in Texas for only about a month when Steve started feeling slight twitching sensations in his right shoulder. He didn't think much of it. He had faced pain and discomfort almost every day of his life as a pro football player. But then his hands started getting weaker and his legs started feeling heavy. Smith went to the hospital. Orthopedic tests could find nothing wrong. Neurologic tests would find something different. On September 11, 2002, doctors told him he had ALS and would most likely die within the next five years.

More than five thousand people a year are diagnosed with amyotrophic lateral sclerosis, one of humankind's most horrible and mysterious diseases. A human being has motor neurons, or nerve cells, that are located in the brain, brain stem, and spinal cord. The cells serve as controlling units and vital communication links between the nervous system and the voluntary muscles of the body. Messages from the motor neurons in the brain, the upper motor neurons, are transmitted to motor neurons in the spinal cord, the lower motor neurons, and then to particular muscles. With ALS, both sets of neurons die off and the messages are no longer sent to the muscles. Unable to function, the muscles gradually weaken and waste away. From there, the ability of the brain to start and control voluntary movement is gone. When muscles in the diaphragm and chest wall fail, those afflicted lose the ability to breathe without a ventilator.

ALS seemingly comes from nowhere, occurring at random. Doctors only have theories on what causes it. Some researchers think it is a gene mutation that produces some kind of harmful enzyme. Others theorize that it related to a high level of a chemical called glutamate in the spinal fluid. No one is close to finding a cure.

What do you do when someone hands you a death sentence? Steve and Chie Smith embarked on a tireless odyssey to save his life.

They spoke with countless doctors. They tried many medications. They visited a variety of hospitals. In Reno, Nevada, the Smiths found a clinic that experimented with alternative medical treatments. The treatments there cost them

$20,000 and were not covered by health insurance. Steve wasn't getting any better.

One day while sitting in a waiting room at the Reno clinic, Chie started browsing through a *People* magazine. She happened upon a story about a man who had been misdiagnosed with ALS. The man was being treated at a suburban Philadelphia clinic when Dr. Gregory Bach determined that the man didn't have ALS at all. He had Lyme disease, an ailment transmitted from a bite by a deer tick that often mimics the symptoms of amyotrophic lateral sclerosis. Bach cured the man with antibiotics.

Smith, who had previously tested negative for Lyme disease, took another test. This one was positive. The Smiths now had hope.

They made monthly trips to Philadelphia to see Bach at the Haverford Wellness Clinic. At the clinic, Chie underwent a three-week training program to learn how to detoxify her husband with something called infusion therapy—a treatment designed to clean and regenerate the motor neurons. Chie had to withdraw Steve's blood into a syringe, mix it with a combination of medicines and nutrients— something called phosphaditylcholine and glutathione—then place the fluid back into his system through a port that had been drilled into his chest.

Smith stayed on the treatment for a year. Still, there was no improvement. The port in Steve's chest became infected. He spent two weeks in the hospital just to treat the infection. Chie Smith explored other alternative treatments. She consulted with other doctors with different alternative treatments. The new doctors also prescribed medications introduced into the body via a chest port. Again Steve's port became infected. Meanwhile, Chie continued speaking with conventional ALS specialists. They told her that tests may have revealed Lyme disease, but that her husband also had ALS, and no amount of medication was going to cure that.

WHEN THE CALL CAME for the teams from Penn State and Miami to perform skits at a welcoming barbeque a few days before the game in Arizona, there was little question as to who would be the Nittany Lions' front man.

John Bruno, Penn State's spunky punter, the kid who would sometimes grab a guitar and start imitating Elvis Presley, would serve as the Lions' master of ceremonies. After all, Bruno was the team's jokester, and the Lions in 1986 really needed some laughter to diffuse the pressure of a run to a national championship.

John Bruno had always been the happy-go-lucky kid with the carefree spirit. And he certainly had Penn State in his blood.

John's father, John Bruno Sr., had played football for the Lions—he was a shifty wingback—in the early 1950s. Rip Engle had just arrived in Happy Valley as the architect of a new Penn State football era. Engle came from Brown University and brought with him to State a young assistant who had played quarterback for him there. The assistant's named was Joe Paterno.

One of Paterno's early recruiting coups as a Nittany Lions assistant was signing a fleet halfback named Lenny Moore, a circumstance that diluted John Bruno Sr.'s Penn State football career. Bruno left Penn State with a degree, though, and began a career in steel. He worked for Jones and Laughlin, a Pittsburgh steel company, which meant moving his wife, Alfreida, and young family—daughter Cheryl and son John Jr.—around the country. The Brunos went from Pittsburgh to Atlanta to Philadelphia and then to Dayton before settling back near Pittsburgh. The constant moving never affected young John—he made good friends everywhere he went and used a love for sports as his balance. For him, the sporting seasons flowed into each other, from football to basketball to baseball and then to golf. And John dragged his older sister into every sport he played.

The two kids made everything a competition. When John was in the fourth grade, he and Cheryl played a punting game his father had made up called Five Up, Five Back. They'd go into the back yard beyond the border of the Bruno home and punt a football to each other. If you caught the ball on the fly, you were allowed to advance five giant steps. If you dropped it, you retreated five steps. First one to cross the boundary line of the house was the winner. Naturally, the Brunos' youngest child would grow up to be a major college punter.

Bruno came to Penn State as a walk-on. He was a three-sport athlete at Upper St. Clair High and loved football the most. A slick receiver who was maybe a tad too slow for the big-time programs, Bruno was the perfect recruit for the Ivy League and maybe some smaller mid-major programs. But he couldn't see himself as an egghead and didn't know if he'd enjoy those smaller programs where the crowds for football games were smaller and to most of the students games were just a diversion from study halls.

John Jr. wanted to play football at Penn State, just like his dad. One Friday his parents drove John to Lafayette College in Easton, Pennsylvania, where John was being recruited. On the way back to Pittsburgh later in the weekend, they stopped at Penn State to see Cheryl, who was a student there. Lafayette soon disappeared from Bruno's radar.

Walking through the ponderous campus, Bruno, in awe, turned to his dad and said, "If they give me a chance to be a walk-on, I'm coming here."

Penn State assistant coach Fran Ganter, out of scholarships but still scanning his lists for players who might have a shot to walk on to the Nittany Lions' football team, had Bruno in his sights anyway.

Ganter called Bruno. "Ever think of coming up here as a walk-on?" he asked John.

"Are you kidding me, Coach?" Bruno replied. "I'd give anything to be with you guys."

Bruno sent in his materials, was accepted to Penn State, and began fall workouts as a freshman walk-on. Being a "recruited" walk-on got him a confirmed spot on the team. The nonrecruited walk-ons were forced to survive a big tryout camp the following February in order to make the Nittany Lions varsity. Joe Johns was one of those. He had been a flanker at Baldwin High near Pittsburgh and knew Bruno from his days of playing against him in high school. Both players had made their all-conference teams. Of the ninety-six players who tried out that winter, the Penn State coaches kept five. Johns was one of those five. That spring, Bruno, Johns, and two other walk-on players, Mike Arnold and Mark Wilcox, would form lasting friendships.

Arnold was a walk-on offensive lineman who brought to Penn State a love of football and collection of record albums that could have started a small radio station. The team was holed up in the East Halls dormitories for practice that fall. Arnold had his dorm door open while his portable stereo blared the Yardbirds with Eric Clapton on lead guitar. He looked up to see John Bruno come dancing into the room, digging the sound. They became inseparable friends from that day on, sharing living arrangements for the rest of their Penn State days and raising hell off the field together.

Bruno was always entertaining. In those days, the freshmen footballers were required to perform a skit for the Nittany Lion upperclassmen. Bruno made it *his* stage, doing a stand-up routine imitating David Letterman cold and cracking up the team. One Saturday night after a game, Bruno and Arnold went down to the Phyrst, an eclectic State College bar where peanut shells decorated the floor and everybody swooned over the music of the regular house band, the Phyrst Family. During one of the band's breaks, Bruno grabbed a stray microphone from near the stage. It was still hooked up to the sound system. He spent the rest of the night conducting interviews with patrons live over the speakers.

Nothing Bruno did ever surprised Ganter. The PSU offensive coordinator first met the kid who would become Penn State's starting punter at a family function in Ohio. Ganter had married into the Bruno family. His wife, Karen Bruno, was John Sr.'s second cousin, and Ganter and his wife had been in the room the night Cheryl Bruno asked her younger brother to do his imitation of '70s soul and gospel singer Billy Preston. John Jr. was ten years old at the time, but he started gyrating and banging on a fake piano and lip-synching Preston's "Nothing from Nothing" as if it were a Las Vegas audition. It was hysterical. Ganter remembered thinking what poise the kid must have had to do such an act even in front of relatives.

Bruno was the guy who kept everybody loose. Football was a game. You were supposed to have fun. He and Johns had been receivers on Penn State's fourth-team offense, the offense to which the coaches didn't pay much attention. At the time, Penn State had a unique huddle where offensive lineman lined up in a V, with the split end and running backs behind them and the players all facing the quarterback and flanker. The quarterback would call a typically conservative Penn State play, and Bruno would hit Johns with a look as if to say, *Boy, that's real fancy.* Bruno could crack Johns up with just a subtle look. When the players broke the huddle and Bruno and Johns had to cross paths to get to their positions, Bruno might try to step on his buddy's heel and make him fall.

But he also got it back. Walk-ons, especially walk-ons who punt like John Bruno, were put to use all over the field at Penn State practices. Sometimes Bruno was called to take snaps at quarterback for defensive lineman drills. Paterno's practices were organized to the second. Everybody had a place to be at a certain time. One day Bruno got caught up talking on the sidelines with his kicking buddy Manca when Paterno was expecting him to be participating in another drill.

"Bruno!" the coach yelled. Bruno quickly grabbed his helmet and ran over to Paterno.

"Goddamn it! This is a football practice, not play time!" Paterno railed. "The next time that whistle blows, you'd better be where you're supposed to be, you hear me?!"

Oh, it was such perfect fodder for Johns and the walk-on Musketeers. Bruno might be lollygagging somewhere else when Johns would yell, "Bruno!" Instantly, Bruno would grab his helmet, turn around, and run toward the center of the field, thinking it a coach calling and if he didn't get to a certain spot on the field right now, it would be his butt. Except there was no drill going on. Johns was just messing with him.

Bruno would rarely get back at them. He was content to take it because that was the way the four of them had the most fun. If he did, Bruno would stick the needle into his buddies gingerly, cleverly.

The team Bruno made as a walk-on his freshman year wound up winning a national championship, beating Georgia in the 1983 Sugar Bowl. It had talent. Kenny Jackson, who would become a No. 1 draft pick in the NFL, was its top receiver. But behind Jackson, the Lions were also loaded with other highly recruited receivers. Bruno came to realize the odds were not good that he would ever catch a pass in a Penn State game. But the kid could really punt. And that's the position on which he would focus. Paterno had signed a highly recruited punter named Greg Montgomery, but he had fallen into disfavor over some disciplinary problems. JoePa dismissed him and Montgomery transferred to Michigan State. By 1984, John Bruno, the walk-on who so desperately wanted to wear a Penn State uniform, was the team's starting punter.

Bruno may have been a jokester, but he was serious when it came to kicking a football. He studied tapes of the great punters, college and pro. He made himself technically perfect. Bruno, who loved golf almost as much as football, likened punting technique to a golf swing. The leg has to be in perfect alignment during its swing toward the football. The football should be imagined to be dropping slowly onto a tee and, as it lies there, should be met squarely, smoothly, by the foot, but at the end of a leg swing—just like the golf ball should be met by the head of the club at the end of the shaft. The length of the leg swing—just like the back swing in golf—determines how far you want to hit the football. Bruno's "pooch" punts, the ones he'd drop inside the 10-yard line and for which he became so famous at Penn State, he likened to the swing of a pitching wedge.

Years later, Ganter would admit to being fascinated by Bruno teaching his techniques to campers at Penn State's scholastic football camps, where Bruno was often invited back as an instructor. "Johnny made it a science," Ganter said. "I had never quite realized punting was that scientific."

The Penn State coaches knew Bruno's punting ability was special; he was able to get the ball off quickly. That played right into their scheme. Unlike most college football teams, Paterno favored his punters only 11 yards back from the center, and with only a two-step approach before they kicked the football. Standard procedure for most punters was to stand 15 yards back from the center and take three steps before they kicked the ball. The Penn State alignment left outside rushers unblocked; they would be free to come fast at Bruno. But it also allowed two extra members of the Nittany Lions' cover team—who now didn't have to stay back to block the outside rushers—to get downfield more quickly to cover the punt. With Bruno's ability to get the kick off swiftly and Penn State's snapper Greg Truitt able to get the ball consistently to his punter at the perfect velocity and height, punting became a clear advantage for the Lions no matter whom they played. In his three years as a Penn State starter, John Bruno punted more than two hundred times and had only one blocked—*none* his senior year.

But Miami had Tom Bradley, Penn State's special teams coach, very worried. The Hurricanes had a crackerjack rusher in Bubba McDowell, a swift, sophomore backup cornerback Miami used as a speed rusher from its right defensive flank. McDowell blocked five punts for the Hurricanes that year and had two blocks each against Texas Tech and Cincinnati. He came like a bullet. In the weeks of practice preceding the Fiesta Bowl, Bradley was constantly on Bruno to waste no time at all, to get his punts off as quickly as he could.

"Here he comes, Johnny!" Bradley would yell the moment after Truitt delivered the snap. Sometimes Bruno would hold on to the ball just to tweak the coach the Nittany Lions called "Scraps."

"Don't worry, Scraps. I got it. Relax," Bruno would assure Bradley.

After Penn State's first series of the game, Bruno dropped back to punt and was standing at his own three-yard line when McDowell came firing. Bruno got off the punt with McDowell not a factor. His second punt of the game was better—a 52-yarder downed at the Miami two-yard line. But this time McDowell, firing from the flank, came within a whisker of blocking it.

After the kick, Bruno came to the Penn State sidelines to a hero's welcome. As teammates offered high-fives, Bradley, in a panic, came rushing down to meet his punter.

"John, he almost blocked that!" Bradley said.

"It's okay," Bruno said.

"What do you mean it's okay? He almost blocked it. You were too slow!"

"What is your problem?" Bruno said.

"John, he almost blocked it. I think the football went right through his hands!"

"No it didn't," Bruno said.

"Are you sure?"

"Yeah. Actually, he ran *past* it. He was *too* fast," Bruno deadpanned.

Bradley shook his head, smiled, and moved away. John Bruno had managed to loosen up his uptight coach.

IN 1984, BRUNO GOT THE STARTING PUNTING JOB almost by default. But that year he fared better than Paterno ever imagined—averaging 41.4 yards per kick, the fourth-highest average in Penn State history. He even set a new school record for number of punts in a season. Paterno had no choice but to give the kid a scholarship.

That was the year they found the mole.

Coming into fall practice just before the start of his junior season, the fair-skinned, blond-haired Bruno went to see Penn State's team doctor, James Whiteside, for a painful lump on his back. Whiteside immediately sent him to a hospital in Pittsburgh where the lump was removed and a biopsy conducted. It was cancerous. John Bruno had melanoma. But doctors felt confident they had extracted all of the cancer. Bruno missed a couple of weeks of fall practice and the team picture, but he was back and ready for the Lions' opener that year against Maryland. He punted four times that day for a 46-yard average. So far as Bruno was concerned, he was healthy and happy, and he spent the next two years cementing his legacy as perhaps Penn State's finest punter ever.

He averaged 42.9 per kick the next year with a nifty 38.2 net per kick—the receiver being able to return his lofty boots for an average of only four yards. Bruno had a 71-yard punt against Boston College; five of his "pooch" kicks were downed inside the other team's 10-yard line, and he dropped ten more between the 10- and 20-yard lines. By his senior year, Bruno and Manca had become a deadly combination. Bruno wasn't overly long, but he was deadly consistent. In Tempe when asked by a reporter why Bruno didn't have a few longer punts on his résumé, Paterno said simply, "John Bruno is a team punter. He doesn't worry about his average."

He was just a kid having fun kicking and winning. The agenda at the Fiesta Bowl called for a get-together several days before the game and a skit to lighten what had been a heavy mood. Shaffer, perhaps the team's most cerebral player, was chosen to plan the skit with Bruno. The punter had previous skit experience. The year before, at the Orange Bowl, Bruno had lampooned his own coach. At a team dinner, Bruno stood up with two glass Coca-Cola bottles, suggesting that the bottles could serve Joe Paterno's sight just as well as his thick, black-rimmed glasses. Even Paterno was amused.

Years later Cheryl Bruno, sorting through boxes of her brother's stuff, found a few pages of notes on the Fiesta Bowl skit. Shaffer had written the main text, but much of his comments are crossed out and edited in red pen by Bruno's handwriting.

"Okay, the thing everybody talks about is Jimmy Johnson's hair," he told a few teammates, including quarterback John Shaffer, who was in on the planning. "We've got to go right after that, no? And those ridiculous fatigues they're wearing. That's fair game. And we'll try to rip them a little on their individuality. They don't seem to be a 'team' as much as us."

After dinner, Bruno, wearing a conservative sweater and jeans, walked on stage and first jabbed Johnson. "Clairol would like to thank him for doubling their hairspray profits," he said.

Then came the comment that touched off the fireworks. Aware that there was a perception that Penn State University didn't have enough black students, Bruno attempted to combine that theme with a mocking of Miami's combat fatigues show of togetherness. "We're close at Penn State," Bruno said. "We even let the black guys eat with us at the training table once a week."

The Bruno family was headed to Tempe in a couple of days, but their son's comment made national news and their home phone in Pittsburgh started ringing off the hook. Miami players publicly interpreted John Bruno's comment as racial. It was just another assault in their weeklong psychological war against Penn State. The circumstance left a bitter taste in John Sr.'s mouth. People who knew his kid knew that John Bruno didn't have a racist bone in his body. In fact, most often

Bruno had been the bridge between black and white on all the teams he played. The comment at the barbeque, John Sr. knew, was his son's way of diffusing any racial tension whatsoever. He was saying that at Penn State there is no division at all. That everything about the Nittany Lions was about togetherness, about team.

"What that Miami team did that day was a very unfair thing to do to a very special kid," John Bruno Sr. says.

"What I remember most about his comment was that the black guys on our team were cracking up," Manca recalled. "The thing about John is that he never, ever saw the world as divided like that. He felt comfortable enough with everybody that it never even dawned on him that his comment could be perceived that way."

As was his personality, Bruno didn't sweat the controversy in Tempe. After the Miami walkout, he moved quickly on his feet. "You'll have to excuse them," Bruno told the crowd. "They have to make the taping of *Rambo III*."

The skit aside, Bruno knew he had to be focused on one thing as game time approached: punting. He was smart enough to understand that the Penn State offense might have a difficult time moving the football against Miami. Bruno knew that the Nittany Lions would have to win the Fiesta Bowl with defense. And good field position would be essential. John Bruno knew he needed to be the best punter he had ever been.

While the rest of the Lions practiced in the cozy confines of their new indoor facility, Bruno spent the month punting *outdoors*, in State College's frigid December weather. The ceiling of the indoor facility was too low to accommodate punts. So when Bruno got to Tempe and its temperate climate, he felt as if he had been sprung from a cage. First day there, he kicked for an hour straight and then woke up the next day with a sore leg. After that he would temper the workouts that preceded the game's kickoff.

Bruno's first punt of the Fiesta Bowl, coming after Penn State went three and out and had *lost* 16 yards, went only 38 yards. Fortunately for Penn State, Miami was penalized 10 on the runback and started its first drive on its own 36. And it was the last break Bruno would give the 'Canes. His next punt pinned the Hurricanes down at their own two-yard line, a 50-yard beauty. He knocked his next one 45 yards to the Miami 22. Miami was moving the ball all game long on the Lions, but they weren't going anywhere because Bruno was making them start from way back.

"Johnny Bruno was our savior that night," acknowledged Sandusky.

John Bruno's finest day as a Penn State punter led to him being drafted in the fifth round that spring by the St. Louis Cardinals, who were still a year away from moving to Arizona, as the first punter taken in the draft. The drafting by the Cardinals caught Bruno by surprise. He had been communicating mostly with the Seattle Seahawks and looked forward to kicking inside their domed stadium. With Bruno snatched from their grasp, the Seahawks wound up drafting Ruben Rodriquez from the University of Arizona a couple of picks later.

The Cardinals, expecting that Bruno would be their punter for the next several seasons at least, gave him a $40,000 signing bonus. But Bruno struggled trying to transition back to the three-step punting approach pro teams used. Going into the final 1987 preseason game, Bruno was neck and neck with Cards incumbent punter Greg Cater, whom the Cards had signed in the middle of their 1986 season. St. Louis coach Gene Stallings flipped a coin and selected Cater to kick in the first half of the game and Bruno in the second. Bruno remembered thinking that he might not even get to kick—the second half of the fourth preseason game is usually garbage time when coaches throw in second- and third-teamers and take chances with trick plays like going for it on fourth down. His instincts were right. The Cardinals never punted in the second half. The following day Stallings called Bruno to his office and cut him.

By then NFL teams had their punters. No one else called him in for a look as the season began. But 1987 was also the year of the NFL players' strike. When the players went out, team owners looked to carry on the season with replacement players. The Pittsburgh Steelers, the team for whom Bruno had rooted as a kid, called and offered him a job. But Bruno's granddad on his mother's side was a staunch union man who had worked all his life in the mines. Bruno called his granddad on the telephone not knowing whether he'd approve.

"If you don't take it, somebody else will," he told his grandson.

John Bruno played in only four games as a Steeler. The regular players would soon come back to their NFL jobs and the replacement players would be cut adrift like expired bait. Bruno's stay in Pittsburgh would become notable only for the time he made stoic Steeler coach Chuck Noll laugh.

When the replacement Steelers arrived at Three Rivers Stadium one day for practice, Noll saw workers preparing a stage on the field.

"What's going on here tonight?" Noll asked.

"Yunz-Two is here," said Bruno, using the Pittsburgh slang term for the word "you" (the rock band U2 was performing that night).

Noll, who smiled about as often as a mannequin, cracked up.

Bruno visited a couple of NFL camps the following season, but neither his leg nor his mind had the same enthusiasm for football. Nobody signed him. His football career was over. Disappointed but still upbeat, John Bruno went on with the rest of his life. He started selling stereo equipment. He learned to play the guitar and formed a garage band with a couple of his cousins. They called the group "Ping and the Ruins" in honor of John Bruno's love for golf. He had a steady girlfriend whom he hoped to marry one day. It was a life that turned out a lot shorter than it should have been.

One night Bruno and Arnold were in the middle of a rowdy bachelor house party for a buddy. At about 10 P.M., John plopped on the sofa and fell asleep. Arnold thought that to be very odd since John Bruno's partying stamina usually went well into the night. In the fall of 1991, Arnold and Bruno traveled to the Penn State–Notre Dame game at Beaver Stadium together. Arnold thought his buddy looked really pale, but he never mentioned it to Bruno.

Then the holidays came.

John Bruno went to his sister's house in Hanover, Pennsylvania, near York, the day before Christmas for a Bruno family holiday party. Cheryl, her husband, Doug Gamber, and their children, Johnnie and Emily, were delighted to see Uncle

John. But as Cheryl Bruno Gamber watched her brother walk from the car to the house, she thought he didn't look well. He was callow and pale.

Bruno returned to the Pittsburgh area, where he celebrated Christmas with his parents at their home in Upper St. Clair. The next day, his dad took John to a hospital for tests. Two days later, he got a grave diagnosis. The cancer had returned. John Bruno had only a few more months to live.

"Get busy living, or get busy dying." It is a line in the movie *Shawshank Redemption* uttered by Morgan Freeman in lament of his sudden and uncomfortable release into the real world from prison. John Bruno was going the opposite way. He had surgery on New Year's Eve to remove a tumor on his colon. He went through several melanoma treatment trials in Pittsburgh. His parents, sister, and friends prayed for a miracle cure that would never come.

Even in the final months of his life, John Bruno never once mentioned dying. He carried on just like before. One night Johns invited Bruno and his girlfriend over to watch a hockey game. Bruno was in so much pain from the tumors on his back that he had to lie on the floor on his stomach. But he never complained. In February 1992, Arnold called him with news of his firstborn child, a daughter.

"What's her name?" Bruno asked.

"Madeline Rose," Arnold replied.

"Madeline Rose . . . what a great name," Bruno said. "That's a name that would make a great song. Hey, we've got to put together some lyrics."

On Sunday, April 12, a close friend of the family's called Johns, Arnold, and another close friend, Mark Wilcox, and told them to come to the hospital, that Bruno might not make it through the night. Other friends started to show up at the hospital, finding out just then that their friend was terminally ill. John Bruno hadn't told anybody. Only those closest to him had known. That's the way he had wanted it. Behind the door of Bruno's hospital room, tears flowed like a water wall.

In the room, Johns, Arnold, and Wilcox tried to lighten the mood as much as they could, even though they hurt badly. Johns told Bruno that a new Elvis stamp had just come out. The two friends had always talked about Elvis and, especially about the different stages of his body. They wondered whether the fat or thin Elvis would be put on the stamp. Bruno smiled. Johns tried to get his buddy to do one more of the Elvis imitations that used to crack everybody up, but John Bruno was tired. He had nothing left. He died the following morning.

John Bruno's funeral drew some four hundred people to the First Presbyterian Church in Irwin, Pennsylvania. Many members of the 1986 Penn State football team were there and so was their coach, Joe Paterno. The Lions sat in the first couple of pews, wearing their navy-blue blazers with the Penn State logo and smart, conservative ties. With watery eyes, Johns couldn't help thinking that somewhere in spirit, John Bruno was giving him that *look* again as if to say, *Gee fellas, lighten up.*

A few days after the funeral, the Brunos received a cassette tape in the mail from a friend who was a radio broadcaster in Pittsburgh. From his radio studio, the friend had recorded a special testimonial for John Bruno:

The Easter lilies stood around the altar like white trumpets. They'd been arranged so that the blossoms pointed right and left and towards us, so that the silent anthem they played would reach everyone in the church. Each of us are in parts of the same song, even though we didn't know each other. Even though many of us were complete strangers, we shared some of the same thoughts that day, because we had something in common. All of our lives had been touched by John Bruno. . . .

The funeral procession that day was a solid line of headlights that stretched over the top and well beyond each hill behind us. The sun was out, the grass was getting green, the birds were singing, there were flowers blooming everywhere. For much of the world, it was a beautiful spring day. The pastor of Westminster Presbyterian Church in Upper St. Clair who gave the eulogy said the funeral procession was the longest he'd ever seen. None of us were surprised. The reception after we all went to the cemetery was more like a party as we celebrated John's life. The room was filled with greetings and laughter, introductions and recollections. But in each group standing there was an empty space. At each table full of people, there was an empty chair. In each conversation there were both happy memories and traces of sadness. Someone said this would have been John's favorite part of the day; all the rest of it he could have done without.

And then as we all started to leave and stood in line to say goodbye to the family, I thought back to the quiet hour we all spent in that beautiful little church, listening to the loud silence of the lilies. How we were all drawn nearer to each other by John Bruno, as we closed in around the space he occupied in our lives.

Then on the drive home, I couldn't help thinking that if we are all creatures of nature, John Bruno was a bird. All the time we knew him, he seemed to float a little above the crowd, just far enough to be able to see over the horizon and still look back and see the rest of us. Never too distant to be out of touch. Just far enough overhead to appreciate things the rest of us can't see yet. And he's looking back on us now.

In 1995, Arnold, Johns, and Wilcox spearheaded a movement to honor the memory of John Bruno. Arnold was working for the Foreman Group, an architectural engineering and construction management firm in Pittsburgh. The firm's president, Phil Foreman, had been a Penn State student and met John Bruno in college. Foreman was looking to put together a charitable foundation. The walk-on Musketeers suggested a platform that would fund melanoma research and heighten awareness of the disease in memory of John Bruno. Through golf tournaments, raffles, and black-tie balls, the Foreman Foundation has raised nearly a million dollars and funded a lab for melanoma research in honor of John Bruno that operates out of the Hershey Medical Center. Each year, at the first Nittany Lions home game of the season, Johns and his buddies walk onto the Beaver Stadium turf between the first and second quarters and present a check to the foundation with the money they have raised.

During the 2006 Akron game, the Foreman Foundation presentation coincided with the honoring of the 1986 national championship team. Johns had casually mentioned to John Shaffer, who sat in a super box that day with many of his '86 teammates, that it would make a great presentation to have the guys flank him during the presentation. Consider it done, Shaffer told him. Strangely, when it was time to walk on to the field, Johns couldn't see any of the players. Then he turned around toward the north end zone and watched Shaffer lead a parade of about twenty guys on to the turf, all of whom wanted to pay their respects to their buddy Bruno.

Joe Johns keeps a photo on his desk at work and looks at it every day. It is a photo of Johns standing in street clothes on the sidelines during a Penn State football game. He was not chosen to dress that day. Next to him in full uniform is John Bruno. Johns recalled, "He wasn't having such a good day punting that day. And he was asking me what he was doing wrong, how he could improve. John Bruno was a star by then, a starting player on a major college football team. And I'm sure he didn't really need my advice on what he was doing wrong. He was down there with me because he wanted me to feel a part of the team. He knew I was probably hurting about not having my uniform on that day. That's the type of guy John Bruno was."

John Bruno is buried in Greensburg, Pennsylvania, some five hundred yards from where his parents, John and Alfrieda, now live. The Brunos moved there recently. It is where they both grew up and it is where their son used to love visiting, hanging out with his football-coach grandfather, and playing ball with his cousins. They know his rest here is peaceful.

Why him? It was a question the Brunos asked for a while. Why would God take a person who had loved life so much, whose good spirit rubbed off and made everyone feel so much better? There are no good answers. The Brunos have simply carried on. They use their son's memory as a beacon.

John Sr. has a letter from Dr. James Whiteside, the Penn State team physician who first found the mole on John Bruno's back and rushed him into the Pittsburgh hospital to have it removed. Whiteside wrote to the Brunos the week John Jr. passed away. "I know you prayed for a miracle all this time," Dr. Whiteside wrote, "but know that you did experience a miracle. That miracle was having John in all of our lives."

STEVE SMITH ARRIVED ON Penn State's campus in August 1982. Only a short few weeks later he began to think that maybe Happy Valley wasn't for him.

Smith had been an All-American scholastic player in high school recruited by hundreds. He was big and fast and tough and smart, a kid from a good family whose parents had both graduated from college. Penn State wanted Smith, and in the end he chose the Nittany Lions. But when he got to State College, things changed. He was no longer the big man on campus but just one of a number of other great high school recruits. The Penn State coaching staff told Smith that he would be redshirted his freshman year. They had a dearth of running backs on the roster. The truth was, Paterno and his crew didn't know what to make of Smith. He was fast, but maybe not fast enough to be a tailback. He was strong, but maybe not big enough to be a fullback. Meanwhile, Paterno decided that Rogers Alexander, who had been recruited together with Smith as a teammate at DeMatha High, *would* play as a freshman.

"Steven called us almost every night," recalled Morris Smith, his dad. "He felt lost. He was extremely homesick. All along his mom and I thought that getting away would be a good thing for Steve in his maturation process. We urged him to fight through it, to stick it out."

Morris Smith and his wife, Norma, had been high school sweethearts. Morris was a star basketball and baseball player at Dunbar High in D.C. Norma was the captain of the cheerleading squad at Cardozo High, Dunbar's inner-city school rival. Friends introduced them one Sunday at church. They were seventeen years old and from that day forward would spend the rest of their lives together. After high school, Morris joined the Army, served in the Korean War, and then got stationed back in the States in Huntsville, Alabama. By then Morris and Norma had married and started a family. The couple moved back to D.C. after Morris's Army stint and both husband and wife earned business degrees at Howard University. Morris Smith entered college ten years after his high school graduation. The Smiths both worked in government service—Norma for the Federal Power Commission and Morris for the Federal Trade Commission—before Morris Smith settled into a long career as an account manager for Xerox.

Steve Smith wasn't as much a child of privilege as he was a kid with a clear-headed direction to success. He was a precocious athlete, the boy who was always bigger and better for his age than the others. His first love was baseball. Morris coached in the D.C. Little League, but he made sure his son played for someone else so he could get coaching that was more objective. Steve Smith also loved basketball. Football was an afterthought; he only played because his buddies did, but he was good at it. Before long, football would become his master.

Steve attended Bishop McNamara High in D.C.'s highly competitive Catholic League. The Smiths were Methodist, but Morris felt that a Catholic education would provide more discipline for Steve than the inner-city schools of D.C. The summer before his sophomore year, Smith needed to take a summer school class to lift up one of his grades. That class was held at DeMatha High, which had developed a national reputation for basketball excellence under a legendary coach named Morgan Wooten. A summer hoop league was going on inside the gym. Steve joined it. An instructor took an interest in his abilities. He was hooked. He wanted to play basketball at DeMatha, and his parents allowed the transfer to a school that was McNamara's bitter rival.

The basketball thing never worked out for Steve Smith at DeMatha. Not good enough to survive on a roster full of major college recruits, he was cut from the varsity that winter. A devastated Smith turned his energies toward football, where he became a superstar. One day Jerry Franks, the head coach at DeMatha, noticed that his assistant coaches had started to refer to Steve as "Sir." When Franks asked why, a coach replied that when you have that much respect for someone's ability and character, you call him "Sir." Steve Smith was a "Sir," an irresistible force and an immovable object.

His junior year, Steve had a 225-yard game against Bishop O'Connell. It was his coming-out party. DeMatha had gleaned a play used often at Moeller High, the nationally recognized football program in Cincinnati that at the same time was molding a quarterback named John Shaffer. The play entailed faking a toss sweep, then tucking the ball into the fullback's belly. Smith, who had great vision, would pound through the hole like a missile, then shift to a clearing created by linebackers who had pursued the fake. Often, he'd take that play to the house. Smith, in fact, had run the play for an 80-yard touchdown to cinch a victory against McNamara. In his headset, Franks heard his assistants in the press box say, matter-of-factly, "He's gone," as soon as the DeMatha quarterback handed Smith the ball.

Franks's daughter Tracy remembers only one player vividly as she lived through her dad's coaching career at DeMatha. It was Smith. "I was eight years old at the time," she says. "I remember he wore number 33. I remember being in the stands yelling, 'Give it to Steve!'"

He was the player everyone else followed, the team leader who could be stoic but also excitable. DeMatha's teams traveled to road games in an old blue school bus they called "Bluebird," a by-product of a parochial school's limited budget. There wasn't enough room on Bluebird for the coaches, so for a night game at Old Mill High, Franks met the team in his own car. As Bluebird rolled into the parking lot, Franks watched Smith get up from his seat and start banging his helmet against the inside steel roof. His teammates followed suit, creating a deafening roar that wafted throughout the school's grounds. DeMatha players filed out frenzied. Old Mill had no chance.

Smith usually saved his best games for his old school, Bishop McNamara. He still had a lot of friends on the other side of the field, including his first cousin Gregory Smith, McNamara's starting quarterback. The cousins had practically grown up together and played side by side in the same youth leagues. When the two schools faced each other, Smith family members scattered throughout the stadium, on both sides of the field. Steve's grandmother, Morris's mother, spent one half on the McNamara side and the other on the DeMatha side. In Steve Smith's senior year, he rushed for 90 yards against McNamara and scored two touchdowns, including one during a kickoff return. After the game, it was business as usual for the Smith family. Everybody congregated near the locker-room doors to await Steve and Gregory. When they both finally came out, Steve was determined to stay humble. He didn't want to rub it in. Greg stared at him, as if to say, *Man, you had to do that?* Steve broke into one of his famous smiles.

There was the game Smith's senior year against John Carroll High. Smith had been nursing an injured ankle and didn't start. In the third quarter, there was still no score. Smith went to Franks and told him he could play. It was as if Willis Reed had come on the floor for the Knicks in the 1972 NBA finals against the Lakers. With Smith in the lineup, DeMatha's level of play magically ascended. They scored two touchdowns in the game's final 12 minutes and won 14–0. By the end of his senior season, Steve Smith had been named Washington's Metro Player of the Year, the D.C. Touchdown Club's scholastic player of the year, and a *Parade* magazine All-American. He gained more than 2,000 yards and scored 224 touchdowns in his two-year career at DeMatha.

At first Penn State was reluctant to recruit Smith because they had already committed to Alexander. John Rosenberg, Penn State's chief recruiter, told the

DeMatha coaching staff that Paterno's policy was not to recruit two players from the same high school for fear of creating uncomfortable situations with playing time.

"But, John, this kid is just too good to pass up," DeMatha assistant Ed McGregor told Rosenberg.

Rosenberg already knew that. Smith was a great football player and a great student who came from a great family. He was the perfect Penn State recruit. Rosenberg went back to Paterno and convinced him that Smith was his man.

Once he committed to Smith, Paterno thought he had the big running back locked up. Smith had narrowed his final two choices to the Nittany Lions and Stanford. Paterno knew Smith was very close to his family and would prefer to stay on the East Coast, where they could watch him play in person every Saturday. But then Bobby Ross stepped into the mix.

Ross, a longtime respected college and pro coach, had just been named head coach at the University of Maryland. Eager to rebuild the Terrapins' program, Ross put a priority on keeping homegrown prospects at home and wanted Smith badly. The new coach got help from an influential Maryland alum named Jay Nussbaum, a corporate vice president at Xerox. Technically, Nussbaum was Morris Smith's boss. The boss asked Morris Smith for a favor: would he and his talented son just meet with Ross? Morris Smith agreed. Bobby Ross's visit went exceedingly well—with Ross's southern gentlemanly style a big hit with Norma Smith.

When Paterno found out about Ross's intrusion, he rushed down to DeMatha the next day. That pretty much sealed the deal for Penn State. Truth was, the Lions were Morris Smith's first choice anyway for his son. The old man loved the fact that Paterno emphasized academics and that Penn State had no athletic dorms. It was important to Morris Smith that his son not be isolated in an athletic environment twenty-four hours a day and seven days a week. Years later Morris Smith would ponder the ramifications of his son going to Maryland. Might it have meant a promotion at Xerox?

He laughs. "Maybe," Morris Smith says. "But for Steve, Penn State was the right choice."

By mid-season of his freshman year, Smith had adjusted to college life in Happy Valley. The Nittany Lions were in dead pursuit of a national championship, which they would win that year in the Sugar Bowl against Herschel Walker and Georgia. After the game Smith, though not in uniform, received some credit for the big win. Paterno had chosen his redshirt freshman, who was built a lot like Walker, to emulate the Georgia star in practice to help prepare the Lions defense for the game. Afterward, a Penn State defensive player mentioned Smith specifically for his practice work. "We beat him up pretty good," the player said. "But he came right back for more."

At the end of the school year when Smith returned to D.C., his parents hardly recognized him. Morris Smith remembers seeing Steve come up the walk after he returned home for the summer. "I turned to my wife and said, 'What have they done to our baby?'" Morris Smith said.

Their son had turned into a man. He was more mature both mentally and physically. Morris Smith couldn't help but feel that tough love, his urging of Steve to stick it out that uncomfortable redshirt freshman year, had paid big dividends.

Meanwhile, the Penn State coaching staff reached a consensus. Steve Smith could be a good tailback, but he'd be a great fullback. The Lions had successfully landed D.J. Dozier, a star tailback from Virginia Beach who had been one of the nation's top-ten high school recruits. They saw a backfield with Dozier at halfback, Smith as the finesse guy who could swing out of the backfield and catch passes, and Pittsburgh recruit Manoa, a bulldozer-type, sharing the spot at fullback. And for the next few years, that alignment would function as smoothly as it was drawn up.

Smith was the kid who played with a pinch of chewing tobacco between his cheek and gum even while he wore a mouthpiece. Chew was acceptable back then. Oddly, that lump of Skoal gave Smith more of an aura, like the toilet-seat neck pad he also wore. It made him appear even more leather-tough. Manoa would fight you in an alley. Steve Smith was just plain tough. The coaching staff was amazed that he could keep the tobacco in there. For the first three years of Smith's career at Penn State, the Lions practiced on a grass field. When their brand-spanking-new Astroturf facility was christened in the late autumn of 1986, Paterno warned Smith not to spit tobacco juice on the artificial surface. One afternoon as he was walking off the field Paterno spied a brown spot on the new carpet.

"Smitty!" the coach yelled. "What's this?"

"Not me, Coach," Smith said.

"Nobody else chews, dammit!"

Paterno had him.

As a sophomore, Smith's moment of glory came in a nationally televised game against Boston College when the feisty fullback rushed 23 times for 126 yards. That year he also scored five touchdowns, which led the team. But that year Paterno wasn't exactly enamored with Smith's work habits. By the end of the season, the coach was often in his fullback's face. The mere suggestion that he was not putting forth his best effort got Smith's attention. It embarrassed him. Smith was determined to prove Paterno wrong, which was precisely what JoePa was after. After the season, Smith became a workout maniac. He came to spring practice that year bulked up to 235 and in the best shape of his life. When the Lions went into the Blue-White game that April, Smith had already been awarded the team's Red Worrell Award, given to the spring's most outstanding player.

His junior year, Steve Smith's best moment was an electrifying 63-yard touchdown run against Rutgers. Steve Smith was not unlike any other fullback that Joe Paterno had ever recruited. He had to be a serviceman, the guy who would throw the key block that sprung Dozier, or catch a pass out of the backfield on a third and four to get Penn State a first down. Smith was a player the others would follow, who the coaches suggested they follow because of his work ethic. As the Lions came into the magical 1986 season, Steve Smith was named a team co-captain.

"The most impressive thing about Smitty was that he played the game the same way every single down," said Ganter. "It didn't matter what the situation was. Whether we were ahead or behind or whatever. He only knew one way to play football. You only coach so many guys who are like that."

Smith just loved everything about the game. He loved playing on Saturdays before a hundred thousand people. But mostly he loved just being part of the team. He loved the camaraderie, the bond that forms within an athletic locker room. It was like having a hundred brothers, guys with whom you went to war, who would have your back and you would have theirs. He loved hanging out and laughing with them and playing practical jokes on them. It was a guy thing.

That senior season when they played at West Virginia, Smith tried to pull a prank on his teammates that backfired. The Lions had just arrived at their hotel and were headed up the elevator in clusters to get to their room. The door slid open and Smith piled in with Dozier and Shaffer and a couple of offensive linemen. Smith figured it was a great time to pass gas. That was always good for a gross-out moment and a laugh with the boys. And boy, did they laugh. But what Smith hadn't realized was that a tiny elderly woman was in the elevator behind him. Smith was mortified. He tried hard to apologize, but the woman didn't hide her disgust, and when the elevator stopped at the next floor, she stormed out. Smith's teammates didn't let him forget about it all weekend.

"Steve felt so bad about it that he pleaded with us to stop razzing him," Dozier recalled. "He really felt ashamed. That was what was great about the guy. He had such a good conscience."

He was an Al Davis type of player. Davis, the owner of the Oakland Raiders, was a rebel among NFL owners who had publicized a saying, "Just win, baby," which reflected his philosophy about football. The only thing that Davis cared about in a player was that he played ferociously and tried to win at any cost. Criminal or choirboy didn't matter to Davis so long as you had the heart to win. After Penn State won the national championship, Nittany Lions players were given a closer look by the pro scouts. Smith had a good showing in the East-West Shrine game, a televised college all-star game, and then excelled at the NFL combine. The Raiders, who had moved from Oakland to Los Angeles only a few years before, had Smith on their radar as a guy who would be perfect as a blocking back for Marcus Allen. They traded up to select Smith in the third round of the '87 draft. Smith was watching the draft with his mom in their Clinton, Maryland, home, but only the first two rounds were televised. When Smith wasn't selected in the first two rounds, his mom left the house to run some errands while Steve went to take a long shower. Nobody was there to answer the phone when the Raiders called.

But the neighbors had heard. Swiftly, they moved into position, tying balloons on planters and draping trees with toilet paper. Someone walked in front of the Smith house with a freshly painted sign that read, "Congratulations Steve, Go Raiders." They did this in the heart of Washington Redskin country. It didn't matter. Steve Smith was one of them.

When Smith was a sophomore, his dad bought him a secondhand car. He was driving that car back up to State College with a couple of buddies after spending the weekend at home when the car sputtered and stopped. It hadn't had enough juice to get up the long mountainous climb to the Penn State campus. He called Morris, who arrived the next day with a tow truck, but the car was shot. The next year Morris Smith bought his son a new car, a Ford sedan. The car was more functional than stylish and it certainly wasn't befitting of a "Just win, baby" Los Angeles Raider. But even when Steve was a rookie with the Raiders and had gotten a signing bonus decent enough to buy a new car, he wanted that Ford with him. It was a gift from his dad. So he asked Morris and Norma to drive it across country for him to Oxnard, California, to the Raiders' training camp. He was that kind of a humble guy.

Smith wound up playing seven years with the Raiders, then two more with the Seahawks. His first *Monday Night Football* appearance came in September of his second year. Morris Smith, an early riser for work, was usually in bed by 10 P.M., but he stayed up late this night to watch his son have a bust-out game. With Los Angeles trailing the Denver Broncos in the second half, Steve Smith ran for one score, then caught a pass from Raiders quarterback Jay Schroeder for another as the Raiders won. In the locker room afterward, he was awarded a game ball. Years later ESPN would name that 1988 Raiders–Broncos game as one of the best *Monday Night Football* games ever. And they would have Schroeder and Smith in the studio to discuss it.

Later when Steve was with Seattle, the Smiths watched him in another *Monday Night Football* game and saw Steve being helped off the field with a leg injury. The announcers weren't giving an update on his condition. It was maddening. About a half hour later, Morris Smith's telephone rang. It was Steve's sister, Cheryl. Steve was all right; it was just an ankle sprain. Cheryl Smith had somehow gotten a phone number that connected to a trainer on the Raiders' sideline. The trainer gave Cheryl the medical update, and she called her parents with the good news. The Smiths were close like that.

It was very rare that Steve Smith ever got the platform to be a star. Mostly, his role was similar to the one he had at Penn State—he was the fullback who would give up his body so the other guy could get the glory. He blocked for Allen, then for Bo Jackson, and then for Eric Dickerson as the Raiders swashbuckled their awesome running attack through the AFC. And Smith became best friends with all of them. Chris Warren had his two best seasons with the Seahawks with Steve Smith as his running mate. In 1994, Warren led the league in rushing with 1,545 yards and took Smith and his family to the Pro Bowl in Hawaii, all expenses paid, as a token of his appreciation.

Steve Smith embraced his role. In the pros, coaches convinced him that he was "the hammer," the blocking back. They even called him "Hammer." If that's what the Raiders coaches wanted him to do—just get up into that hole and block defensive linemen or linebackers—by God, that's what he would do. He was a team player. And he would do it just as hard in practice as in the games.

Winston Moss, who had played against Smith in the 1987 Fiesta Bowl, joined the Raiders in 1991. By then Steve Smith was fully established as one of the best blocking backs in the league. Smith became best friends with Moss, who was a hard-hitting linebacker. They hung out off the field, and Moss and his wife often socialized with Steve and Chie Smith. But when Steve Smith was on the field, he didn't have any friends. Often, as the Raiders practiced their running game, Smith would head up into the hole and try to knock Moss, the linebacker closing on the play, into the next county. Then after the play, he would simply help Moss up, return to the huddle, and wait for the time when he could do it again.

"If you weren't ready for Steve Smith, he would just mash you into the ground," Moss said.

Blocking was a role that Smith almost relished *too* much. His running backs coach with the Raiders, Terry Robiskie, constantly reminded Smith that he also had the ability to make some plays on offense, that he was a pretty good athlete who could break an occasional long run or make a big play catching a pass out of the backfield. Robiskie looked at Smith as a guy who never got as much out of watching film as he could have; he'd watch for hours but not really understand what it was he was watching. So Robiskie began sitting in on film sessions with his fullback, going over things together.

Prepping for the Bears during one week of the 1992 season, the banged-up Raiders inserted into the lineup Nick Bell, a big but practically untested tailback from Iowa. Robiskie sensed that the game plan would thus include a few more carries for Smith. The two converged in the film room with Robiskie tutoring Smith on some defensive alignments he might face, but specifically discussing the symmetry he needed to have with Bell.

"Steve, you've got the tailback's back, but you also have to make sure he's got yours," Robiskie told him. "You're his lead blocker. But we're going to call this play where he's *your* lead blocker. And you can't let him off the hook. You've got to make sure he knows that.

"So we get to the game. We're running Bell and Steve's just killing people in there for him. And Bell is having a pretty good game. All of a sudden we call Steve's number and Bell misses the block and Steve gets hammered. After the play, he grabs Bell by the facemask and just goes off on him. It was like he was telling him, 'Why, you son of a bitch, I'm busting my ass for you all game long and we call one play where you have to come up big for me and you do that?' I knew it came from the film sessions we had had during the week. And I loved it. I wanted Steve to be a little more selfish out there. And I'll tell you one thing: Nick Bell never missed another block for him the rest of the year."

The coach and the player formed a special bond. Robiskie had coached football for more than thirty years and could count on one hand the number of players who were totally dedicated to *team*. Smith was one of them. If Steve Smith only had a small role on a team, he was determined to perform that role the best he could.

The Raiders wanted him to be a blocking fullback so one year he came back after having spent an entire off-season in the weight room. He had gained ten more pounds, all of it muscle. He looked like Adonis. The weight gain worried Robiskie a little bit because he thought it might slow Smith down. It never did, but that didn't stop Robiskie from razzing him a little.

Robiskie started calling Smith "Fat Boy," a reminder to his fullback that he should not let his weight get totally out of control. It drove Smith crazy. In an offensive meeting one day, Robiskie was going over some film with his backs and he began specific instructions to Smith by saying, "All right, Fat Boy, when they line up this way. . . ."

When the instructions were over, Smith replied, "Okay, I got you, Fat Boy." It was Smith's way of reminding Robiskie that he wasn't too svelte himself and that maybe it wasn't a good idea to call him "Fat Boy" in front of his teammates. Robiskie got the message. For the rest of their time together in Los Angeles, Smith and Robiskie called each other "Fat Boy," but the name was merely a joke between them.

Terry Robiskie had come to see Steve Smith as more than just another one of his players. He had become his *friend*.

Smith played until a disc problem in his back allowed him to play no longer. He retired from football after the 1995 season with the Seahawks. It was the start of Steve Smith's new life, the life of a family man, the life of a successful business-man. He was ready to conquer the world. And then, after all those years of fighting and winning on a football field, he was taken down by illness.

In September 2002, Smith called his parents and asked them to come to Texas. There was something he needed to discuss with them. He wouldn't tell them anything more. When the Smiths arrived, Steve started to tell a story about playing tennis one day. His opponent served. Smith's brain told his body to move to a certain spot and try to return it, but his body didn't move. It didn't respond. He had been having these periodic minor twitches in his body, but this was different. He went to the hospital for tests. Now that his parents had come, he needed them to be by his side when he got the results.

Morris Smith remembers the day as if marked by a lightning strike or an earthquake. He remembered a neurologist telling them that there were some "abnormalities" in Steve Smith's test results. The neurologist told Steve Smith that he had ALS. Walking out of the hospital that day, Morris and Norma Smith felt as though they'd been hit over the head with a brick, but Steve was surprisingly upbeat. He turned to his parents and said that he was going to beat it, that he wasn't willing to accept that he'd only be on earth for such a short period of time and he didn't want anyone to feel sorry for him.

A couple of years later, when Steve was trying to work his weakening limbs in a rehabilitation clinic in Dallas, a staff psychologist came in the room. He told Steve Smith that it was in his best interests to deal with the reality of his situation. He told him that the nerve damage within his system could not be undone and that he needed to understand that his health was deteriorating rapidly. Smith looked to his dad, who was in the room, gave him a look as if to say, *I'll show them*, and then smiled.

"As parents, whenever your child falls down, your instincts are to reach down, pick them up and make them better," Morris Smith says. "To know that my son is going through this and that I can't reach down and pick him up, that I can't make it all better, makes me feel as helpless as I've ever felt."

STEVE SMITH LIES IN A RECLINER in the living room of a well-apportioned home in a suburban Dallas development. A breathing machine flanks him on the right from which thick, plastic accordion tubes protrude and attach to his body. The flickering computer screen sits on a stand a little to the left of the ventilator. Behind his chair is a bookshelf on which some football memorabilia sits— Raider and Seahawk helmets, game-worn and paint-smeared from games when Smith likely blasted into a hole as the lead blocker. The memorabilia serves as monuments to what his life had been. Just below is a neat little row of game balls Smith received for his play: the game in '88 against the Broncos; October 10, 1990, versus the Jets; December 30 that same year against the Chargers; and October 11, 1992 versus the Buffalo Bills. It is hard to fathom that the person lying prone, helpless, prisoner in a reclining chair was once Steve Smith, world-class football player.

He awakens each morning at 6:15. His wife and children, with the help of an automatic lifting machine, move him to a wheelchair and roll him to the living room and to that ominous apparatus where he receives his first dose of liquid food and medication. Then they strain to get Smith to his recliner and in front of a television, which provides Steve Smith his only access to the outside world. Chie Smith would like to take her husband for an occasional walk, but it would be such a chore—the machines would have to go with him. How could she wheel him around by herself? Who would help her if Steve should fall over and out of his chair?

Take away the machines and the constant whirring and beeping, and it is by most accounts a normal existence. Suburban home, beautiful wife, two beautiful children, two dogs—one a pit bull terrier named Shaq that Smith has had for fourteen years—and two cats. But it is so far from normal. The friendly cat, Nonna, occasionally climbs on top of Steve Smith, rubs into his lap, and then looks up at him, perhaps wondering why he won't—*can't*—pet back.

His mind is still as sharp as a razor. People in the room with Smith sometimes have conversations *around* him as if he's just another piece of furniture. But he hears everything. He's part of the conversation. He just has a difficult time being *in* the conversation.

The visitor in Steve Smith's home is speaking with Chie about Penn State football. He's telling her a story about the Penn State baseball team being prohibited from using the football team's brand-new Astroturf field even during a day when inclement weather made the baseball field unplayable. The visitor looks over at Steve Smith's computer. He has written with the mouse pouch he works with the tiny bit of strength in his knees: "Do you not know that football pays for all the other sports at Penn State?"

A few minutes later, Chie and the visitor are in conversation about Joe Paterno. She asks how old the Penn State coach is and how long he has coached. The discussion turns to the age-old question raised by Penn State football fans and practically everyone who follows college football: When will Paterno retire? Ten minutes later, the visitor again looks over at Steve and his computer. He has typed out, "He is scared of dying . . . when his arch rival bear bryant retired he died."

The irony hits the visitor as if a goalpost has just fallen on his head. Steve Smith is talking about other people being afraid of dying. *He* is not afraid.

Steve Smith will watch just about any sport on television. The sight of athletes running and jumping does not make him angry or bitter or envious that he can no longer do that. On this day he is glued to the screen and the U.S. Open tennis tournament. His left eyebrow rises as Maria Sharapova whistles home a forehand winner. It is the way Steve Smith expresses approval or affirmation. When his football playing days ended, Smith took up tennis and became an accomplished player. He taught Chie to play. Husband and wife would play at least twice a week at the local courts. The visitor sits and watches tennis on TV with Steve Smith for a couple of hours. He asks him who is his favorite tennis player. He types out, "Chie." His wife is in the kitchen preparing dinner for her children, who will be home shortly. When the visitor tells her what Steve has just written, her eyes well with tears.

Chie Smith mostly misses the hugs. She was his baby doll. The big fullback would often pick up his slightly built, 5′3″ wife and whirl her around like she was Audrey Hepburn. He'd hug her so tight some days she felt as if her ribs would crack. She is a remarkable woman. Her role in life with husband Steve, once so glamorous, has become merely custodian. She can hug him, but he can't hug back. She can't sleep in the same bed with him anymore.

Where does she go from here? Chie Smith doesn't really know.

Her husband desperately wants to live. He's willing to try anything, any possible treatment that can help him meet that goal. She just wants him to live the rest of his days comfortably. The expenses of caring for an ALS patient are tearing a large hole in the family finances. The Reno treatments cost $20,000 alone. At that clinic they had injected Smith's legs with some kind of herbal solution. It reduced some of the swelling in his legs, but it didn't do much to retard the symptoms of ALS. Chie is paying $3,000 a month in insurance premiums. But even with that, many of the treatments aren't covered by insurance since some alternative treatments are not endorsed by the American Medical Association. Chie estimates that her husband's medical attention costs the family about $250,000 a year. Some of those costs are defrayed by contributions from the Smith Foundation. The NFL has kicked in some aftercare money. Mostly, money Smith saved from his football days, money that was earmarked for his children's college education, pays for the treatments. And Smith never made a superstar's salary in the league.

In February 2004 the family got help from his old team, the Raiders. An alumni group headed by NFL Players' Association president Gene Upshaw, a former Raider, and former Raider executive Mike Ornstein formed the Black and White Club, a charity arm designed to help struggling ex-Raiders. The first player the club needed to help was Steve Smith.

Several of Smith's former teammates flew to Burbank to stage an autograph and memorabilia show. There was Marcus and Bo, Tim Brown, Howie Long, Art Shell, Willie Gault, and Tom Flores. Even Rod Woodson, who had no connection at all to Steve Smith, showed up. The show raised some $180,000 to help defer the Smiths' medical costs.

"He never asked, his wife never asked, but I told her, 'Steve laid his life out on the line for me for four years straight, every Sunday,'" Bo Jackson told an ESPN interviewer there to record the event. "The least that I can do is get on a plane and come and help out."

Later Jackson said that when he first saw Smith, he had to turn away because he didn't want to start crying in front of him. Allen had a similar reaction. "I was shoulder to shoulder, behind, in front, of a guy who was a physical specimen, like a fire hydrant," he said. "And now, he was in a wheelchair. It was hard."

In one camera shot, Jackson and Allen are surrounding Smith in his wheelchair. Smith speaks in a slow and lilting voice, "I love you all and I'm so thankful that I had the opportunity to play with the Raiders because the best thing that came out of it was the people I met."

Eight months later, in October 2004, ESPN visited Smith at his home to finish its piece. By then Smith could barely be understood and his words had to be translated by Chie. He was asked about the autograph show where he got to spend time with his Raider teammates. "For . . . them . . . to . . . make . . . me . . . feel . . . important . . . to . . . them . . . it . . . felt . . . beautiful."

He keeps a photo in his bedroom to remind him of the old days. In it he's flanked by Long, Gault, Brown, Allen, and Jackson. Smith is flashing a big smile.

Just two years later Steve Smith could no longer voice any words. He no longer has control over his voicebox. His condition requires constant care. The Smiths have nurses living in their home from 10 A.M. to midnight. A respiratory therapist visits Steve twice a day. The therapist exercises Smith's dormant lungs by pushing hard on his chest. It is an uncomfortable process for Steve; his body contorts and his facial expressions give off a look of terror. The therapist pushes air out, allowing the lungs to replenish that air and give the organs the impression they are still somewhat alive.

This is the type of prison in which Steve Smith now lives. When he came home following the surgery, his buttocks were riddled with bedsores, which formed because nurses didn't rotate his prone body often enough. One night his trachea tube came out of his slot and he was forced to breathe on his own—a tremendously difficult activity at this stage of his ALS—for nearly an hour in the middle of the night because nurses on duty never discovered it. Smith had to wait until he got home, in front of his computer, before he was able to communicate the abuses to Chie.

Steve Smith just wants to live. It is bothersome that he must rely on others to feed him, to clean him, to supervise his water and bowel movements. A couple of years ago in the early stages of Smith's ALS, when he was just confined to a wheelchair and could still move, he had come back to Penn State with his family for a football game. He was in the Lettermen Club at the new Bryce Jordan Center, across the way from Beaver Stadium, visiting with some assistant coaches, including Ganter. Someone suggested a photo. Dante Smith, then thirteen, moved around to the front of the wheelchair and extended his hands, offering to pull his dad up. Steve waved him away, preferring to pull himself out of the chair. Ganter remembers that it took Smith about thirty seconds to stand, but he did it. When he stood, he smiled. Now he was ready to take the picture. He didn't want it to be with him in a wheelchair. He wanted his coaches to see that he still fights.

Smith knows that his condition shocks the people who knew him when. Before the ALS had gripped his body, he returned to DeMatha with Chie. The principal was walking him through the halls during the school day, showing him the renovations, showing how the all-boys school had grown. Word spread like wildfire. Steve Smith was back. And walking with him was this beautiful woman. Students started following Smith as if he were a flag bearer in a parade. He was a conquering hero.

Just a couple of years later, Smith came back to DeMatha to accept his entry into the school's sports hall of fame. By then the ALS started to grip his body, so McGregor and Morris Smith helped Steve walk to the podium. He was taking four-inch steps. When he finally got to the microphone, his speech was slow and stuttered. It broke McGregor's heart. Most of the audience—parents, teachers, former and current DeMatha players—had tears in their eyes.

Steve Smith's wife just wants him home with the family and to live as long as he can. She wants him to see their children graduate from high school. She has seen cases of people with ALS live well beyond the five-year period normally predicted for them.

Sweat is beading up on Steve Smith's forehead. He is listening to the conversation the visitor is having with his wife. He types, "You are just taking her viewpoint." He wants to tell the visitor his thoughts. He asks the visitor to be patient and wait for him to tap out his thoughts on the computer screen. The visitor curses himself for being afraid to ask for *his* viewpoint on *his* condition. It has never occurred to the visitor that this man, this proud former football star, may not want to think of himself as an invalid.

Steve Smith is asked why he wants to continue with the intravenous treatment that has caused infection and so much misery without seeing any evidence that the process is healing him.

"I wasn't getting better . . . but I wasn't getting worse. . . . I felt over time that I would improve."

He's asked whether he thinks he can beat this. He raises an eyebrow, his signal for a yes answer, and then types: "You cannot think anything but success or else you will fail."

The computer screen flashes. Steve Smith tests his body strength again. He wants to answer more questions. He needs to answer more questions. It doesn't happen like this for him anymore. Visitors look at him with a detached curiosity. They don't look him in the eyes anymore. Some people worry about how *they* feel inside when they see Steve Smith. They feel bad. Whatever problems they have pale in comparison to a man who lies motionless, strafed with ALS. They protect themselves by not looking into his eyes.

The visitor asks Steve Smith why life is so worth living.

"My children . . . whenever I feel like I'm dying I think of me and my son playing basketball and my strength to fight what is impossible for man but not for god."

He's asked if he feels that he just has Lyme disease, not ALS, and that's why he feels he can be cured.

"I don't care what I have . . . my god can beat it."

The visitor is asked whether he has ever pondered the question "Why me?"

"In the beginning . . . yes . . . but you can't question the fight you are in . . . you just have to fight to win."

It is taking Steve Smith about fifteen minutes to answer each question, to use the mouse that's velcroed between his knees and attempt to find the right words, the right letters. He is straining, probably putting in more effort than he ever did in a football weight room. Maybe he doesn't feel like talking about living or dying anymore. Maybe he would like to talk about football. Maybe he'd like to talk about the night Penn State—with Steve Smith, the co-captain who wore number 33—beat Miami.

The visitor asks what it was like playing football at Penn State. An answer forms quickly in Steve Smith's head.

"It was like being in the military . . . they tell you when to wake . . . eat . . . work . . . and sleep . . . and you adapt or you are out."

Did he like Joe Paterno?

"When you are there you hate him . . . but when you get out in the real world and you start getting shit on . . . you say this is just like school . . . so you know what to do."

Smith had a modest Fiesta Bowl. He carried the football only four times for 13 yards, including one 10-yard gain, the night Penn State beat Miami. Someone sent him a copy of that game redone on DVD. As he sat with Chie and their children, watching the television screen, Steve Smith often broke into beaming smiles. He was reliving a time of innocence, a time when he was big and strong and spry. He was reliving the night a team of which he was a major part pulled off one of the great college football victories of all time. As he watched the television screen, Chie noticed that Steve was smiling almost constantly.

The visitor asks Steve Smith what he most remembered about the game. He looks at his computer screen again.

"I remember the sense of invincibility . . . of not being denied . . . they were more talented than us . . . but we would not be denied."

Down the stretch, when Miami was driving toward the Penn State goal line in the final frantic moments, was he afraid the Nittany Lions would lose?

"They made us so mad . . . we did not care who won . . . we just wanted to kick their ass."

The visitor looks at the computer screen and laughs. Smith smiles and strains to write again, readdressing the question of Miami's final drive.

"We did not care . . . we were in a fight . . . we knew we would win . . . if you are in a fight with someone who does not respect your manhood . . . you will die proving your point."

8

THE BROADCAST

THAT'S HOW A YOUTHFUL-LOOKING
Bob Costas began the most historic broadcast in college football. More than 70 million viewers tuned into the Penn State–Miami game on January 2, 1987. The game wound up pulling a monstrous 25 rating, meaning that 25 percent of all households in America had the game on, and a whopping 38 share—38 percent of all the televisions in use at that time were tuned into the broadcast. It would be the most-watched college football game in television history. By today's TV standards, the Penn State–Miami game had a primitive look to it. The graphics were simplistic, the background lead-in music was somewhat cheesy but it was a telecast that would stand the test of time.

Ken Schanzer, NBC Sports executive vice president at the time, had come to the network in 1981 from a stint as senior vice president for the National Association of Broadcasters. In 1983, he was appointed the right-hand man of venerable NBC Sports president Arthur Watson. Schanzer, who had graduated from Colgate and had a law degree from Columbia, was young, bright, energetic, and, most of all, savvy.

A year ago at the Orange Bowl, a national title is within Joe Paterno's grasp. But it was not to be. Oklahoma rides off with a 25–10 win. [*Cut to Barry Switzer being carried off the field on his players' shoulders, and to Joe Paterno, with a forlorn expression on the sidelines.*]

That same night in New Orleans . . . the Sugar Bowl . . . Vinny Testaverde sacked eight times . . . with three interceptions . . . three fumbles . . . Tennessee 35, Miami 10.

Both disappointments are placed aside as the sun rises on a new season. In the next four months, all the contenders will be tested. But only two will run the gauntlet without a loss. Only Miami and Penn State greet the New Year with a chance to be No. 1.

Two separate paths [*Cut to Testaverde walking through airport wearing combat fatigues and combat hat; cut to Paterno and his players walking down the steps from their airplane wearing conservative blue sports jackets and ties.*] . . . one destination . . . the steps along the way to a showdown.

And now as the sun sets on the college football season, all that remains is one game . . . one game for the national title.

🎙️ The first time Miami had the ball on offense, a chyron (on-screen graphic) flashed across the screen with the Hurricanes starting offense, which showed stars such as Testaverde, Highsmith, Bratton, Irvin, and Blades. Jones read off the names. "Offensive firepower, oh-ho!" he exclaimed.

After an early completion to Irvin, the announcers gushed about the ability of the 6´2˝, 190-pound wide receiver.

"Tell the people that I run a 4.4 40-yard dash," Jones quoted Irvin as telling him. "That's all they need to know."

Cefalo corrected, saying that Irvin was timed at 4.6 seconds.

"Last night Irvin told us that he ran a late 4.49," Jones said.

"Yeah, but he didn't say how late that was," quipped Cefalo.

In 1986, NBC was strictly a pro football network, dabbling only in college sports at New Year's time with telecasts of the Orange and Rose Bowls and an upstart bowl game out of Phoenix called the Fiesta Bowl.

As the college season unwound that year, and Miami and Penn State rolled through their seasons unbeaten and eventually into their No. 1 and No. 2 rankings, Schanzer saw an opportunity to make TV sports history. The Hurricanes and Nittany Lions were independents. They had no particular bowl associations. The winner of the Big Eight Conference was locked into going to the Orange Bowl. The winners of the Big Ten and the Pac-10 had to meet in the Rose Bowl. The SEC winner was already ticketed for the Sugar Bowl. But Penn State and Miami could pick and choose any bowl they wanted. Schanzer wanted that bowl to be NBC's Fiesta.

Schanzer had had past dealings with Miami athletic director Sam Jankovich and liked him very much. He knew Jankovich, a slight man with a grizzly edge, as a bit of a rebel, a riverboat gambler type who was determined to turn Miami into the kind of football powerhouse that wouldn't have to take a back seat to the traditional stars that had long dominated college football. But getting the Hurricanes to the Fiesta Bowl would be easier said than done.

First, Schanzer needed to keep his efforts quiet. In 1986 networks tried to avoid matchmaking. Schanzer knew that the viewing public was still a little uncomfortable about television controlling sports—especially college sports, which still smacked of innocence and purity in the face of professional greed.

What's more, the Fiesta Bowl was considered a stepchild of sorts of the college bowl season. It was a bowl normally reserved for "leftovers," the teams without conference affiliations, or those who didn't win their conference championships or usually didn't appear in a national championship picture. The Fiesta Bowl paid out less per team than most of the others. And new bowls were springing up all over the place, such as the Citrus Bowl, born out of the rapidly growing area of Orlando, Florida.

To get Miami's and Penn State's attention, Fiesta Bowl organizers knew they had to find more cash—to more than double the million or so dollars they had previously paid their teams. The month before the game, Fiesta Bowl executives announced they would pay the teams who played there a whopping $2.2 million each, commensurate with the richest payout of any bowl that year. Years later, Fiesta Bowl chairman Bruce Skinner would say that he was helped financially by NBC, a statement that Schanzer would neither confirm nor deny.

"I really don't remember whether we helped in that way or not," said Schanzer, now the president of NBC Sports. "What I remember was that the Fiesta Bowl people were cowboys. They wanted to be a major bowl."

It was a bowl that had already made great strides since its birth in the early 1970s. The Fiesta Bowl originally was played on Christmas Day. But bowl founders knew nobody really paid much attention to the college games played before New Year's; those were the also-ran teams. But the Fiesta Bowl had a wonderful hook. It was played in a warm location, where fans could include it in their winter vacation schedule. And it was totally independent. It could match up any of the top teams not already committed to playing elsewhere. In some years, if they got lucky enough, they just might be able to match the top two ranked teams in the country.

After a Miami first-quarter penalty and some activities among a couple of linemen, Jones said, "There's some pushing and shoving. There's been a lot of cross talk this week between the ball clubs."

"In fact, it continued coming into the stadium," Cefalo added. "As Penn State was getting off their bus, Miami was waiting on them, yelling and screaming. So it continued right up into game time."

Fiesta Bowl organizers also understood the value of the lobby. While other bowl games thought of themselves as the mountain Moses came to, the Fiesta Bowl took the mountain to Moses. They made a regular practice of inviting coaches and athletic directors down to Phoenix, all expenses paid, for off-season functions. In many ways, they were the runts of the litter, the pups who had to burrow through the others to get to the teat. By 1982 they had garnered enough clout to have the game approved by the NCAA for New Year's Day.

It wasn't until 1985 that the Fiesta Bowl took its leap into the upper tier. That year, it produced one of the most exciting games of the college postseason when UCLA beat Miami, 39–37. But nobody talked much about it afterward because neither UCLA nor Miami had been ranked in the top ten and because the Fiesta was still considered bargain basement—it was only paying out $600,000 per team, considerably less than any of the major bowls. No major team was going to come, even an independent, unless it upped the ante.

In the early 1980s bowl games sprouted plentifully. And all of these new bowls had found a formula to keep them afloat—corporate sponsorship. There was the Sea World Holiday Bowl out of San Diego and the John Hancock Sun Bowl. Even the Sugar Bowl got into the act, altering its name to include banking sponsorship as the United States Fidelity and Guaranty (USF&G) Sugar Bowl.

The Fiesta Bowl had reached out to Sunkist Growers of Sherman Oaks, California, which had been one of the original sponsors of its bowl game. Sunkist, a cooperative of more than six thousand independent business people in Arizona and California, agreed to throw in some fresh cash to help sponsor the game so long as the game would thereafter be known as the Sunkist Fiesta Bowl. That boosted the 1986 game payout to $1.1 million for Michigan and Nebraska but Fiesta Bowl folks knew they would need to more than double that to ensure the participation of Miami and Penn State to play for No. 1.

Griese, who in his pro career had the reputation as a cerebral quarterback, chose to analyze the early moments of the game that way. After a pass in the flat to Highsmith, Griese remarked, "One thing the Hurricanes are doing is throwing short passes. And they're doing that not to get Vinny Testaverde into the game, but doing it to ease their offensive line in.

"They knew that Paterno was going to try a lot of different blitzes. He went back and got the game film of the Sugar Bowl last year where Tennessee used all kind of blitzes against Testaverde. They want to ease their offensive linemen in. [Paterno] thinks he has some mismatches on the offensive line of the Hurricanes with his first seven players."

A little later, Griese expressed surprise at Penn State's decision to pass the ball early against the Miami defense instead of relying on its usual grind-it-out running style when Shaffer completed only one of his first five passes. "Penn State has come out doing the exact opposite of what they normally do," Griese exclaimed. "They normally come out and run the football. The reason Shaffer has not started off hot is that he is trying to do something that may not be natural to him."

Schanzer knew that Penn State would be a sure thing for the Fiesta. Paterno, long a proponent of some kind of a college football playoff, desperately wanted to play the Hurricanes to decide the national championship. Paterno had already told Skinner that he would play the Hurricanes in a parking lot, if that was what it would take. The problem lay with Miami.

Jankovich knew that a game with Penn State would raise awareness for his program, but he also knew his coaches didn't want to go to Phoenix. The national championship was the Hurricanes' to lose. They could stay in their home state, go to the Orange Bowl right at home, or the Gator Bowl up in Jacksonville, or the Citrus in Orlando, beat up some hapless opponent, and win a national championship with minimal effort. Why did they have to travel all the way across the country and risk a game with Penn State to do it? They just didn't feel there was that much to gain.

But by then Schanzer had come up with a perfect sales pitch. The NBC Sports VP suggested to Fiesta Bowl executives that they move their game to prime time on the night of January 2, a Friday night, when people stayed glued to their sets. NBC already had two hugely popular back-to-back shows on Friday nights—*Miami Vice* and *Crime Story*. They already had a programmed audience. Skinner and his Fiesta cohort, Don Meyers, loved the idea. It would separate the Fiesta Bowl completely from the others. They already had the marquee game. Now they would have their own night. They would dominate the Cotton, Sugar, Rose, and Orange Bowls. It was perfect.

That's the angle Schanzer would use to convince Jankovich. What better exposure could Miami's football program receive than by playing on prime time on a separate night when there was no other competition, where viewers couldn't change the channel and find another game? It was an offer that Jankovich couldn't refuse. His football coaches saw only the present. Jankovich was looking into the future. That's why he was hired to come there in the first place. Miami's president, Tad Foote, had been concerned about football growing so big that it would overshadow Miami's academic reputation but how could he turn down $2.2 million in the school's coffers?

It was a win-win for everybody. Penn State would get a chance to win a national championship in a game that resembled a football playoff system that Joe Paterno coveted. Miami would get a prime-time chance to show how powerful its football program had grown. The Fiesta Bowl would take a huge leap out of the shadows of the other, more traditional bowls. And NBC would get a prime-time football game that would generate huge advertising dollars because it might set a record for viewership and share.

It was all good. Only a few minor details remained.

Schanzer had vacillated on whom he would choose to broadcast perhaps the biggest college football game in history. NBC's top announcing team at the time was Dick Enberg and Merlin Olsen, who had teamed together on the network's AFC telecasts. Enberg, the network's venerable play-by-play man, and Olsen, the former Los Angeles Rams great and popular spokesperson for such brands as Hallmark and FTD Florist, had also been the regular announcers for NBC's Rose Bowl broadcasts. The Rose Bowl was considered in the college football bowl world to be the so-called granddaddy of them all. But this was one year the game—played in Pasadena—would not have nearly as much impact on the college football world. Schanzer considered switching things up by moving Enberg and Olsen to the Fiesta.

Cefalo was at his effusive best in describing a Testaverde scramble late in the first quarter. Penn State had the Miami quarterback trapped in his own end zone, but somehow he wriggled out of an inevitable sack by Bob White and came roaring out, gaining nearly 20 yards.

"Testaverde, not with his arm but with his legs!" gushed Charlie Jones. "All right!"

Said Cefalo, "This is why he's the Heisman Trophy winner. Some guys can throw it. But he throws it better than anyone else and he's got great strength to get away from a couple of people in the end zone! If Testaverde doesn't live in the weight room in the off-season, he's tackled in the end zone for a sack. But he gets away and gets a lot of yardage and a first down and gets Miami out of trouble deep in their own end zone!" Later Cefalo would reveal that Testaverde bench presses 325 pounds and squats 525.

"The problem was that we had had this long-standing association with the Rose Bowl, and at the end of the day, we thought that the Rose Bowl people would take it as an insult if we pulled our main announcers from their game," Schanzer said.

In the end, Schanzer decided that Charlie Jones, who had been the play-by-play man for all previous Fiesta Bowl telecasts, would continue with the bowl. Jimmy Cefalo, the ex–Penn State star who was just finding his stride in the broadcast business after a fairly successful pro football career with the Miami Dolphins, would be Jones's partner. Jones and Cefalo had been the second team on NBC's AFC telecasts. The other man in the booth would be Bob Griese, the former Dolphins quarterback who had been a color analyst on NBC's Sunday pro football telecasts. That three-man crew—with help from Ahmad Rashad as the sideline reporter—would be the guts of a broadcast supervised by the game's main host, Bob Costas.

His Fiesta Bowl coup already in hand, Ken Schanzer, in December 1986, married his girlfriend, Lisa Sherman. For their honeymoon, the Schanzers went

After Highsmith pranced for a good gain, Jones told how the Miami fullback complained about getting beat up all season long. "Look at these hands!" Jones said Highsmith said to him. "I have the hands of a sixty-five-year old man! And they just keep getting beaten up more."

Griese, watching Testaverde overshoot his intended target Bratton on one play, said, "Paterno wanted to get into the mind of Testaverde. One of the ways he's doing that is taking away anything deep. He has three men sitting deep. Testaverde would have to wait eleven seconds for his receivers to get by them."

skiing in Aspen, Colorado, then took in the Rose and Fiesta Bowls from seats in the stands. As he sat with his new wife in Sun Devil Stadium, Schanzer couldn't help but think that this game, the monumental clash of Penn State versus Miami, the game that would make television history, was his baby.

BOB COSTAS HAD BEEN WITH NBC for only six years but had emerged as the network's signature sports announcer. Though serious and knowledgeable about the subject matter, Costas had a soft edge that allowed the viewer to like him, to not feel threatened by his intelligence. That's why NBC had recently locked him up in a long-term contract.

Schanzer's blueprint for the Fiesta Bowl had Costas as a sort of broadcast overseer. Costas would open the broadcast, handle halftime duties, and then close it up. And he would handle all the important pregame taped interviews. Days before Penn State left for the West Coast, Costas made his way to State College to interview Paterno. From a seat behind his office desk, JoePa was cordial, Costas remembered, but not overly expansive, and certainly had no desire to wade into the undercurrent that Penn State and Miami would be a matchup of good versus evil.

Schanzer knew that with this Fiesta Bowl he had a goldmine. He didn't need his network to hype the obvious subplot. That took take care of itself as the fatigue-clad Miami players walked off the plane in Tempe and then later hooted at Penn State's team bus and generally acted like reform-school refugees as game time approached. Instead, Costas worked the Italian American angle with Paterno and Testaverde, both of whom were born in Brooklyn and both of whom came from supportive parents and immigrant grandparents.

In Costas's interview, Paterno talked about his father being disappointed that he had become a football coach. The elder Paterno had worked as a clerk in the New York court system. His son had just started out as an assistant football coach when Joe Paterno Sr. passed away in 1955. "He kept waiting for me to get out of coaching," Paterno told Costas, "and go into something more meaningful, like going to law school. He had a great love for the law and always envisioned the great lawyer son. He never really was crazy about my coaching."

In the interview, Costas asked Paterno what he thought made up a good coach.

"I think a good coach has got to stand for something and how he can get what he stands for across to people depends," the Penn State coach said. "Some need you as a friend. For some you need to be a real SOB. You've got to be tough; you've got to make them do things they may not want to do until you think they refine their character, until they learn to go to class. If they don't go to class, they don't play."

Only a couple of weeks before the interview with Costas, Paterno had been named *Sports Illustrated*'s Sportsman of the Year, becoming only the second coach in that magazine's history to be so named. UCLA basketball coach John Wooden had been the other.

"I was in awe of it," said Paterno of the SI feat. "I went to bed thinking about it, and then I checked myself and said, 'Hey, relax.' My wife tells me to look in the mirror when I ask her how many great coaches are out there in the world. She says, 'Well, there's one less than you think there are.'"

Since winning the Heisman Trophy, Vinny Testaverde had been put on a media blitz, moving around the country like a whistle-stop tour. To interview the Miami quarterback,

After Cobbs intercepted Testaverde at the beginning of the second quarter, cameras caught a shoving match among Giftopoulos, a couple of Miami offensive linemen, and Testaverde. "What's Vinny Testaverde doing in there?!" screamed Cefalo. "The shoving matches, that's supposed to be the big guys, linebacker types. But I told you, he's an athlete and he can mix it up in the middle."

Jones asked Griese, "Did you ever help any of your offensive linemen out like that, Bob?"

"My offensive linemen were big enough to take care of themselves, Charlie," Griese said with a laugh.

Costas was forced to wait until the Miami team arrived in Tempe. He did so two days before the game on a barren practice field. Testaverde, dressed in a dingy gray practice tee shirt with the right sleeve ripped off, seemed reclusive in the interview. Following the Italian American storyline NBC had already created, Costas asked Testaverde a question about playing against Paterno.

"I like Coach Paterno a lot," Vinny said. "I respect him a great deal, but that will not put me in awe."

In Tempe, Costas was incredulous over Miami's antics. He saw the combat fatigues and wondered why the Hurricanes would give Penn State any further incentive. On paper, Miami was certifiably the best team in the Fiesta Bowl. They were heavily favored, with a roster of future NFL stars. Costas had cut his teeth broadcasting games of the Spirit of St. Louis, a team in the old American Basketball Association whose star was Marvin (Bad News) Barnes. Barnes was terrifically talented, but a career troublemaker. The negative attention that Barnes created for himself swallowed up a once-promising career. Great players didn't need to talk, Costas learned then. And as Miami did that week against Penn State, walking out of a steak fry, disrespecting their opposition, Costas thought that the boorishness would come back to haunt Miami.

"I just thought their shenanigans were stupid," Costas said. "Miami was a terrific team. Jimmy Johnson was a great coach. I don't know why they just didn't let that speak for it. They bought into that good guys–bad guys theme and I think it just sucked some of the energy out of them."

Costas had been involved in a minor controversy himself a couple of weeks before the Fiesta Bowl. Broadcasting as host of NBC's Sunday pro-football studio show *NFL '86*, Costas aired an "exclusive" report that Johnson would leave Miami after the Fiesta Bowl to become the head coach at the University of Texas. The

🎙️ Shaffer, continuing with the game plan to pass first, then run, fired a long pass that overshot an open Ray Roundtree on a fly pattern.

"This doesn't look like Penn State," exclaimed Jones.

"No, it doesn't," added Cefalo. "Those wide receivers, they have the black shoes on. I don't think anybody told them that they're not supposed to run past cornerbacks."

But a couple of plays later, Griese was critical of Penn State's decision to go with play-action after Shaffer misfired on another long throw.

"Going with a play-action fake on third down I just don't understand," said Griese. "How are you going to fake anybody if you're not running the football?"

Testaverde, meanwhile, continued with his short-passing game plan. After he completed one to Brian Blades near the right sideline and after Duffy Cobbs made the stop, Jones wondered if Miami was picking on Cobbs.

"I don't know if they're picking on him; he's also 20 yards off the ball!" Cefalo said. "He's not going to allow anyone to run past him. Penn State is playing that gambling type of defense, saying, *we'll give you those short-passing things. We're going to come up and make the tackle and, hopefully, make you cough up the ball*. But I don't know if that's good enough to beat Miami tonight."

report sent ripples through the television sports world. At CBS, which was airing a competing pregame football show entitled NFL *Today*, the producer, George Veras, was informed of Costas's report. Veras ordered his staff to chase the story. CBS quickly made calls to Texas, to Johnson, and to Miami and was able to snare an interview with Jankovich.

The story was wrong. Opposing networks piled on NBC. A couple of weeks later Costas ran for cover, telling Madison Square Garden network host Greg Gumbel that the story wasn't his—it was a product of network producer John Filippelli—and that he had merely "conveyed it." Costas recalled, "We aired that report over my strenuous objections. We got it something like second or third hand. Somebody had overheard Tad Foote [Miami's president] tell it to somebody on a golf course, or something like that. I argued that it wasn't a story, or if it was, it certainly needed further confirmation. But there were a lot of dynamics at work. I was told to go on the air with the story and I didn't really have the clout, especially back then, to refuse. Something like that would never happen today."

At halftime Costas presided over one of the most unusual TV breaks of any college football broadcast: a live newsbreak. NBC News had been No. 3 among the three networks at the time. Knowing there would be a huge national viewing audience, the NBC News department had decided that sending anchor Tom Brokaw to the game would give the network—and Brokaw—some needed exposure.

Costas quickly wrapped up the first half, teased upcoming Rashad interviews with former Penn State star Curt Warner and former Miami star Jim Kelly, then turned it over to Brokaw by saying, "Now we give you a chance to catch up on some national and international headlines with broadcaster and football fan Tom Brokaw."

With the Penn State Blue Band playing and marching in the background of the television shot, Brokaw, sitting right next to Costas in his booth in the stadium, dove immediately into somber stories about a heavy death toll in a Puerto Rican hotel fire, student protesting in Beijing, China, and a hurricane that was battering the East Coast. But the sound of the band was drowning out the news anchor and he appeared to be shouting the stories into his lapel microphone just to be heard.

"It was one of those train wreck moments," recalled Michael Weisman, the game's executive producer, "and I didn't even know how the thing came out until the next day. After the game, we're all patting ourselves on the back for doing a good broadcast. And then you wake up the next day and everybody in the world is panning you for the halftime thing."

Following a package of first-half highlights and Rashad's interviews with Warner and Kelly, Costas took back the microphone and shared a split screen with then-President Ronald Reagan from the White House. Costas, referring to Reagan's early days as a sports broadcaster, asked him to critique the work of Jones and his play-by-play crew.

"I don't envy those fellows because I liked it better when the audience had to wait to find out from you what was going on," the president said with a smile.

Reagan delivered a long-winded story on his first job in the business—broadcasting the Iowa–Minnesota homecoming game after a successful job audition where he re-created a football game in his head. Reagan went on to extol the virtues of the student-athlete. He told a story of becoming aware of a quarterback from a big-time football school who quit the team and transferred to tiny Eureka College— Reagan's alma mater—in order to enjoy more of his college experience. It was a poignant tale, but rather long-winded. And Costas suddenly had to deal with some TV time issues.

"In my ear, the guys in the truck were telling me to 'wrap it up, wrap it up,'" Costas recalled. "Now how in the world are you supposed to wrap up the president of the United States?"

CHARLIE JONES HAD BEEN the regular play-by-play man for the Fiesta Bowl since its inception, but he was well aware that politics were

🎙️ Early in the third quarter, Shaffer completed a short pass over the middle to Dozier.

GRIESE: "What you like to do is throw short and try and beat this gap-8. What you do is fake, look downfield, and try to hit the tight end, Siverling. If you don't have that, Shaffer likes to go to his halfback. This is a halfback–tight end offense."

JONES: "Go back and explain what a gap-8 defense is."

GRIESE: "It's simply a defensive man in every gap of the offense—between the guard and the tackle, between the guard and the center, and all the way down the line so it's tough to get any blocking lanes and it's tough to run the football."

Shaffer's downfield pass was deflected and intercepted by Miami's Selwyn Brown. After the play, the cameras showed Dozier stamping around, speaking with one of the game's officials.

"Dozier's upset about something," Cefalo said. "He was on the sidelines. He was not on the field of play for that particular down, and ran on to the field, wanting to give his opinion to the officials."

An NBC replay showed a Miami player crash into Penn State receiver Eric Hamilton, who had crossed in front of intended receiver Ray Roundtree.

"He's complaining about an illegal chuck on Hamilton," Cefalo said.

However, after the game Dozier said he was complaining that officials didn't throw a flag for unnecessary roughness of Shaffer, who was blocked to the ground on Miami's interception return.

playing a part in the choice of announcers for the 1987 game of Penn State and Miami. Cefalo, a star football player at Penn State, had badly wanted to be in the booth for the Fiesta Bowl. Handsome, well coiffed, and articulate beyond that of the normal ex-jock, Cefalo, who had just finished a decent career with the Miami Dolphins, was on his way to becoming a sports broadcasting superstar. And he felt a game this visible could only enhance his profile.

Jones knew that Cefalo was on pins and needles waiting for the NBC honchos to make their decision on the broadcasters. He had become fast friends with Cefalo. Jones was twenty years older than Cefalo and had willingly served as his mentor. The two also had a decent enough rapport to be able to pull off some practical jokes without hurting each other's feelings.

Jones received a call from Weisman, the game's executive producer, telling him that the Jones–Cefalo team would indeed be calling the '87 Fiesta Bowl. Charlie immediately called Cefalo.

"Jimmy?" he said.

"Tell me we got it," Cefalo said excitedly.

"We didn't get it," Jones said.

There was silence on the other end.

"Just kidding. We got it," Jones said.

"You SOB," Cefalo said, nearly dropping the phone.

Schanzer and Weisman knew, though, that they might have some credibility problems with Cefalo because of his Penn State roots. They feared that the viewing audience might perceive him as biased for that reason. The truth was that Cefalo had a rocky relationship with Paterno while he was a player at Penn State and had not been that prideful of his Nittany Lion background. Still, Weisman felt as if he had to balance the broadcast with some Miami flavor and settled on Bob Griese, the former Dolphins quarterback, as his third man in the booth. Griese had been under contract for NBC anyway, broadcasting Sunday AFC pro football for the network.

Bob Griese had come a long way from his early days as an analyst. When Griese, the quarterback of the Miami Dolphins' historic undefeated season in 1972, first retired from pro football, NBC grabbed him. He was a cerebral quarterback when he played, and network executives thought he'd be a natural in describing football action. NBC honchos figured they could easily pair up Griese with Jones, the veteran play-by-play man, and have perfect broadcaster symmetry. One Sunday, the Chargers were playing the 49ers in San Diego, where Jones lived. So NBC arranged for Griese to fly there and meet up in the booth with Jones to perform a practice broadcast. They did the first three quarters of the game into a tape machine before Griese had to leave to catch a flight back to Florida.

"Bob was just terrible," Jones said. "They wound up pairing him that year with another one of our broadcasters, Jay Randolph. I was thinking, 'There is no way that this guy is going to make it.' He just couldn't describe the action succinctly and quickly enough. He was stammering all over the place.

"So the next year, I go to New York where the NBC folks are going to tell us what the announcing teams will be for the upcoming season. I'm paired with

The most compelling part of the broadcast, as far as the NBC commentators were concerned, happened after Miami took over following Manoa's fumble with about four minutes remaining in the third quarter. Testaverde lofted a long pass to Michael Irvin near the Nittany Lions' goal line. Irvin tripped and fell as he pursued the ball and officials called pass interference on Penn State's Ray Isom. Several replays revealed later that the call was a correct one—Isom had inadvertently nudged Irvin's ankle as both pursued the ball, forcing Irvin to trip himself. Jones and Cefalo discussed the play for several minutes as replays flashed across the screen. Several minutes later, Griese joined the fray.

JONES: I must tell you, I'm not sure of that call. I thought it was an inadvertent trip.
CEFALO: When you're a receiver, there is no such thing as inadvertent tripping. You can see it appears that way, though no one was going for the football. A little bit overthrown. They just got tangled up at the end.
JONES: He just tripped over himself! Now, what you're looking at here is the reason there is instant replay in the National Football League. He trips himself! How they don't have instant replay in college football, but that's the kind of call that instant replay was created for.
CEFALO: Let's take another closer look. Little rough to see, but it does not appear that Ray Isom, number 22, ran into him at all.

JONES: Do we have another angle? Here it is. Now watch his feet. He trips himself!

The broadcast turned back to the action on the field. Miami now had a first down at the Penn State 17-yard line. Warren Williams rushed for three yards. Then the discussion in the booth continued.

JONES: All right, we're going to take one more look and then we're going to bury this one.
CEFALO: Is there any action between the two? There doesn't appear to be. It just appears to be Michael Irvin tripping himself.
JONES: Bad call. Oh, you hope the No. 1 doesn't come down to that one call.
GRIESE: Charlie, I disagree.
JONES: Okay.
GRIESE: I think Isom did trip him. And if we can get another look at that at some time, I think there was some tripping and Irvin did not trip himself.
JONES: Did my eyes deceive me?
GRIESE: If we can get another look.
JONES: They're looking for it in the truck. Okay, here we go. Bob?
[A replay comes on the screen again.]
GRIESE: Right . . . next step . . . right there! See it? Isom, number 22, hit his left foot and tripped him.
JONES: No, I think he hit Isom's left ankle.
GRIESE [laughing]: Well, whatever. You always did have those good eyes, pal.

But a closer look at the replay would reveal that Griese's analysis was correct.

Griese. I'm saying to myself, 'You've got to be kidding me! This is going to be a disaster.'

"So the season starts and we start doing the first game together and Bob Griese is terrific! I mean, just great. Finally, there's a commercial in the third quarter

Two plays after Bratton was tackled for a loss, Miami got a first down on an eight-yard run by Highsmith. Then Highsmith broke up the middle for 21 yards. After the play, he lay on the turf in agony with a leg cramp.

"Who else to go to but Alonzo Highsmith?" Cefalo gushed. "You want to know who Vinny Testaverde's vote for the Heisman was? That man right there sitting on the ground with a leg cramp—Alonzo Highsmith. He thinks he's the best football player in the country."

Said Griese, "Gary Stevens, [Miami's] offensive coordinator, told me that Miami can run the ball, but they don't like to do it too much because then we take the ball out of Testaverde's hands. Well, they may wind up winning a national championship with the running game."

and I have to ask him. I say, 'Bob, what has happened? You started off so rocky and now you're just one of the very best I've ever heard. What happened?' He turns to me and says, 'Well, it was the same way when I broke in as a football player in the NFL. My rookie year, I was just lost. So that off-season, I took home a bunch of tapes and started analyzing every play, trying to figure out what the coaches wanted me to see. And I did the same thing with broadcasting. I finally saw the game the way they wanted me to see it and tell it.'

"It was one of the most amazing transitions I'd ever seen."

The hierarchy in NBC's broadcast booth allowed for Cefalo as the main analyst with Griese adding thoughts here and there. Though Cefalo's work during the game appeared solid, later he would tell Jones that he never felt as though he was on his game. Griese had been his quarterback in the first couple of years Cefalo played for the Dolphins, and his old football mentality had kicked in to respect his leader. Cefalo didn't want to get in Griese's way. He had too much respect for him. Consequently, after the broadcast he told Jones that he had held back.

JIMMY CEFALO CAME FROM PITTSTON, PENNSYLVANIA, in the heart of the state's coal mining regions, where he had been one of the most recruited scholastic football players in history. Strong and swift, Cefalo was a state sprinting champion as well as a record-setting running back—every big school in the country wanted him. As a senior at Pittston Area High School, Cefalo had averaged an astronomical 17.9 yards per carry, a total that had broken O.J. Simpson's national record. He gained 1,949 yards that senior year with 28 touchdowns. He had 312 yards rushing and six touchdowns in a game against Dallas High that year and followed that up with a 273-yard, four-touchdown game against Meyers the next week. That senior season, Cefalo received letters from some 150 schools and was contacted by six U.S. congressmen on behalf of their states, the governor of Maryland, and baseball great Hank Aaron, then playing with the Atlanta Braves, who pitched the virtues of schools from Georgia.

Also a good student at Pittston Area High, Cefalo was interested in journalism. He wanted to go to the University of Georgia, a school with a good journalism reputation, which he felt would give him the perfect combination of football and academics. He took a weekend visit to Athens, Georgia, and returned home on a

Sunday night. Cefalo had expected his parents to pick him up, but no one greeted him at the airport. He wound up taking a taxi home. Lugging his duffel bag up the walk, Cefalo could see clearly through his screened-in porch that a man was sitting with his parents at the dining room table. As he got closer, he saw that it was Joe Paterno.

"Mrs. Cefalo," he heard Paterno say to his mother, "your spaghetti sauce is even better than Mrs. Cappelletti's."

Jimmy Cefalo wound up selecting Penn State.

The times playing for Paterno were anything but smooth sailing. Cefalo was a star, the most celebrated recruit in the country, and Paterno treated him just like everybody else. Cefalo didn't think Paterno was using him enough. He wasn't letting him carry the ball twenty times a game like the other schools had promised. He didn't throw the ball to him enough. Cefalo thought Paterno was wasting his talents.

The two battled constantly. Cefalo missed time with nagging injuries that Paterno thought he should have played through. Cefalo considered transferring. In the end, he stayed a Nittany Lion. After a decent senior season, Cefalo was drafted in the third round by the Dolphins and had a decent pro career. But there was always a little edge between Cefalo and Joe Paterno.

Besides that, many residents of State College considered Jimmy Cefalo persona non grata. Several years into his Dolphins career, Cefalo decided to marry his fiancée, State College native Suzie Baker, who had been his girlfriend since college. But Cefalo suddenly got cold feet. Friends attending the rehearsal dinner in State College the night before the wedding noticed that Cefalo wasn't himself and wasn't exactly immersed in the evening's revelry.

Early the next morning, Cefalo went to the church in which he was to be married, told the minister that he wasn't coming for the ceremony, and left town. The story made a small headline in the *New York Times*, and Suzie Baker's father blasted the former Penn State football star publicly.

Those circumstances didn't make for a smooth path to inside information on the Fiesta Bowl broadcast. Fortunately for NBC, Cefalo still had good relationships with several of Penn State's assistant coaches and he had gleaned enough pertinent information out of them to make for a good broadcast.

JONES REMEMBERS THE 1987 FIESTA BOWL BROADCAST for its importance and its bloopers.

Two nights before the game, on New Year's Eve, NBC asked Jones and Cefalo to record a promo teasing the Fiesta Bowl, which the network planned to use some-

🎤 Miami took a 10–7 lead on a 38-yard field goal by Mark Seelig. Penn State got the ball back with 11:44 remaining, trailing by three points.

CEFALO: And now we find out what kind of winner John Shaffer is. We mentioned 65–1 since the seventh grade. You know, they said about him in the past, he doesn't throw very well, doesn't run very much, but he does win football games. The same words were used by Rip Engle when he was at Brown, when he was describing a skinny, little, scrawny, left-handed quarterback by the name of Joe Paterno.

On a second down and six with less than ten minutes remaining, Conlan intercepted Testaverde with a brilliant over-the-shoulder catch and then returned the ball 38 yards to the Miami five-yard line.

"Remember when you were a kid growing up you dreamed about things like maybe playing in a national championship football game?" Cefalo said. "Fourth quarter, you're down by three points and you make a big interception. That's exactly what Shane Conlan did and his dreams of his youth may come true tonight."

A couple of plays later, Dozier scored, knelt down in the back of the end zone, and prayed as teammates surrounded him with congratulatory pats.

"D.J. Dozier, a very religious young man," Jones said. "On Sunday, we were shooting some head shots of the teams in groups of five. He was in the last group of five because he had come back from church."

time during its telecast of the Orange Bowl, held New Year's night. So Jones and Cefalo (Griese was committed to another event) made it to Sun Devil Stadium and stood at the 50-yard line to begin what was supposed to be a one-minute recording. On the first take, Jones got down to the final twenty seconds of the spot when he unrepentantly began to laugh. That triggered similar moments on successive takes in which even Cefalo caught the laughing bug. In the end, Jones and Cefalo needed eighty-two takes to complete the one-minute promo. They had been at Sun Devil Stadium for two hours.

"I still think that's an NBC record," Jones said.

In fifteen years of broadcasting the Fiesta Bowl, Charlie Jones had built up enough goodwill with the Fiesta executives to feel like part of the family. And Miami's act that week sickened him. In the early days of the Fiesta, organizers almost had to beg for press coverage. Jones had been the master of ceremonies of the first Fiesta Bowl pregame luncheon, which consisted of thirty people in the dining room of a cheap motel. For the '87 game, the dais was 50 yards long—Jones paced it out with footsteps—and some three thousand people crowded the ballroom of the most exclusive hotel in Phoenix. Floats paraded down the streets of Tempe to denote the game. Jones and the broadcast team rode on one that celebrated the Special Olympics. Then there were the Miami Hurricanes walking around like Genghis Khans in their black sweatsuits instead of the more respectful outfits of coats and ties, throwing stuff at Fiesta Bowl organizers, walking out of barbeques, and, in general, acting like, Jones felt, hooligans.

"They fucked up the whole week," Jones said of Miami. "They alienated everybody there. They put a damper on everything. I never did understand it."

Jones had hardly slept the night before the game. The broadcasting team was well aware of how many potential viewers this game had. Just as there was this distinct pressure for the Penn State and Miami teams to perform well, so was there on Jones, Cefalo, and Griese. They would get this one shot. The game was live. Nothing could be erased.

As the beginning of the game approached, the NBC cameras caught some interesting shots. Testaverde warmed up on the sideline, throwing a football with a teammate. Instead of having another teammate receive the return throw, the

Hurricanes' quarterback snared the return one-handed, with his left hand, before transferring it to his right.

It was the twentieth bowl game as play-by-play man for the bass-voiced Jones and he made sure he found the necessary hype. "This ball game is entirely different than any of the games I've covered," Jones said on the telecast. "The reason? This is for a national championship. Usually, a bowl game is a reward for the players. Have a good time. Enjoy yourselves. And then, try and win the ball game. But with a national title on the line, this week everybody's uptight. It's been more like a Super Bowl week."

NBC mostly let the pictures tell the story. As Miami kicker Mark Seelig waited for the okay to kick off, director Andy Rosenberg cut to several different shots—Paterno and Johnson on their sidelines, the crowd, Testaverde, Dozier—with Jones, Cefalo, and Griese silent for thirty-five seconds.

As the game unfolded and Penn State stayed in it, contrary to what most football experts had predicted, Jones realized what was at play. The 1987 Fiesta Bowl had the potential to become one of the most memorable upsets of all time. During commercials, and then at halftime, Jones, Cefalo, and Griese talked about it.

"Can you believe this is happening?" they mused. "It's got to change, right?"

🎙 Fueled by the touchdown that put his team ahead, Manca knocked the ensuing kickoff through the end zone and Miami had to start its drive at the 20-yard line.

GRIESE: There is no question at this point in time Vinny Testaverde is confused. Now the teams exchange all eleven game films for this year, but the one Joe Paterno wanted was last year's Sugar Bowl. He called Johnny Majors at Tennessee. Tennessee beat the University of Miami, 35-7. Johnny Majors was once at Pittsburgh. But Johnny Majors said, "I can't do it." Last year's Sugar Bowl game, Testaverde threw three interceptions and was sacked eight times. Paterno called Majors and he said, "No, I know Jimmy Johnson." Paterno turned to his assistants and said, "I want that film. Just get it. I don't care how you get it." Paterno said the other day, "Well, we got it, but I don't know where we got it from."

The emphasis shifted. When Jones, Cefalo, and Griese first took to the air, they were programmed to describe how great Miami was, how Testaverde was the greatest quarterback they had seen in college football in years. Now Penn State had a 14–10 lead and the announcers were poised to speak of a great comeback from a team that shouldn't have needed a great comeback.

In the production truck, Weisman was doing handsprings of delight. The perfect broadcast, he reasoned through the years, was the one that pulled viewers along with a consistent, compelling tug. Through the first quarter, Weisman knew that viewers would stay tuned to NBC because Penn State was staying in there with Miami; the Hurricanes weren't pulling away early as expected. By halftime he knew the game had hooked them even more. Through the third quarter the game's outcome was *still* in doubt. How could anybody leave now?

Weisman implored his crew, "Don't miss anything! Stay focused on the action! We're coming down the stretch!" Prior to the game, Weisman had instructed

🎤 As time ran down on the fourth quarter, the broadcast ran a graphic on the many postseason awards won by Vinny Testaverde.

JONES: Look at Vinny's awards. The Heisman, Maxwell, Davy O'Brien Award, Consensus All-America, Touchdown Club Athlete of the Year. And now, time is running out to be No. 1. Let's see what he can do from his own 23-yard line.

GRIESE: Penn State has played the Heisman Trophy winner three of the last five years and has beaten them all three times.

On the next play Bauer nearly intercepted a Testaverde pass.

GRIESE: He's seeing linebackers all over! They're coming from nowhere. He is the man who has to bring Miami to a national championship. And their leader is shaken!

director Andy Rosenberg to focus camera shots on the game's most compelling participants: Testaverde and Jimmy Johnson from Miami, and Shane Conlan and Paterno from Penn State. In those faces, Weisman figured, viewers would see most of the drama.

Rosenberg had directed many important sporting events for NBC, but he noticed a special aura around the Fiesta Bowl even in the days that preceded the telecast. Rosenberg remembered going over to meet with the Penn State players and coaches at a team breakfast at their hotel. There was the normal cacophony of sound as hungry athletes devoured stacks of pancakes and breakfast meats, telling stories and laughing. Then Joe Paterno walked in. Rosenberg was stunned at how silent the room suddenly got; Paterno's presence stopped all the foolishness. It said volumes about the enormous respect the Nittany Lion players had for their coach. Moments later, Penn State's players would line up in orderly fashion for their NBC headshots. They were all business.

The next day, when Rosenberg took his staff to the Miami hotel for headshots, he noticed the exact opposite behavior. Jerome Brown had collected all his teammates' gold chains and stockpiled them so he could adorn *all* of the Hurricanes with jewelry to accompany their NBC still shots. The only player who did not accept Brown's offering was Testaverde, who figured a big gold chain did not jibe with his soft-spoken style.

"Come on, Vinny, be a man!" Brown implored. But Testaverde didn't give in.

Brown wound up supervising the entire shoot, yelling to his players, "Now don't you smile, man! Remember, this is war!" Meanwhile, Jimmy Johnson walked around, patting his players on the back and seemingly endorsing the behavior.

"I thought to myself, 'Boy, if this isn't a case of the inmates running the asylum,'" Rosenberg recalled.

By the game's end, Rosenberg, the man responsible for getting his cameramen keyed on the important action, then calling for the proper camera to red light, was running purely on adrenaline as if he was on the field playing the game himself. NBC had some fifteen cameras—an extremely high total back then for a college football game—stationed all over Sun Devil Stadium, covering every angle of play.

"Down the stretch, we wanted to show the emotion; who was keeping their cool and who wasn't," Rosenberg said. "I ordered a lot of shots of Jimmy Johnson. He

With the clock closing in on two minutes remaining, Miami faced a fourth down and six at its own 27-yard line.

"Do you take a big gamble with 2:24 left?" Jones asked.

"I don't think so," answered Cefalo. "Miami has two time-outs left. Their defense has been playing fairly well. I think you kick it away and try to come back and give it to Vinny Testaverde with a little time left. He's got the arm to get a touchdown and a national championship in one series."

"It shouldn't be any other way: a good defensive team versus a good offensive team in the last minute of a game for the national championship," gushed Griese.

Miami did go for the first down and Testaverde completed a pass on the left sidelines to Blades, who nearly broke the play for a touchdown before being stopped by Penn State's Marques Henderson at the Penn State 43. Testaverde proceeded to complete five straight passes, the last one going to Irvin at the nine-yard line with 1:01 left.

CEFALO: Let's talk about Vinny Testaverde. Down here fourth and six, not completing a lot of passes. He's got the guts to stand up and get the first down and then take them down the field! That tells you a lot about that young man.

GRIESE: He's throwing to the outside, on the corners who are playing one on one on the wide receivers. When he's gotten in trouble, he's thrown the ball to the middle of the field, and linebackers that he did not see have picked the ball off.

Testaverde would complete his final pass on the next play, hitting Irvin for four yards to the five. Tim Johnson blasted through and sacked Testaverde on the next play. On third down, he was rushed out of the pocket and threw incomplete to the right side of the end zone. And then, on fourth down, Giftopoulos made the interception that shook up the world. Jones, Cefalo, and Griese let the television audience hear the excited buzz of Sun Devil Stadium but appeared speechless at the shocking conclusion. Griese mumbled something about having to give credit to Joe Paterno and his staff for shutting down Testaverde and winning a national championship. The director cut to the sidelines where Ahmad Rashad was interviewing Shane Conlan.

"They talked about our defensive backs being too short; man, they didn't want to catch the ball," said Conlan through an upper set of teeth where one was missing. "They rocked 'em, man. That was the key to the game. They didn't want to catch the ball!"

Rashad then moved to a soaked Paterno.

"We beat a great football team tonight," the Penn State coach said on camera. "I think our defense played about as great a college football game as I've ever seen."

had this look of bewilderment on his face. He was coaching the team that was supposed to win, but this other team was staying right there with them. Who *was* this other team?"

But Miami was coming back. The Hurricanes had converted a fourth down way back in its own territory and were now moving toward what would be the game-winning touchdown. The Hurricanes were at the Penn State five-yard line. Charlie Jones was mentally rehearsing how he was about to describe the final scoring play.

Then "The Play" happened—the pass was intercepted.

"The emotions we went through in those final seconds were incredible," Jones recalled. "To be honest, I wasn't expecting the interception; I was expecting the touchdown. And so maybe I didn't give that Giftopoulos interception the call it deserved. First Miami wasn't going to win the game, then they were going to win it, then they didn't win it. It was really a wild ride down toward the end."

The next day Charlie Jones ran into Vinny Testaverde at the airport. Vinny had been so guarded during the week, so surrounded by Miami people and network producers who had to take care of things like taped interviews and still head shots that would appear on the telecast, that there had been no time or availability for Jones, Cefalo, or Griese to talk to the Hurricanes quarterback directly.

"He seemed to be a really nice kid," Jones said. "And I didn't think he was that devastated over the loss. It's amazing how quickly athletes recover from things like that. Of course, Vinny could have been that way because he knew he was about to make millions in the NFL."

Life in broadcasting continued on for Charlie Jones until he retired in 2002. He continued to be the main voice of the Fiesta Bowl, except for the one played in 1991. That year NBC lost the Rose Bowl telecast to ABC. The '91 Fiesta Bowl had a matchup similar to the Miami–Penn State game of '87, pitting two highly ranked teams against each other. Dick Enberg, now without a Rose Bowl to broadcast, lobbied to broadcast the Fiesta with his usual partner Olsen. NBC executives acceded. Jones remembered not being happy, but he was under contract to NBC. What could he do if they wanted someone else?

That lesson resounded in his head a few years later at the Olympic Games held in Atlanta, Georgia. Jones had always held important assignments at the Olympics. At the Barcelona games, he covered the incident where American diver Greg Louganis slammed his head on the platform in the middle of a dive. But just four years later, in Atlanta, he was dispatched to cover rowing, one of the least watched events.

A novice of that sport, Jones asked competitors basic questions mostly because he needed to learn more.

"What happens when you break an oar in the middle of competing?" he asked one rower.

"That's outside my boat," the kid replied.

"What happens when the water that day is a bit too rough and it throws off the rhythm?" he asked another.

"That's outside my boat," the rower replied.

It occurred to Charlie Jones that these young kids were telling him, in so many words, that they could only deal with the things they could control. Everything else didn't matter. It was "outside their boat." From that moment on, Jones looked at his broadcast career like that. He had to let go of the things he couldn't control, such as Dick Enberg getting the 1991 Fiesta Bowl.

"And I can tell you that the last few years of my professional life were a lot happier than some earlier years," Charlie Jones said.

9

HURRICANE FALLOUT

AFTER PETE GIFTOPOULOS MADE his interception and Shaffer ran out the clock, bedlam reigned in Sun Devil Stadium. Isom went running around like a madman. The team hoisted Paterno on its shoulders and carried him off the field, the Penn State coach pumping his fist into the air. Sandusky hid on the bench and cried.

Walking off the field toward his locker room, Miami cornerback Bennie Blades, Brian's brother, fired his helmet. It broke apart with the innards caroming off the stands' scaffolding underneath. Blades stormed into the locker room, where he saw Testaverde, normally the picture of cool, finally break. The quarterback sent his helmet into the lockers. Several other teammates kicked over some Gatorade buckets.

The next day several Penn State players rolled their eyes at a comment by Melvin Bratton published in the *Arizona Republic* newspaper. "We're better than Penn State just like Oklahoma was better than them last year," Bratton insisted. "We beat ourselves."

Days later, after Miami had gotten blasted by the national sports pundits for their

Alonzo Highsmith couldn't believe the play his quarterback had just called in the huddle.

It was second down for Miami at the Penn State five-yard line. There was only about a minute left in the game. The Nittany Lions defense was gassed. Miami had moved into position to score the game-winning touchdown. Highsmith had done most of the damage, blasting through Penn State like a hot knife through butter. He had gained more than 100 yards in the game and figured it would take only about one or two more carries to get his team into the end zone.

But Testaverde, on second down at the five, called a pass play. And after taking the snap, he had gotten himself sacked. With only two downs left and the team backed up to the Penn State 10, Miami would have to pass the ball now. Highsmith would not carry the football again. Two plays later it was over.

Afterward, Alonzo Highsmith, one of the toughest players on the field, sat in front of his locker and cried.

rowdy behavior and questionable fashion statements, Jimmy Johnson issued a public apology—after being *encouraged* to do so by university president Foote. Highsmith, however, continued a defiant stance.

"I apologize for nothing," he said. "The only thing I apologize for is losing the game. That's it. If Foote is so concerned about our dress, why doesn't he come out of his air-conditioned office and pay for our suits?"

Jimmy Johnson, the man who had been hired to bring Miami a national championship, had now lost two straight New Year's bowl games. The quarterback he had groomed for those championships, Testaverde, had thrown for a combined thirteen interceptions in those two games.

Said Johnson, "The loss was not a matter of us not moving the football. It was a matter of Penn State making big plays. It was just a matter of Vinny not being on. He was not executing the way he normally executes. There's no doubt in my mind that all of the distractions [on Testaverde] in the past month—even though they were positive—had some effect."

Sixteen of Miami's starting twenty-two position players on the night of January 2, 1987, would go on to the NFL: Testaverde, Highsmith, Irvin, Bratton, Brian Blades, Brett Perriman, tight ends Charles Henry and Alfredo Roberts, and center Gregg Rakoczy on offense; and Jerome Brown, Daniel Stubbs, Winston Moss, Bennie Blades, Rod Carter, Dan Sileo, and George Mira Jr. on defense. That list doesn't even include punter Jeff Feagles, who wound up playing in the NFL longer than them all.

Perhaps the biggest collection of talent on one college football team in history, the 1986 Miami Hurricanes, the big, bad boys in the flashy orange, green, and white uniforms, the football version of the James Gang who took your town and then bragged about it afterward, for the most part ended up hardly provident and somewhat star-crossed.

The coach, the irrepressible Jimmy Johnson, would drown out an untidy 0–3 record in bowl games with a national championship the following year when Miami beat Oklahoma, 20–14, in the Orange Bowl. Johnson would go on to achieve great success as an NFL coach, winning two Super Bowls with the Dallas Cowboys, before becoming a successful broadcaster. Irvin became a Hall of Fame receiver with the Cowboys, continuing his brash act in the NFL where he would overcome several brushes with the law. The loss to Penn State that night in Tempe seemed to cause a hangover for many others.

Vinny Testaverde wound up playing nearly twenty years in the NFL but never quite achieved the success that was predicted for him. The No. 1 pick in the 1987 draft by the Tampa Bay Buccaneers, Testaverde became a fan punching bag as the Bucs existed as one of the worst teams in the league. It wasn't until 1998 with the New York Jets that Testaverde finally put up some eye-popping statistics. That year he threw for twenty-nine touchdowns with only seven interceptions and had a 61 percent completion rate.

Highsmith, who was drafted third that year by the NFL's Houston Oilers, played only a couple of seasons before banging up his knee. He was out of the league a few years later and then tried to begin a career as a heavyweight boxer.

Jerome Brown was on his way to a star-studded career as a Philadelphia Eagle. But on June 25, 1992, Brown took his young nephew for a ride in his new Corvette and crashed the car, killing them both. Brian Blades, a popular player with the Seahawks, wound up on trial in 1996 for manslaughter after an incident at his home in Florida when a gun was fired and killed Blades's cousin. He was found guilty, but a circuit court judge overturned the verdict and acquitted Blades.

ALONZO HIGHSMITH IS BACK in football. He says it is where he was meant to be, where he belongs. He spends most of his days on the road as a pro football scout, scanning the talent of hundreds of college football players a year. He's not that scientific. He's not blown away by statistics. Highsmith knows a football player when he sees one. Usually, he looks for someone like himself.

A couple of months after the 1987 Fiesta Bowl, the night Highsmith was arguably the best football player on the field, he cashed in. He was the third player selected in the 1987 NFL draft, taken by the Houston Oilers. Highsmith reminded the Oilers of Earl Campbell, the big, fast wrecking ball who had terrorized the NFL in the early 1980s.

For the most part, he has had a very successful life. Although his football career was cut short because of knee injuries, Highsmith made a few bucks in the NFL before turning to boxing. His body was shot. He went into Houston's famed Main Street Gym just to try to get back in shape. He became good at it, and perhaps could have become a contender were it not for his desire to work somewhere in football.

Miami's Fiesta Bowl loss is more than a few decades old, but for Alonzo Highsmith it still burns inside as hotly as ever. "Had we won that one game," he says. "We would have been considered one of the best teams in college football history."

Five more carries. That's all Alonzo Highsmith says he would have needed for Miami to beat Penn State. Five more carries, and just two more when the Hurricanes got to the Penn State five-yard line in the game's final minutes. Like many others who saw the 1987 Fiesta Bowl, Highsmith thinks he could have dived over the line twice and gotten those final five yards. He dreams about that sometimes. Or, rather, he has nightmares. The nightmare is that Vinny Testaverde has called his number in the huddle and then when the ball is snapped, Vinny goes back to pass and throws an interception.

The 1987 Fiesta Bowl was *his* night. All year long the season had belonged to Testaverde, his cannon arm, and his receivers, Irvin, Blades, Perriman, Roberts, and Henry. But on this night, Alonzo Highsmith was having the game of his life. He had come to the University of Miami wanting to play linebacker. He was a good running back in high school, but a great linebacker, and that's the position where he began his Hurricanes career. Had he stayed at that position, Alonzo Highsmith thinks he could have been one of the best college linebackers in the country. But a few years into his Miami career, the Hurricanes coaching staff asked him to switch permanently to running back and he made that sacrifice. His dad, who had coached him growing up, always told him to do what was best for the team. Here he was in the college football season's final game, the most important cog in the Hurricanes' backfield.

He was running over people, through people, around people. Penn State couldn't stop him. Cramps couldn't stop him. In the fourth quarter as the perspiration drained out of his pores, his calf muscles bunched up, causing Highsmith searing pain. He merely took those massive hands of his and rubbed those cramps out. He still had plenty of spunk. He had already gained over 100 yards. He yearned for the touchdown that would give his team the national championship. In the end he stood by idly, an ornament watching for an oncoming rusher he was called on to block as his quarterback desperately tried to find an open receiver. All he could think about as he sat stunned on the Sun Devil Stadium turf, with Penn State players and fans dancing around him like drunken sailors was that his sacrifice at Miami had all been for nothing.

Alonzo Highsmith feels cheated. All along he had looked at the Nittany Lions as the inferior opponent. If Miami had played Penn State ten times, he reasoned, the Hurricanes would have won nine of them. Why did this Fiesta Bowl have to be the *one loss?*

The combat fatigues had been his idea. When the Miami–Penn State matchup was officially announced, Highsmith saw the game as an opportunity to finally establish his school's football dominance. He had come to the university as a sort of mercenary. A star player at Christopher Columbus High in Miami, Highsmith was one of the cornerstones of a building process put forth by new Hurricanes' coach Howard Schnellenberger.

Schnellenberger had come to the university after a long stint in pro football. He was the offensive coordinator under Don Shula during the Miami Dolphins' perfect 1972 season, returning to the Dolphins after a short and failed stint as the head coach of the Baltimore Colts. Before going to pro ball, Schnellenberger had been Bear Bryant's longtime offensive coordinator at Alabama, where he was a large part of the Crimson Tide's three national championships in the 1960s. The Hurricanes' football program was on unstable legs when Schnellenberger took over in 1979, having almost been eliminated by the university administration a few years before. Drawing from the disciplined style fostered by his mentors, Shula and Bryant, Schnellenberger also brought a pro-style, pass-oriented playbook to Miami that had not been the norm in Division I college football. At Miami the new coach's plan was to secure every great local player in talent-rich Florida. Recruiting Highsmith in 1982, Schnellenberger told the running back that if he could get every local Florida player from Orlando down through Belgrade, south of Miami, the Hurricanes could dominate college football. Highsmith wanted to be a part of it.

In just his fourth year as Miami coach Schnellenberger brought the Hurricanes a national championship. With Bernie Kosar at quarterback, the Hurricanes defeated Nebraska to win the 1983 season title. But then the pioneering coach left, taking a job as coach and general manager of a USFL team. Miami turned to Jimmy Johnson, who had previously rebuilt a program at Oklahoma State.

Johnson, a longtime assistant to Barry Switzer at Oklahoma, did not downplay individuality. The way the new Miami coach saw it, if players were having fun, if they played without fear of making mistakes, they would be more efficient. It wasn't like Johnson had given his Hurricanes free rein. He was a bit of a taskmaster, but he didn't want his players to be robots out there.

But even with the national championship forged by Schnellenberger, Miami's football program was still considered something of an upstart. It was a young program, lacking the tradition of the big-time football powers. And the college football literati looked at the Hurricanes as a bit of a fluke. To that end, Jimmy Johnson figured it wasn't a bad thing to promote an us-against-the-world attitude to facilitate its path to respect.

By the time Alonzo Highsmith was a senior, the running back had grown weary of the national hype of the big-time college football programs. He was tired of hearing about how great Notre Dame was and about how Miami would never be Nebraska or Oklahoma or even Penn State. Miami's image was that of a "party" school whose students liked going to the beach more than they did a football game. At Miami the campus was a lot smaller than the big football schools; the student body was a lot smaller. There was no unified audience that followed the Hurricanes. It wasn't like 90,000 people would show up on Saturday and pile into a campus stadium. They didn't even have a campus stadium. They had to commute to the Orange Bowl just like everybody else. Support for college football in Miami was thinly scattered. It was hit or miss.

"When I came to Miami in 1983, I remember my friends and all the coaches from other schools saying to me, 'The only bowl you're going to see is a salad bowl,'" said Highsmith. "The fact that there was always these so-called football schools around and we were the little school looking up at all of them, we were jealous of that. We needed our own identity, so we just kind of fell into this image as the bad guys."

Politics had been involved in Miami's selection of a bowl game. While the school's administration was being pulled to stay in Florida, Highsmith says the team unanimously wanted to play Penn State. It was the game that would most exemplify their image. It would be a classic storyline of the good guys versus the bad guys. And the Miami players reveled in that possibility.

When it was finally settled that Miami and Penn State would play for the national championship in the Fiesta Bowl, Highsmith, whom many Hurricane players saw as the team's best leader, thought the team could be better motivated with a gimmick. Two weeks into the team's preparation for the January 2 game, Highsmith, walking with Brian Blades, turned to Blades and said, "Time to go to war!" *War.* The concept stuck in his head. So after practice, Highsmith and Blades grabbed Testaverde, Bratton, and Brown. The five of them went into downtown Miami, found an Army Navy store, and bought full sets—shirts, pants, hats, and boots—of combat fatigues.

He did it as a joke. Highsmith figured that Jerome, Vinny, Melvin, and he would wear the fatigues on the plane to Phoenix and they would get a laugh or two from their teammates already seated on the place. But then a few other players found out about the caper, and word spread to a few others. By the time the 'Canes were ready to go west, about twenty of them had dressed in combat fatigues.

Johnson hadn't known anything about the fatigues. He left for Phoenix two days before the team arrived to handle some media and pregame bowl duties. As he watched his team come off the plane, he thought it was great. He loved brash. He wanted his team confident. This wasn't false bravado. He knew his players were good, and *they* knew they were good. The way Johnson saw it, if his players wanted to talk the talk, they *had* to walk the walk. With such bravado, they couldn't risk losing.

Years later Miami players swear they weren't *overconfident*, just *confident*. They had watched Penn State on film for nearly a month prior to Fiesta Bowl game day and reasoned that there was nothing the Nittany Lions could do to stop them. They didn't think Penn State could even *score* on their defense, not with Brown and Stubbs on the defensive line, Winston Moss and George Mira at linebacker, and Bennie Blades in the secondary. And how was Penn State's tiny secondary going to stop Vinny Testaverde and Irvin, Brian Blades, and Brett Perriman?

Penn State wasn't Florida State or Oklahoma or any other college football team that had speed and athleticism. Only those kind of teams could even stay in a game with the 'Canes. They just didn't see that the Nittany Lions had *that* kind of talent. Highsmith thought he'd be able to run for 200 yards in the game.

The Hurricanes came to Tempe with an attitude and soon developed an even bigger chip on their shoulders. Fiesta Bowl organizers had issued brand-new sweatsuits to the Miami and Penn State players. The Nittany Lions got blue and white sweatsuits, their colors. Miami's sweatsuits were all black. Highsmith resented that. The Hurricanes' colors were orange, white, and green. Why were the sweatsuits black, Highsmith wondered? It was okay for the Miami players and coaches to foster that bad-boy image, but what gave anybody else the right to exploit it?

A banquet was given in a fancy Phoenix hotel a few days after the teams arrived. Fiesta Bowl people told Highsmith and the Hurricanes that the teams were supposed to wear the sweatsuits. The 'Canes rolled in wearing their black issue, accessorizing with sunglasses and gold chains, and saw Penn State players seated at their tables wearing navy blue blazers and ties. Later that night Paterno took the podium. The Nittany Lions coach praised Miami as a "fine institution." But Highsmith seethed as JoePa asked his team to stand up and show the banquet attendees "what kind of guys we have at Penn State."

There was no way Penn State was going to stop Alonzo Highsmith that night. As the game moved along and Testaverde struggled, Highsmith kept carrying the load. He was over 100 yards for the game. Thoughts whirled through his head. It was *his* night. Vinny Testaverde was still the Heisman winner. Michael Irvin was still going to be considered the best receiver in college football. But this was Highsmith's night. This was the one night *he* was going to carry Miami to a victory, to the national championship.

In the final moments of the fourth quarter, Testaverde caught fire. Completing a desperate fourth down and six at his own 27 to Brian Blades for 30 yards, he gave Miami a second life. And a few plays later, after a couple of completions to a suddenly resurgent Irvin, the Hurricanes had a first and goal with two time-outs left at the Penn State five-yard line with just thirty seconds remaining on the clock.

In the huddle, Highsmith turned to his backfield mate, Bratton. "We gotta go I-formation here, Melvin," he told Bratton. "I'm going right over the top."

But his number was never called. On the sideline, Testaverde had talked Johnson and offensive coordinator Gary Stevens out of a running play. Tim Johnson burst through and sacked the Miami quarterback as he looked into the end zone for an open receiver. On third down, Vinny tried to throw again, got chased out of the pocket to the right, and was incomplete. And then on fourth down with Alonzo Highsmith, the man who had carried Miami that night, in the backfield blocking for Testaverde in maximum protection, Vinny was intercepted by Pete Giftopoulos.

Highsmith was stunned. He sat on the turf as if comatose. Then he started to cry. Minutes later, managing to pull himself up, he walked to the Miami locker room but really couldn't feel his legs. Once there, he thinks he said something like, "Hey guys, hold your heads up, we're still the best team in college football." But Alonzo Highsmith sat up in his hotel room until five in the morning just staring at the television. He doesn't even remember what was on the screen.

Ironically, a few days later at the Japan Bowl, a college all-star game in Tokyo, he was paired up as roommates with Penn State's Johnson, the same guy who had sacked his quarterback on the game's third-to-last play.

"And Tim Johnson swiped my sweatsuit," Highsmith recalled. "He wanted it as a souvenir."

Professional football never worked out that well for Alonzo Highsmith. He was the third pick in the NFL draft but injured his right knee his rookie year trying to dive over a pile into the end zone for the Oilers. It was the same play he thought he would be called on to run in the final seconds of the Fiesta Bowl the year before. His anterior cruciate ligament (ACL) was stretched and pulling cartilage away from the bone. It probably should have been operated on right there, but Highsmith was young and hearty and both he and the Oilers figured he could overcome it through rehabilitation and exercise. It never quite worked out that way.

He lasted only three years with the Oilers. In his best year, 1989, Highsmith rushed for 531 yards and four touchdowns. But he was no Campbell. After that '89 season, he finally had the knee surgery. Doctors found that he was trying to run on a knee that was practically bone on bone. His old college coach, Jimmy Johnson, now with the Cowboys, took a flyer on Highsmith, signing him to a contract in 1990. He played in seven games for Dallas that year and lasted only two the following season. He told Johnson to release him; he just couldn't run anymore and he didn't want to cheat his old college coach.

Highsmith returned to Florida and hooked up with the Tampa Bay Buccaneers. If someone was with the Bucs back then, either he had been drafted or he was on his way out of the league. They were that bad. Alonzo Highsmith closed out his football life with two lackluster years with Tampa Bay, where he carried just thirteen times for a combined 44 yards.

His knee was killing him. So he went to see famed orthopedic surgeon Dr. James Andrews in Vail, Colorado. Andrews told him that he must have one of the highest pain tolerances of any player he had ever examined. His knee was a mess. Andrews couldn't understand how Highsmith was walking, much less playing football all these years. The doctor suggested microfracture surgery, a relatively new procedure where small holes are bored into the bone to generate new cartilage development. The surgery gave Alonzo Highsmith back a somewhat normal life.

Highsmith was disgusted by how beaten up his once-stout body had gotten, which is what brought him to the Main Street Gym in Houston. Many of the hot heavyweight boxers were training there—Evander Holyfield, Andrew Golota, Michael Grant, and Hassim Rahman. Highsmith picked up the sport like it was second nature. He could hit like thunder. He soon realized from sparring sessions with the likes of Holyfield that he could also take a pretty good hit. Al Bolden, a well-known trainer who had been instrumental in the development of welterweight champ Thomas (Hit Man) Hearns, agreed to take him on. In one of his early bouts, Highsmith went up against former NFL lineman Mark Gastineau, who had been getting major publicity in his quest to start a boxing career. Highsmith took him out in the second round. He was on the undercard of an Oscar de la Hoya fight in Las Vegas. He fought in Japan and Argentina. When Highsmith looked up, he was 27–1–1 with seventeen knockouts.

"Getting in that ring was the scariest feeling in the world," he recalled. "But it was also a turn-on. In football, there may be 75,000 people in the stands rooting for you. But those people aren't focused on one guy; they're rooting for everybody. In boxing, it's just you and the other guy, mano-a-mano. It's the closest thing to being a gladiator.

"When I first started, I was full of anxiety. I was fighting out of anger. I was just pissed off, trying to beat up the other guy. I didn't know how to go about it. What you learn is that it's nothing about anger. You find a medium. You learn control."

He was on his way to a big payday fighting George Foreman, but the bout fell through. And, really, no fighter wanted any part of him. They had everything to lose and nothing to gain fighting an ex-football player. Highsmith tired of the training and the roadwork. So when the Packers called and offered him a scouting job, he took it.

These days he watches a lot of football and plays a lot of golf. There are moments of regret in everyone's life, moments that, upon reflection, cause sharp pains in the belly. Alonzo Highsmith can never forget how it felt sitting on that field moments after Miami had lost to Penn State.

"I hadn't talked about it; hadn't even thought about it until you called," Highsmith said. "Now it's going to take a long while for me to get over it again."

VINNY TESTAVERDE SAID ALL the right things after Miami lost to Penn State, 14–10, in the 1987 Fiesta Bowl. The Miami quarterback praised Penn State's defensive effort and acknowledged that he did not have the best game of his stellar college career. And then he put the game away for good.

Years later when ESPN was producing a replay of that Fiesta Bowl, they invited several players from Miami and Penn State to be studio cohosts for the rebroadcast on its ESPN Classic network. Testaverde declined.

It was not until many years after that when Fox Sports Net produced a *Beyond the Glory* feature on Testaverde that he had even a small comment on the '87 Penn State game. Said Vinny in that feature: "It was something that stuck with me for a long time. It was just a sick feeling inside, not playing well enough to help my team win."

Vinny Testaverde was bred to be a quarterback. His father, Al Testaverde, was a maniacal supporter, following his son from the sidelines in youth league, high school, Miami, and then pro ball. In his first varsity high school appearance at Sewanhaka High in Floral Park, Long Island, Testaverde, then just a fifteen-year-old sophomore, was called off the bench in a championship game when the starter was injured. He promptly threw a 45-yard touchdown pass to win the game. He was precocious, a surefire star.

Al Testaverde worked in Manhattan right next door to the Heisman building. He would sit down to have lunch and dream that one day his son would win that trophy. Al Testaverde told his wife, Josephine, that if his son ever made it to the Super Bowl, he could die right there and know his life was fulfilled. Dad would see his son win the Heisman, but a Super Bowl would stay out of his reach.

After being the No. 1 pick in the draft, Testaverde had a nineteen-year career in the NFL. Many football experts felt the Fiesta Bowl was a foreshadowing of what was to come—that despite his overwhelming physical talents, Vinny Testaverde would never break through to greatness.

With the Tampa Bay Bucs, Testaverde signed a contract guaranteeing him $8 million, making him the highest-paid player in the NFL at the time. But his years in Tampa were miserable. The Bucs were a bad franchise and their hotshot quarterback struggled. In his first full year as a starter, Testaverde threw for 13 touchdowns but had a whopping 35 interceptions. In his six seasons there, Vinny never finished with more touchdowns than picks. In 1991, with the Bucs drifting into another woeful losing record, a Tampa radio station rented a billboard with a special message for the city's quarterback. Testaverde was colorblind. The radio station savaged the Bucs quarterback with a billboard that had a picture of Vinny superimposed in front of a blue backdrop.

"Vinny thinks this is orange," the billboard read.

He went to the Cleveland Browns in 1993 and had a few decent years there. After that he played two seasons with the Baltimore Ravens, where in 1996 he threw for 4,177 yards and had 33 touchdowns to 19 interceptions. It wasn't until 1998 with the New York Jets that the Brooklyn-born Testaverde finally fashioned a season that many people thought would be his norm. That year he threw for 29 touchdowns to just seven interceptions and had a completion rate of 61.59 percent. But the Jets failed to get to the Super Bowl, losing in the AFC championship game.

Testaverde tore his Achilles tendon the first game the following season and was out for the year. But in 2000 he returned to quarterback what Jets fans call the "Miracle of the Meadowlands" game in October. In that game, the Jets fell behind the Miami Dolphins, 30–7, going into the fourth quarter, but came back to win the game, 40–37, as Testaverde threw five touchdown passes. In 2001 Vinny led the Jets to the playoffs again. Chad Pennington, a Jets' high draft pick from Marshall University, replaced him the following year.

Testaverde spent a year with the Cowboys in 2004 pressed into emergency service by his old coach with the Jets, Bill Parcells, when Quincy Carter was bumped from the league for drug problems, before ending his career with stints with the Jets and Patriots.

On December 26, 2005, during *Monday Night Football* against the Patriots, Testaverde, with the Jets, set a new NFL record for the most consecutive seasons throwing a touchdown pass—nineteen. In his career he threw for 45,252 yards but had just eight more NFL TD passes in his career than interceptions. Some football experts have predicted that Testaverde will be the only quarterback in history to throw for more than 40,000 yards and *not* be elected into the Pro Football Hall of Fame. Other quarterbacks in NFL history to reach that lofty plateau—Johnny Unitas, Fran Tarkenton, Joe Montana, Dan Fouts, Warren Moon, John Elway, Dan Marino, and Brett Favre—are either already in the Hall of Fame or are sure locks to be elected there.

SAM JANKOVICH WAS SITTING calmly at a Fiesta Bowl banquet when an aide rushed into the dining room and nudged him on the shoulder.

"Did you hear what they did?" the aide asked him.

"No, what?"

"They came off the plane wearing combat fatigues."

"Please tell me you're kidding," Jankovich pleaded.

It had been an already stressful season for Jankovich, who was in his fourth year as the Miami athletic director after coming in from more conservative Washington State. While the Hurricanes were sweeping to their undefeated season, they also left a trail of broken glass. Linebacker George Mira Jr. was slapped with allegations of steroid use and suspended for a couple of regular-season games. Jerome Brown was caught on campus with a handgun. Winston Moss used a car that had been leased by an assistant coach, an NCAA violation. Daniel Stubbs was caught siphoning gas from someone else's car for his personal use. And only a few weeks before the Fiesta Bowl, Melvin Bratton got into hot water when he—inadvertently, he said—walked out of a convenience store with a $2 pair of sunglasses.

Jankovich had the Miami administration breathing down his neck. The school's president, Edward (Tad) Foote, implored his athletic director to help clean up the football program's unruliness. Foote thought his team's rebel image was diluting Miami's academic reputation. Jankovich hired Jimmy Johnson on his pristine credentials as a football coach, but he also knew Jimmy, who had been tutored by Barry Switzer, was a bit of a risk in that he wasn't as discipline-oriented as his predecessor, Schnellenberger. In a bright national spotlight, where Foote and the whole football world were paying attention, Miami players landed in Arizona and came off the airplane wearing combat fatigues. Jankovich said, "If there is one thing that I could change in life, it would be that our players never walked out of that plane with fatigues. But nobody knew. Jimmy had come a day early with me to Tempe and so there was nobody to stop them from getting on the plane that way. And then, how do you clean it up after the fact? The damage was already done.

"When I look back at it now, what it did was foster this horrible misconception about our players at that time. We had a few rambunctious kids. But the truth was, they were all pretty good people who turned into outstanding citizens."

In 1986, Jankovich found that being the athletic director for a major college football team ranked No. 1 in the nation was not an easy gig—and that was just in the selection of a postseason bowl game. All along Jankovich had wanted his team in the Fiesta Bowl. The reasons were simple. First, it was where the Hurricanes could make their biggest statement. Second, it was paying the most money. Fiesta Bowl organizers realized they had a goldmine because they could match up the two highest-ranked teams in the country and put together the cash needed to attract Miami and Penn State in a dream game.

Jankovich entertained overtures from the Citrus Bowl, an upstart bowl that played in Orlando. The Citrus Bowl wanted Miami badly. It had even solicited help from Florida governor Robert Martinez. Jankovich was having dinner with Fiesta Bowl execs Skinner and Meyers one night when a waiter came to their table to inform the Miami AD that there was a telephone call for him from the governor.

"You know, Sam," Martinez began, "You can do your state a huge service by keeping this game in Florida. It's in the best interests of the state."

"I appreciate that, Governor," Jankovich replied.

Jankovich was just playing a bluff. The Miami athletic director had kept open the possibility of playing in either the Citrus or the Gator, but that was only to make his playing hand appear stronger and to force the Fiesta Bowl to raise the ante. In truth, he had no intention of sending the Hurricanes to a bowl game where the stadium seated only 35,000 fans and the payout was not nearly attractive enough for the No. 1–ranked team in the country. In the end, Jankovich and Miami would choose the Fiesta Bowl even though Martinez had called him again.

"Governor, I don't want to disappoint you, but we're going out west," Jankovich told Martinez in their second telephone conversation. "Now what I suggest you do is get back to the Citrus Bowl folks and tell them that when they build a big-league stadium, we'll think about going there one day."

The riverboat gambler had won the hand and had the guts to rub that in the face of a governor. But once Sam Jankovich got to the Fiesta Bowl, he would have to put out many fires.

Fiesta Bowl organizers gave Miami the smaller locker room at Sun Devil Stadium. When Jimmy Johnson found out, he freaked.

In luring the Hurricanes to Tempe, Skinner had promised that they would be considered the home team. As the home team, the 'Canes expected the bigger locker room. But Skinner would have explain to Jankovich that Penn State needed to use the Sun Devil Stadium locker room as its practice locker room since they had been prohibited by Arizona State to use the Sun Devils' practice-facility locker room. The Lions thus had to change at Sun Devil Stadium and walk a few blocks to the practice field. As a compromise, Skinner told Jankovich that they would give Miami's locker room new carpeting, but that didn't appease Johnson or Jankovich, who began to think that there was some orchestrated effort by the Fiesta Bowl people to favor Penn State.

"Is new carpeting going to make our locker room bigger?" Jankovich asked cryptically.

A few days later Jankovich was sitting with Paterno at the hotel bar and shared with the Penn State coach Jimmy Johnson's discomfort.

Paterno was a couple of drinks into the evening when he said to Jankovich, "I've got eighteen guys here with me from the Bronx. Tell Jimmy to meet us downtown and we'll beat the hell out of him."

Jankovich assumed the Penn State coach was joking, but he wasn't sure.

To Sam Jankovich, the loss to Penn State on January 2, 1987, was like a "sword through the heart." Like everybody else who watched the game that night, the Miami A D figured the Hurricanes would score on their final drive of the game. Like everybody else, he thought Alonzo Highsmith would get the call to run the football into the end zone for the 'Canes' game-winning touchdown. After the game, he was told that Gary Stevens, the offensive coordinator, had called a running play, and that Vinny Testaverde had insisted the Hurricanes throw. He closed his eyes in disgust. When Miami lost, Jankovich knew that he would be called on the carpet. He knew that only winning the game would have diluted the upcoming discussion he would have with the Miami administration about the program's lack of discipline.

The next day Jimmy Johnson flew to Japan to be a coach in the Japan Bowl, which meant that Jankovich alone had to face the music of his president and the Miami board of trustees when he returned to campus. Two days later Foote called him into his office. One of the suggestions at the meeting was to fire Johnson.

"I said to them, 'You had better not. You're not going to like the end result,'" Jankovich recalled.

Johnson wound up keeping his job, but at that meeting Foote laid down some rules pertaining to conduct that were designed to tighten up the Miami program. The following year the Hurricanes beat Oklahoma to win the national championship.

Jankovich left Miami three years later to take the job as CEO of the New England Patriots under Victor Kiam, the Remington Shaver heir. He left there in 1993, became a consultant to various college athletics fund-raising programs, and then landed as the general manager to the Las Vegas–based team in the Arena Football League. He says he still feels the effects of the sword that went through his heart the night Miami lost to Penn State.

"It was one of those wounds where you know you're not going to die quick," Sam Jankovich says, "and it's still dripping out of me."

Sam Jankovich had come to Miami in 1983. Jankovich was born in Butte, Montana, a nice, conservative community and a great place to raise a family, but about the most exciting thing that had ever happened were blowing tumbleweeds. He had started out as a high school teacher there and his college coaching career hadn't progressed beyond Montana State. He then took over athletic director at Washington State, where the job seemed to fit his northwestern personality perfectly. To Jankovich, Miami was a world away.

Miami's administration reached out hard for him. They had determined that Jankovich had the perfect attributes to be their athletic director—he was sensible, but also a man of action. They saw the big splash he made at Washington State and they wanted him to do the same thing at Miami.

For his part, Jankovich thought that Miami's athletic programs had huge potential. In football, he felt that the Hurricanes could be "the USC of the East Coast." He saw that as an independent, Miami could pick and choose its opponents and therefore orchestrate big TV matchups in order to bring the program more notoriety. Eventually, he wanted to bring back the school's basketball program, which had been eliminated in 1978, and then gain entry into the powerful new Big East Conference. But still, the job was a big jump from Pullman.

To help make up his mind, Jankovich sought the advice of friends and colleagues—specifically, Don Canhan, the longtime, well-respected athletic director at the University of Michigan.

"Sam," Canhan told him, "if you want to stay at Washington State the rest of your life, you can do that and probably be happy. But if you want to really make an impact on college athletics, you have to take this job at Miami."

So Sam Jankovich did.

The U was already in the midst of a football renaissance. Schnellenberger had coached the upstart Hurricanes to the national championship in 1983. He had uplifted the program from nowhere. Jankovich knew that it would only be a matter of time before Schnellenberger got a better offer. Always meticulous, Jankovich even at Washington State had a handle on the hottest coaching names in the country. And when Schnellenberger jumped at the chance that spring to be chief executive of a new Arena Football League team that was being created in South Florida, Jankovich reached out for Oklahoma State head coach Jimmy Johnson.

Johnson had an impressive résumé. A star player on Arkansas's 1964 undefeated national championship team, he began his coaching career at Louisiana Tech right out of college in 1965. A few years later, at twenty-five, he began a coaching career that would be influenced by some of the sport's coaching legends. Johnson got a job as the defensive coordinator at Iowa State under Johnny Majors. He then worked, in succession, under Chuck Fairbanks at Oklahoma, Frank Broyles at Arkansas, and finally Majors and Jackie Sherrill at Pitt in the late 1970s when the Panthers were building their program into a powerhouse.

Johnson had modest win–loss records at Oky State, but Jankovich saw that in only five years he had raised the Cowboys' program from the doldrums and wound up getting into some bowl games. His last year at Oklahoma State, the

Cowboys finished 8–4, one of their best records in years. Moreover, Johnson's intelligence was well regarded in coaching circles—he was said to have a Mensa-level IQ of 152. Jankovich noticed that Johnson's teams seemed to be the kind that didn't beat themselves. His players were fundamentally sound and they were focused. Jankovich called Gil Brandt, the Dallas Cowboys director of player personnel, to ask him about Jimmy Johnson, and Brandt told him that Johnson wouldn't be interested in the Miami job because he had had his sights on bigger football schools. Even if Johnson was interested, Brandt told Jankovich, he would just use Miami to get to a bigger job. Jankovich didn't care about that. He just wanted someone worthy enough to maintain what Schnellenberger had created. So he called him.

"Who else are you considering?" Johnson asked him.

"John Cooper," Jankovich said. Cooper was making noise as the head coach at Tulsa at the time.

"Well, I'm a better coach than Cooper *and* I like the water," Johnson replied.

Jankovich took Johnson. Cooper wound up at Arizona State.

When he came to Miami, Jimmy Johnson knew that he had just tapped the mother lode of talent. As a state, Oklahoma had great linemen, linebackers, and some skilled people. But in Florida, Johnson knew he could shake a tree and some of the best athletes on the planet would fall out. The new coach's methodology for success at Miami was simple. His offense would be of pro style with a stud quarterback and receivers who could outrun the coverage and break games open with big plays for touchdowns. His defense would be quick. Johnson didn't care if his down linemen didn't have girth. He wanted them to be able to move, to slide off blocks, to pursue and get to the quarterback quickly.

If there was a knock on Jimmy Johnson, it was that he allowed his players too much freedom. In the Johnson reign at Miami, the Hurricanes brought on-field celebration to an art form. They danced, they saluted, they talked trash, and they intimidated. The coach wanted his team to have fun. Johnson was cautious not to stifle their creativity. He didn't want them focused on things they *couldn't* do. If it got out of hand, he would deal with it later.

Said Art Kehoe, Miami's offensive line coach under Johnson, "He was an awesome evaluator of talent. Our practices were unreal. We had studs going against each other out there. Our backups were future NFL players. I mean, look what Jimmy did when he went to Dallas. When he finally left, Barry Switzer, who had been dealing cards in Oklahoma, came in and was able to win a Super Bowl with Jimmy's talent.

"But he also had this incredible ability to squeeze every ounce of effort out of his players. He got deep into their psyche, their minds. He was so smart. He knew exactly how to challenge a kid.

"And strategy-wise, he was ahead of his time in that he really valued special teams. A lot of coaches put emphasis on special teams now. But Jimmy was doing it way back when. He understood how a blocked punt or really good kickoff coverage could influence a game your way."

Johnson inherited a team that had just won a national championship and suffered from attrition. It was up to Johnson to restock the cupboard. Fortunately, he still had the cornerstone—Bernie Kosar, the quarterback recruited by Schnellenberger who had broken in his career at Miami by guiding the Hurricanes to the 1983 national championship as a *freshman*. He threw for 300 yards and two touchdowns as the 'Canes shocked Nebraska that year in the Orange Bowl. Kosar also carried Hurricanes the following year. He threw for 3,642 yards and twenty-five touchdowns as Miami finished a respectable 8–5 in 1984 and then got back into the national title's on-deck circle the following year, finishing 10–2.

Kosar was also a good student. In 1985 he managed to graduate a year early from Miami with a double major in finance and economics, but he still had one more year of college eligibility. Rather than stick around campus as a graduate student, Kosar decided to go to the NFL. Johnson never said so publicly, but the Miami coach was devastated. He thought with Kosar the national championship was a lock for 1986. Yes, in Testaverde, Johnson still had a talented quarterback who could take over. And, yes, Testaverde would get the Hurricanes into the big game. But there they would fail. Miami's loss in the 1987 Fiesta Bowl made Johnson's record in bowl games a disappointing 0–3.

The coach had a hard time forgiving Kosar. A couple of years later when Miami wanted to retire Bernie Kosar's number 20, Johnson refused, saying that retired numbers should come from players who played all four years as a Hurricane.

Cocky and stubborn. That was Jimmy Johnson in a nutshell.

ART KEHOE WAS SITTING in the Miami coaches' lounge sorting the bags that would go with him to Tempe, Arizona, for the Fiesta Bowl and waiting for the chartered bus to arrive to take the Hurricanes to the airport when a coaching buddy came into the room with the news: several of the Miami players were wearing combat fatigues.

Kehoe, the Miami offensive-line coach who primarily associated with the guys who played in the trenches anyway, smiled. "I thought it was cool as heck. The guys who were dressed up like that—guys like Highsmith, Bratton, Jerome Brown—these were guys everybody had respect for, guys who brought it every-day at practice and in the games. They weren't trying to be disrespectful by any means. They were sending out a message to the coaches and the rest of their team-mates that they were dead set on kicking somebody's ass. It was the media who portrayed that the other way."

Kehoe had been raised in suburban Philadelphia, within the reach of the very long tentacles of Penn State, where young high school football players dreamed of becoming Nittany Lions. He had come to Miami as a player in the late 1970s, then served as a graduate assistant coach under Schnellenberger before Johnson gave him his first full-time coaching job. He was Miami through and through. But now, among his eastern friends, he was the enemy, a coach from a rebel team that was the antithesis of Penn State pride.

Kehoe had been besieged with telephone calls all week from friends who were actually wishing him bad luck. It was nothing personal, they told him, but they hoped Kehoe's offensive line would have a meltdown and not be able to protect Vinny so Penn State could knock the snot out of him.

Kehoe's sister Grace asked Art for eight tickets to the Fiesta Bowl. Kehoe arranged for the tickets but didn't know that Grace would be bringing seven rabid Penn State football fans. Sitting right in the middle of the Miami section of Sun Devil Stadium, which included many university dignitaries and guests, Grace Kehoe's Penn State partisans cheered loudly and obnoxiously for the Nittany Lions, talking trash and taking names.

"Before the game, I saw where they were and I walked over to the stands and said, 'Grace, are you out of your mind? Are you trying to get me fired?'" Kehoe said.

As did most of the Miami coaches, Art Kehoe figured Penn State would be no match for the Hurricanes. On film the Lions were just too slow. There was no way, Kehoe figured, that they'd be able to stop Testaverde and his talented receivers. But deep down inside, Kehoe also worried about Vinny. The motorscooter accident that felled Testaverde had become public. He had missed Miami's final game of the season against East Carolina because of it. What most people didn't know, however, was that at the Fiesta Bowl the Miami quarterback was still a walking brushburn from his ankles to his shoulders. Kehoe said, "He had really gotten banged up a lot more than people knew. He was so sore and those wounds took so long to heal that he missed a lot of practices because of it. And then, he missed even more because he was flying around the country getting all those awards. Gary Stevens was really pissed about that. He wasn't sharp in the game. Was he not sharp because of all those missed practices? Who knows? But, certainly, it didn't help things."

What's more, the week of the Fiesta Bowl as the Hurricanes enjoyed a vibrant social life in Tempe and Phoenix, Testaverde met a girl and coaches felt the new romance was just another distraction their quarterback didn't need. Earlier in the week, Stevens, the offensive coordinator, had told his team that Penn State was tough, but Miami had the better athletes, and the only way the Hurricanes could lose the game would be by not taking care of the football. In the end, with Testaverde throwing five interceptions and the 'Canes losing some fumbles, Stevens would prove clairvoyant.

Still, the game came down to Miami's final possession at the Penn State five. On second down, the Lions, panicking because they weren't in the right defensive formation, called a time-out. Testaverde came to the sideline to talk to his coaches. Kehoe, on the outskirts of a huddle between Vinny, Johnson, and Stevens, clearly heard the two coaches tell Vinny to call for a run. Testaverde told them he wanted to pass and walked back toward the huddle. When Johnson screamed for his quarterback to come back, Vinny made a dismissive motion with his hands back at his coaches.

After the game, several Miami offensive linemen told Kehoe there was nearly a mutiny in the 'Canes huddle when Vinny returned and called a pass play.

"Let's run the ball, Vinny!" center Gregg Rakoczy said.

"Shut up, we're throwing it," Vinny snapped back.

After the game, there was so much mayhem in the Miami locker room, so much equipment strewn along the floor, players lying face up with their eyes closed in disbelief and crouched in a fetal position bawling that Kehoe reasoned he'd never be able to get to the showers. The Miami coach snatched his suit, hanger and all, and walked to his rental car, where he sat with thousands of other cars trying to leave the stadium. He doesn't remember how long it took him to get back to the team hotel. For Art Kehoe, time stood still.

The next day he ran into Joe Paterno at the Phoenix airport. A group of Miami coaches, including Kehoe, was scheduled to depart for San Diego for a coaches' convention, but the plane had been oversold. The Miami coaches were forced to take the next flight out and were standing around miserable from the disheartening loss the night before. Kehoe had blanched all week listening to Paterno espouse righteous rhetoric. He thought that JoePa was piling on, that the Penn State coach was making an overzealous attempt to discredit Miami simply because the Hurricanes did things a lot more loosely than Penn State.

In the airport, Paterno saw the Miami coaches and started walking over to them.

"Hey, fellas, I know you're probably not feeling too good right now, but for what it's worth, you guys are a hell of a football team," Paterno said. "My staff has been together for a lot of years. They've watched a lot of teams. But when we watched film on you guys, to a man, everybody said that this was the best college team they'd ever seen. The only chance we had to win was to win the way the game played out last night."

Kehoe looked up at Paterno and said to himself, "Damn."

"When he did that," Art Kehoe said. "Joe Paterno showed me that he was a hell of a man."

GARY STEVENS REFUSES to throw Vinny Testaverde under a bus.

Miami's offensive coordinator in the 1987 Fiesta Bowl knows what happened in the final seconds that night. He was there. But he's not sharing anything. That stuff stays on the sidelines and in the locker room. Football coaches are supposed to have a code. They're supposed to stand by their players in good and in bad.

"Ah, you can say we should have run the ball more that night, we should have run it when we got down to the five-yard line, we should have done this, we should have done that; what the hell difference does it make?" Stevens says.

Gary Stevens is one of those crusty football warriors. An assistant coach his entire life, he had a dream one day to be the headman, the chieftain, and mold a program the way *he* saw best. But it never happened. In 1995 he was among three finalists for the head coaching job with the Philadelphia Eagles. Instead, team owner Jeffrey Lurie chose a defensive man for the job, Ray Rhodes.

Stevens left the University of Miami after the 1988 season to take a shot at pro ball. Jimmy Johnson had already gone to coach the Dallas Cowboys. Stevens had been passed over for the Miami head coaching job in favor of Dennis Erickson.

Stevens wanted to stay in Florida, so he took a job on Don Shula's staff with the Miami Dolphins. He would spend nine seasons there. During the last two, he was the team's offensive coordinator under his old college boss, Johnson, who had come out of retirement to succeed Shula. But Johnson's tenure with the Dolphins was shaky; the offense was under fire and Stevens became the fall guy. Johnson had to let him go. The NFL is a little different from college ball. It is a business. There are no loyalties. Not even from a guy whom he had served well at the university.

Stevens went to the Oakland Raiders for three years. And then he spent a year as an assistant with the Atlanta Falcons. But he never again got a sniff at a head coaching job. In retirement he returned to Miami, where he plays a little golf, occasionally goes out for a few beers with his buddies, and watches football, constantly building on the offensive concepts in his head in case he gets the urge to come back and coach again.

He had come to the Sunshine State way back in 1980, lured to the University of Miami by Howard Schnellenberger. Stevens, a curmudgeon-like personality who spoke with a rawness that reflected his native Cleveland, had been an offensive coach at West Virginia under Frank Cignetti, who was considered one of the most brilliant offensive minds in college football. Schnellenberger, who wanted to build an offensive powerhouse, thought Stevens could help bring that kind of flavor to Miami.

In 1983 Stevens helped design a game plan that enabled a freshman named Bernie Kosar to pull off one of the great upsets in college history as the Hurricanes won the national championship by shocking heavily favored Nebraska to win the Orange Bowl. After that season, Schnellenberger left for pro ball. Stevens would have a new master, a hotshot coaching prospect named Jimmy Johnson. Johnson was different from Schnellenberger—a little cockier, a little more brash and stylish. But when it came to the offense, he was on the same page. Teams won with great quarterbacks and athletic skill people. And that's how they would continue to build the mighty Hurricanes.

But there was a problem. After the '84 season, Kosar came into the Miami coaches' office to inform Johnson that he was leaving school before his eligibility ran out to enter the NFL. Johnson was pissed.

"And I was, too," says Stevens. "Anytime you build an entire offense around your quarterback and you have this comfort level with him, and he tells you he's leaving, well, it's a jolt. We had expected to have a great season in 1985 with Bernie. But I tried to tell Jimmy, 'Hey, you can't blame the kid. He's going to make a lot of money. How can we hold him back from that? Let's just make due with what we have.'"

What they had was Testaverde. He had come to Miami the same year as Kosar and had been beaten out for the starting job by Bernie. But Vinny was no slouch. He was big and tough and could throw. And the Hurricanes had a plethora of talent surrounding him—Highsmith, Bratton, Irvin, Blades, and Perriman. All he had to do was let loose back there. Somebody would always make a play.

But deep inside, Stevens worried. Sometimes Vinny was careless. He relied a little too much on his bazooka-like arm and tried to force the ball into receivers who may have been too well covered. Miami's offensive coordinator feared that in a big game against a very good defensive team, Vinny might throw a few picks and that could be the difference between winning or losing a national championship.

The night Miami lost to Penn State in the 1987 Fiesta Bowl, Gary Stevens remembered being "as sick as a dog." After the game he just kind of walked around aimlessly, knowing that the Hurricanes had squandered a big opportunity. This one was worse than losing the year before to Tennessee in the Sugar Bowl when Testaverde again had been a goat. This Miami team was supposed to be invincible. It was a team loaded with stars who had talked trash all week and had boasted about its greatness. And though Stevens and Johnson would team up to win a national title the following year, they both knew that college football fans would never be able to forgive this loss. It would overshadow any accomplishment the program could ever have in the future.

"Had we won that game," Gary Stevens muses and then stops abruptly. "I mean, people can't imagine how good this football team was. And the shame of it was, contrary to what people believed, that was a team of great character kids. People can think what they want about all the stuff they did, the fatigues and all that crap. Truth was, those guys were as highly competitive as any group I ever coached. They brought it every day, in practice and in games. Every college coach in the country wanted his team to play like we did. We played an exciting, enthusiastic brand of football and we had fun doing it.

"And one game, one moment, put a damper on all of that."

GEORGE MIRA JR. REFLECTED ON the whole combat fatigues issue. Years later he's still aggravated by it, still thinks people blew the whole thing way out of proportion.

"We were kids," said Mira. "We were eighteen to twenty-two years old. You weren't dealing with a bunch of grown men. We were just out of high school. We were just having a little fun.

"And I'll tell you something else. Had we won that game, sports stores would have made millions selling camouflage stuff. But because we didn't, everybody turned on us."

Mira is a fireman now, a captain in the Dade County (Florida) Fire Department. But in 1986 he was Miami's starting middle linebacker, the son of George Mira Sr., a legendary former University of Miami quarterback, who had come to the U to continue the Mira legacy. Controversy swirled around him all season. In addition to getting caught in possession of steroids, Mira had been arrested for disorderly intoxication for an incident with his girlfriend and, on the same incident, charged with battery on a police officer and fleeing a police officer.

He was wild, but George Jr. could also play. One of the subplots of the 1987 Fiesta Bowl was the question of who was the better linebacker, Mira or Shane Conlan. Mira had been in on 117 tackles for the Hurricanes that year, nearly 40 more than Conlan, and was determined to prove his worth.

Mira said, "What I remember most is that the week leading up to the game, we were very relaxed. A lot of people have the impression that we had all this pressure on us and we were tight. I think the opposite was true. We didn't feel any pressure. We weren't nervous at all. We were confident without being overconfident. We didn't think Penn State could do anything against us. We practiced and prepared really hard for that game.

"We knew their formations inside and out. I remember during the game, we'd line up and look at their set and all of us would yell, 'They're going to run this,' or, 'They're going to run that.' We were calling their plays for them before they ran them.

"I remember having a talk with my dad before the game. He really knew how to read defenses. He looked at Penn State's defense and said, 'You're going to kill these guys.' But in the end, what happened is that we fell right into their trap. Their defensive coaches out-coached our offensive coaches."

The 1986 Miami Hurricanes were swashbucklers. Off the field they may have run pretty hard, but on the field they were always prepared. Johnson allowed his players some freedom, but he also drilled them unmercifully in practice. Some of the Hurricanes' practices that year were harder than the games themselves. Everybody was so talented. Mira and his defensive mates were lining up every day against quarterbacks such as Kosar and Testaverde and running backs like Highsmith and Bratton. There was no easing up in a Miami practice. Mira would see Highsmith flashing through a hole right at him and he would relish the forthcoming collision. Sometimes Highsmith got the best of him. Sometimes Mira got the best of Highsmith. But it always cranked everybody else up. It was the way Highsmith and Mira led.

One day Johnson was running the 'Canes into the ground in practice. Mira tackled Highsmith on an off-tackle play.

Highsmith got up from the pile and asked Mira, "You tired?"

"Yep," Mira answered.

Highsmith hauled off and punched the linebacker in the head. They scuffled. Johnson sent them to the sidelines. The running back had orchestrated an incident to get Mira and himself a break. They were on the sidelines, drinking cups of water, and made the mistake of laughing at what they had just done. Johnson saw it, ordered them back on the field, and drilled the team for another good hour.

They were kids having fun. Since Testaverde was colorblind, his teammates occasionally snuck into his locker and switched his clothes around, matching colors that didn't go. Testaverde never knew it until he was walking out of the locker room and players and coaches would point and him and laugh.

The night of the barbeque when the Hurricane players walked out Mira happened to be standing on a chair right next to Jimmy Johnson, craning his neck to see what Jerome Brown was planning to do for the team skit. The only thing Mira knew was that none of the players wanted to be there. They didn't want to associate with Penn State and pretend they were friends with the opposition when only a few days later they were expected to bang heads with them. But Mira didn't expect Brown to say, "Did the Japanese sit down with Pearl Harbor before they bombed them?" When Brown ordered his teammates to walk out with him, Mira turned to Johnson.

"What do you think, Coach?" Mira asked.

"You guys do what you need to do," Johnson told him. So Mira walked with the rest.

When the game started, the team that was supposed to win by two or three touchdowns unexpectedly struggled. Mira noticed early on that Testaverde didn't seem to be in sync. The middle linebacker went up to Stevens, Miami's offensive coordinator, and suggested he pull Testaverde for a series in favor of Geoff Torretta so Vinny could study from the sidelines what Penn State's defense was doing to confuse him.

"I'm the coach. I'll make the decisions around here. Go sit down!" Stevens snapped back at him.

So Mira did. From the bench he watched Highsmith riddle Penn State in the second half. Mira says, "We just needed to ride Alonzo. Just give it to him until they stopped him or he collapsed. He kept getting these cramps on the field. I had gone over to him and said, 'I don't care how you feel right now, Alonzo. You've got to stay in this game. We need you to stay in this game.' I stayed there and stretched him with the trainers.

"And then we get down to the five-yard line and we don't run him. Penn State was so spread out; he could have walked into the end zone. Vinny's dropping back to pass and I'm saying, 'What the fuck?' Hey, I can't blame Vinny. He was the quarterback. He wanted to throw it. He threw an awful lot of complete passes that year. He felt confident. Any athlete would feel the same way. But the coaches should have said, 'No, Vinny, not now. We're going to run this baby right down their throats and score.' But we never did."

After the game, Mira didn't want any part of locker-room misery. On the way to Miami's dressing room, he saw his father. George Sr. and Jr. found a quiet place to sit down and talk.

"I wanted to be with somebody who had been through it," Mira Jr. said. "My dad had played thirteen years of pro ball. I knew he knew what to say. I didn't want to hear our coaches talk about how hard we played, or because I was a junior, how I'd have another chance next year. We had just lost a game we should have won and I was hurting."

Mira and Testaverde were the last to leave the Miami locker room that night. His hair still wet from a long shower, Vinny walked over to Mira and said, "I blew it, George."

"I told him that he didn't blow it, that he shouldn't put the whole weight of the team on his shoulders. I told him that he did the best he could and for him not to let anybody tell him that it was his fault. It was everybody's fault."

George Mira Jr. came back the following year to win a national championship as Miami beat Oklahoma. He was drafted by the San Francisco 49ers in the twelfth round after that season, but he never hooked on in pro ball. The 49ers cut him and he tried another camp with the Atlanta Falcons, who also cut him. While in the Falcons' camp, he ran into Stan Clayton, Penn State's starting offensive tackle in the 1987 Fiesta Bowl. The loss still burning in his soul, Mira told Clayton that Penn State had no business beating Miami that night in Tempe.

"You can't change history, George," Clayton replied.

ASIDE FROM VINNY TESTAVERDE, Winston Moss had the most successful pro career of any player produced by the vaunted 1986 Miami Hurricanes.

After being drafted by the Tampa Bay Buccaneers in the second round of the 1987 NFL draft, Moss wound up playing eleven years in the league—with the Bucs, Raiders, and Seahawks—as a swift and tough impact linebacker. He has remained in the NFL as a defensive coach. In 2006 he joined the staff of the Green Bay Packers as linebackers coach after spending six seasons as a coach with the New Orleans Saints. He teaches the same lessons he learned way back as a linebacker at the University of Miami—go hard on every play.

Like nearly every member of the 1986 Hurricanes, Moss has still has a hard time dealing with the Fiesta Bowl loss to Penn State.

"Whenever I run into anybody with a Penn State connection, they tease me about that game," Moss says in a resigned tone.

Like many of his teammates, Winston Moss thought Miami in that 1986 season was unbeatable. Yes, the Hurricanes had watched Penn State on film and thought the Nittany Lions were unimpressive, especially on offense. But to Moss, it didn't matter whom Miami was playing in that game. Their opponent that night could have been an NFL team and the Hurricanes would have thought they would win. They were that confident. They had prepared that well.

Like Penn State, Miami had also lost a high-profile bowl game the year before. They had been embarrassed by Tennessee in the Sugar Bowl, even though the 'Canes were the favorite. They vowed it would not happen again—that 1986 was *their* year, their year to run the table and win the national championship by winning their final game.

"At the Sugar Bowl, we had partied too much," Moss acknowledged. "I mean we were on Bourbon Street. We had never seen anything like that. We thought we were going to handle Tennessee easy that year, so we went out every night and had a good time. And then we got beat. We learned a tough lesson.

"We got back to campus, I looked at Jerome and we both got this look like, 'All right, that's enough. We've got to do this thing now.'"

Away from the coaching staff, Moss formed a small posse with Brown, Alonzo Highsmith, and Testaverde to lead the Hurricanes in off-season drills to prepare them for the 1986 season. They ran running and weightlifting sessions. They ran brutal one-on-one blocking drills and seven-on-sevens. They got *after* each other with a goal in mind that when the regular season began, the Hurricanes wouldn't just beat teams, they'd demolish them. They'd make folks *remember* the 'Canes.

Moss had also been part of the combat-fatigues brigade. He loved it. Highsmith came to him with the idea and it was just supposed to be a couple of guys. Then right before the bus was about to take the Hurricanes to the airport for the flight to Arizona, about twenty more guys showed up in fatigues. Some of the coaches were stunned. But it was too late to order the players back to their dorms to change clothes. The thought never even crossed Winston Moss's mind that walking off an airplane wearing camouflage would be in poor taste. It was Miami's statement to the world that they had come to Tempe determined to *win*.

Then it all backfired.

Moss remembered the Miami locker room being like a morgue. It was total depression. It was surreal. Had they just lost to Penn State? He didn't know what to do, what to say. Winston Moss never got closure. The next day he had to get on a plane to travel to a college all-star game. He knew he was going to get drafted and play professional football, but he still needed to talk about this loss with his teammates, to get it out of his system. Instead, over the years it festered inside him, a bad moment in his life he knew he might have to purge eventually with a psychologist.

The thoughts still rattle around in his mind. Testaverde had a great arm. He was confident he could throw a football into any tiny spot. He probably thought that because he had just been anointed with the Heisman Trophy that he, by himself, would have to win this game. Miami should have loosened up Penn State more by running the football. That would have opened more passing lanes for Vinny. They should have run Highsmith down there at the end. The Miami defense with Moss and Jerome and Bennie had dominated the Nittany Lions. They walked out of Sun Devil Stadium that night with nothing to show for it.

Strangely, the loss has followed Winston Moss like a ghoul on Halloween. After being drafted, Moss went to his first Buccaneers training camp to see that the Bucs had signed as a free agent Ray Isom, the Penn State defensive back who had caused Testaverde and Irvin such nightmares in the Fiesta Bowl. A few years later with the Raiders, Moss met Steve Smith, the Nittany Lions fullback who had also played in that game. Though Moss and Smith would become the best of friends there, the former Lion was sure not to spare the former Hurricane any feelings.

"Steve brought a poster into the locker room one day," Moss recalled. "It was a enlarged photo from the 1987 Fiesta Bowl, an action shot of some Penn State players with some corny, moral message on it about team unity or something like that. And he just hung it up at his locker. He didn't really say anything about it. He just put it at a place where he knew that I would see it. Every day."

ON PENN STATE'S FIRST PLAY from scrimmage, Miami defensive tackle Dan Sileo burst through the middle of the Nittany Lions' offensive line and buried quarterback John Shaffer for a 14-yard loss. Sileo had talked trash all week. He had entertained reporters with daily diatribes ripping Penn State as a team and as a school. Just two days before the game, Sileo told reporters that the Lions' one main weakness was Shaffer. And here he was, standing like a big-game hunter over his conquered prey on the first play of the game.

"I turned and looked at Jerome Brown and yelled, 'Rome, we're gonna fucking kill these guys!' I still can't believe we didn't."

Today, Sileo is an even larger man than he was with about 50 pounds tacked on to the 285-pounds he carried as a Hurricane tackle. He is a radio sports talk-show host in Florida, still as outspoken as he was the week of the Fiesta Bowl when reporters lined up at his press table like pigeons waiting for crumbs.

There was a story written about Dan Sileo a few years ago in a San Francisco newspaper claiming that being a talk-show host has made him so prone to exaggeration, his radio listeners should never trust what comes from his mouth.

As a host in San Francisco, the story said, Sileo had referred to his playing days with the Dallas Cowboys. In truth, the Cowboys had cut him before the actual season began. Sileo said he also played for the Detroit Lions and was on the field when Joe Montana played his final game for the 49ers in 1992. But Sileo never played for the Lions—they allocated his contract rights to the Orlando Thunder of the World Football League. Sileo also said on his radio show that on his first play in the NFL with the Tampa Bay Bucs in 1987 he had sacked Montana. In truth, he had only played as a sub with the Bucs—and in only ten games total with them—and never recorded a sack.

When asked about the discrepancies, Sileo told the reporter who did the story that they were the result of a two-year bout with meningitis brought on by heavy steroid use—when he was a player at Miami and then in pro ball.

"Yeah, I did steroids," Dan Sileo says. "Everybody back then did them."

Dan Sileo has lived a pretty full life. When his football days were over, he banged around the country, from the West Coast to the East, getting various on-air radio jobs where he traded sports stories with friends and teammates and listeners. The stories come and they go, either accurate or totally exaggerated, through the microphone and into the airwaves like so much confetti. But the one story that remains, the one that he cannot shake from his soul, is the night Miami lost to Penn State. Sileo's mind might be a blur these days—he may not be able to recall some of the great moments he had as a player, the great victories he shared in as a Miami Hurricane—but he says he remembers everything about that bitter loss in the Fiesta Bowl.

At the end after Pete Giftopoulos intercepted Testaverde's final pass, there were a few seconds left on the clock. The Miami coaching staff didn't want to send its defense back out there. The game had been lost. They didn't want their players to have to withstand further humiliation as Penn State knelt on the football for one more play. Reluctantly, the Hurricanes came back on the field.

Sileo recalled, "They snapped the ball, Shaffer knelt and Steve Wisniewski, who was one of their offensive lineman, yelled out, 'Look at them, look how pathetic they are, we beat them, they're done!' And then I heard someone else say, 'We beat the beast!' We just stood there. We couldn't say anything else. It was like someone had hit us over the head with a sledgehammer. We all started walked off the field muttering to ourselves, 'I can't believe we lost.'"

This kind of thing didn't happen to the Miami Hurricanes. They had cultivated an image where they did this kind of thing to the other team—stomped on them, humiliated them, and then talked about it in glee afterward. They were Darth Vader's team, a collection of black-hooded ninja assassins.

Sileo had come to Miami to win national championships. He was a tough kid from Brooklyn whose parents sent him to prep school in Connecticut so he could get good enough grades to be eligible for a football scholarship somewhere. He chose Miami because he wanted to be part of the new football tradition it was trying to build, a transformation to the most feared college program in the country. Penn State recruited Dan Sileo. Paterno, who was a paisano from Brooklyn himself, came to see him play at Stamford Catholic. He was thrilled. Then they looked at his grades and decided suddenly that Sileo wasn't a Penn State player after all.

"I told Joe, 'Yeah, well fuck you. I'm going to Pitt," Sileo said.

The rejection from Penn State burned in Dan Sileo, and when his Miami team got a chance to play the Nittany Lions for a national championship, it fueled in him an intense desire. He had wanted to *annihilate* the Lions. He said, "John Shaffer had an arm like my sister. I wasn't saying anything that wasn't true. Reporters kept coming up to me and saying, 'Well you know, the guy is something like 88–0 as a quarterback in his life, and he went to Moeller High School,' and all that. And I'm saying, 'Moeller High School? Where's that?' Whatever. Who cares? This ain't high school.

"Jimmy Johnson came over to my table and said, 'Why are you doing this?' And then, as he's walking away, he winked at me. Jimmy didn't even think we were in any trouble."

All season long Sileo and Brown created their own terror squad in the middle of the Hurricanes defensive line. Sileo often stood over a fallen offensive lineman he had just pancaked and say, "Don't worry about it, son. Everybody gets an asskicking sometimes." If Sileo was having a particular good game, if he was smashing the center and guard and getting into the opponent's backfield to either sack the quarterback or throw the halfback for a loss, Brown would turn to him and say, "Yo, can I get some of that?!" If Brown was having a good day, he would turn to Sileo and yelp, "I am just kicking this guy's ass!" They played with anger and energy and passion.

And they also did so the night of the Fiesta Bowl. Miami held Penn State to just 162 total offensive yards. Sileo and Brown combined for 16 tackles and a couple of sacks. But the game trudged along at a snail's pace and Penn State was hanging in there. According to Sileo, when Miami's defense would take the field after the offense had turned the ball back over to Penn State, the guys in the huddle, instead of focusing on their defensive calls, were questioning what the offense was doing.

"Why are they fucking throwing it?" Sileo would say to anyone within earshot on the Miami sidelines. "Why aren't they just giving the ball to Alonzo?"

Then the game came down to the final few seconds. After Testaverde hit Irvin for a five yard-gain that put the ball at the Penn State five-yard line, Brown nudged Sileo on the sidelines.

"You think they'll throw it?" he asked.

"No way," Sileo said.

After the game, Sileo said, Highsmith stood on a stool and said, "There are twenty guys in this room who played their asses off, but I can't say that everybody else did." The implication was clear. The Hurricanes were blaming Testaverde.

Years later Sileo can't help but think that had Bernie Kosar been the 'Canes' quarterback that year, Miami, not Penn State, would have won the 1986 national championship.

Sileo recalled, "Vinny was a great athlete, but Bernie was way smarter. He would have checked off into a lot more running plays. And the thing people forget is that Vinny hadn't had a lot of practice time coming into that game. He had that motorcycle accident and then he had been on the road a lot with the Heisman thing and everything else. I just don't think he was that prepared for the game."

BRIAN BLADES MADE the biggest offensive play for Miami that night. On a fourth down and six as the clock neared the two-minute mark of the fourth quarter, Blades turned a quick out to the left sideline into a blockbuster 30-yard gain that nearly went for a touchdown. Marques Henderson and Ray Isom eventually tracked down Blades at the Penn State 43-yard line. But the play had given Miami some hope bordering on assurance that the Hurricanes, trailing 14–10, would win the national title after all.

Miami didn't win the game. Brian Blades would just miss being a hero, which is exactly how his professional life turned out to be.

In 1988, the year after Miami finally won its national championship, Blades had a great year and was drafted in the second round by the Seattle Seahawks. In an eleven-year career in Seattle, he caught 581 balls for 7,650 yards, had two seasons with eighty or more grabs, and became one of the town's most popular athletes.

But in 1995 tragedy hit Brian Blades when he was convicted of manslaughter in the shooting death of a cousin, Charles Blades, in Plantation, Florida, a small community outside his native Fort Lauderdale. The conviction, which would have put Brian Blades behind bars for at least ten years, wound up being overturned by a sympathetic judge.

In the shooting, an argument apparently erupted between Brian's younger brother, Bennie, who had played with him on the 1986 Miami team, and Bennie's ex-girlfriend. Bennie, Brian, and Charles Blades returned to Bennie's townhouse. When Brian tried to intercede in the matter, the brothers fought and Brian said he was going home a few doors down to get his gun, according to case testimony. The two cousins scuffled over the gun at Brian's townhouse. Charles Blades wound up getting hit by a single bullet that killed him.

After the shooting, Brian Blades dialed 911 and repeatedly told the operator: "I need you to come right now." When the police dispatcher asked him what happened, Blades said he had gone "to stop my brother from fighting with a girl and the gun went off and shot my cousin."

The prosecution contended Blades was guilty of a crime because he angrily went for his gun after a shoving match with his brother. Charles Blades, trying to play peacemaker, struggled for the gun and was shot dead. Prosecutor Peter Magrino pointed out that for the weapon to fire, it had to be loaded, the safety had to be off, and the trigger had to be pulled. Defense attorneys countered by saying the shooting was an accident and that an intoxicated Charles Blades caused it by grabbing his cousin's gun.

In the spring of 1996, Blades, still on trial, signed a three-year extension contract with the Seahawks for a reported $4.5 million. The contract was contingent on Blades being able to play. On June 14, 1996, Brian Blades was found guilty of manslaughter. But circuit judge Susan Lebow overturned the verdict and acquitted Blades, saying the state had presented no evidence that Blades acted recklessly or negligently in the accident that killed his cousin.

When the judge announced her decision, Brian Blades looked to the sky and raised his left arm. Facing reporters, he said, "The victory is not mine, it's the Lord's. It is a tragedy, a tragedy I'll have to deal with the rest of my life. I do have faith in the man above, and I'm going to keep serving him."

After his trial, Blades returned to the Seahawks and played three more seasons, but he never achieved quite the same success. In the 1996 season, he played in only 11 of the Seahawks' 16 games, catching 43 passes. The year before, he had caught 77 balls for Seattle for 1,001 yards. In 1997 Blades caught 30 passes. The following season, in which he played in 16 games but caught only 15 passes for 184 yards, would be his last in the NFL.

ROD CARTER, Miami's hard-hitting linebacker who had a monster game in the 1987 Fiesta Bowl, became nationally known several years after that game but not for football.

After a short-lived career with the Dallas Cowboys (he was their tenth-round pick in 1989), Carter joined the working world. In 1999 he was a driver for United Parcel Service when the Teamsters union ordered a national strike against UPS. Carter ignored the strike and continued to work, saying in a television interview that he needed to support his family. Following his comments on TV, Carter and his wife, Emily, received a threatening phone call, which phone records showed came from the home of the president of Teamsters Local 769 in Miami.

The following day Carter was stopped in his UPS truck by another vehicle, assaulted, and stabbed with an ice pick.

Attorneys for National Right to Work, a nonprofit legal arm, took up Carter's case and filed a lawsuit against the International Brotherhood of Teamsters. The complaint alleged that a group of union militants pulled Carter out of the truck and began punching, kicking, and beating him. During the beating one of the men produced an ice pick and stabbed Carter six times. The union, the complaint said, bailed out the assailants.

In the end, Carter received a monetary settlement from Teamsters Local 769. The man who stabbed him was the only one to receive jail time in the incident.

MICHAEL IRVIN SITS ON the makeshift set of ESPN's *Monday Night Football*. The Philadelphia Eagles are playing the Green Bay Packers. He's watching guys get hit, laughing, and appreciating the fact that he doesn't have to do that anymore. He can just watch the brutality from afar. He's a survivor. He's been through some wars on the field and off. And he's living to tell about it wearing fancy $2,000 suits and dispensing football bravado each week to millions of television viewers.

Everybody's All-American? More like everybody's All-American Bad Ass. That's what Michael Irvin was in 1986 when he was playing for the Miami Hurricanes and that's what he was for most of his professional career. For Irvin years have clicked by like the chamber of a gun. Click, click, click. People have come to expect that, eventually, Mike Irvin will come to a cylinder that's loaded.

Just a few months after Irvin was hired by ESPN to be one of the network's football analysts, he was arrested for having drug paraphernalia in his car. Irvin said the marijuana pipe found in his Gucci sunglasses case belonged to a friend he was trying to help get straight. Whether the story was true or not didn't matter. The charges were dismissed because prosecutors felt police didn't have probable cause to search his vehicle. In this way, he's been charmed. Unlike a lot of Miami Hurricanes who played in the 1987 Fiesta Bowl, Michael Irvin's star keeps on shining. Rarely does it seem to matter what kind of trouble he gets into. He always seems to find his way out.

The discovery of a pot pipe in 2005 came only a couple of years after Irvin had claimed to be a born-again Christian. Sports fans in Dallas wonder whether he'll be able to build up enough credibility to make Saint Peter disregard the lengthy rap sheet he'll have to produce at the Pearly Gates.

In 2000 he beat a pot charge, though Fox Sports wound up firing him as an analyst over the incident. In 1998, there was a scuffle with a Dallas Cowboys teammate named Everett McIver. Irvin, who had a pair of scissors in his hands at the time and opened up a deep gash on McIver's neck, eventually paid a six-figure settlement to have the matter go away. In 1997 he allegedly assaulted a man in a San Francisco nightclub.

But the granddaddy of them all came in March 1996, when Irvin was pinched for felony cocaine possession. He was in a hotel room at the time, near Texas Stadium, celebrating his thirtieth birthday with two strippers and Cowboys' teammate Alfredo Roberts, with whom he had also played at Miami. The hotel owner called the police, suggesting that drug activity and prostitution was going on in Irvin's room. Police found 10.3 grams of coke, more than an ounce of marijuana, and sex toys. Irvin showed up for his grand-jury appearance later that spring with huge diamond studs in his earlobes and wearing a full-length mink coat. One of the strippers in the hotel room, Angela Beck, told the grand jury that Irvin had pulled her aside and instructed her to tell the police that the drugs were hers. If she did that, he had promised to treat her like "a princess." After that, he allegedly pulled one of the officers aside and said, "Do you know who I am?"

From there, the case just got weirder.

One of his running buddies who said he wanted to expose Irvin to help him get his life back in order agreed to let a Dallas television station put a hidden video camera in his car to film Irvin attempting to purchase cocaine, then sold the video to the TV tabloid show *Hard Copy*. Then, during the middle of jury selection for the case—Irvin had pleaded no contest to the charge—Dallas police arrested a former officer named Johnnie Hernandez. Hernandez's girlfriend was dancer Rachelle Smith, who had spent a few nights in hotel rooms with Irvin and Beck. Smith told police the drugs were Irvin's. Irvin then allegedly made phone calls to Smith threatening to harm her if she testified against him. Hernandez, meanwhile, tried to hire someone to kill Irvin to get him off his girlfriend's back. The man he tried to hire, however, just happened to be an undercover Dallas officer.

And then, later that year, Irvin found himself in another public controversy. A stripper named Nina Shahravan claimed that Irvin and Dallas teammate Erik Williams had held a gun to her head, sexually assaulted her, and videotaped the assault as the three did drugs in a hotel room. Shahravan was later charged with filing a false complaint, and Irvin and Williams wound up suing a Dallas TV station for reporting the matter as true.

"I've accepted the fact that I have been a lightning rod for controversy," Irvin said.

Michael Irvin came to the University of Miami in 1985. One of seventeen children, he was a football star at St. Thomas Aquinas High in Fort Lauderdale. Unlike a lot of the older skilled players on the Miami roster who had been brought to the U by Schnellenberger, Irvin was one of Johnson's earliest and most famous recruits. And Jimmy attached a longer leash on Irvin than some others. He was running a pass-oriented offense and he knew he had on his roster one of the best receivers in the country—a surefire NFL star in waiting.

In 1986, when Irvin was just a sophomore, he set a school record with 53 catches for nearly a thousand yards and 11 touchdowns. He was big, 6′2″, 205 pounds, rangy, and had long arms to outreach any college cornerback who tried to check him one on one. It was a mismatch.

Meanwhile, Irvin flashed the confidence card to the hilt. He was brash. He trash-talked before, during, and after games. And that's how he came to Tempe as Miami prepared to play Penn State in the Fiesta Bowl.

Irvin wasn't one of the Miami players who wore fatigues. "I would have, but I couldn't afford them," Irvin says. "Back then I was poor."

But Irvin had no problem inflaming the Nittany Lions in other ways. He made a point of condescending to the Lions defensive backs. They couldn't cover the great Michael Irvin. They were too tiny. They were in the big leagues now, covering real receivers. And they were in over their heads. A few days before the game, he laughed in Ray Isom's face. And he carried the abuse right up to game time. Moments before kickoff, Jerry Sandusky saw Irvin standing with Jimmy Johnson, watching Penn State's defensive backs go through pregame drills. They were both smirking.

"We were just really confident," Irvin said. "We just thought we were so superior. We watched them on tape and there wasn't one guy on the team who didn't think we wouldn't run through that team like nothing. I still can't believe we lost that game."

Irvin has a simple answer for why Miami came out on the short end that night: the Hurricanes did too much partying. They had lost their focus for football. Johnson let his team run wild the first few nights in Tempe and they complied. The 'Canes would go out in packs of thirty, find Phoenix's hottest nightclubs, and just take over.

"We're walking into clubs and walking right past the guy at the door who's collecting the cover charge," Irvin said. "We're going, 'The guy behind me got it.' And that guy is saying, 'The guy behind me got it.' Now, the last man is Jerome

Brown. He's saying, 'I ain't got shit.' Now, who's going to argue with Jerome Brown?"

The last few nights, Johnson finally slapped a curfew on his team. The Hurricanes would make it into their hotel room by the required 11 P.M., but then they'd stay up all night playing poker. Irvin remembered having to sneak through the halls at 5 A.M. to get back to his room and pretend he'd been asleep the whole time. The way the 'Canes figured, they could stay up all night and still beat Penn State.

The walkout at the barbeque was a planned deal, Irvin said. The Hurricanes wanted to eat dinner and scram out of there. The outrage about John Bruno's comments about Jimmy Johnson's hair and then his alleged racial remarks meant nothing to the Hurricanes. They weren't rebels with a cause. They just wanted to get out and party.

"Truth was, there weren't any girls at the barbeque," Irvin says.

Irvin and the rest of his Miami teammates *loved* the concept of being the *evil* team while the opponent was the *good*. In Irvin's career at Miami, the Hurricanes thrived in that environment, especially when they played teams like Notre Dame and the football world was printing up T-shirts hyping "Christians versus the Convicts." The Miami Hurricanes were Tony Montana and his crew before there *was* a Tony Montana. "Say goodnight to the bad guy." But it never dawned on Irvin that that kind of attitude could backfire. He certainly couldn't imagine it happening against a team that the Hurricanes were so much better than.

When Michael Irvin made it a point to look down at Penn State's defensive backs when it was reported in Tempe that Irvin ran into Ray Isom near the practice fields and sniffed, "You're Isom? Oh, man," George Mira Jr. cringed. Defensive players crave an extra incentive to punish a playmaker. It's what gets them noticed.

"That was a big mistake," Mira said, "because they rocked him. I really think that when they hit him early in that game, Michael lost his focus a little."

Years later Michael Irvin is unwilling to surrender to that. It was nothing new that a defensive backfield wanted to hurt him. He had to face that in every game Miami played. He still can't remember the names of the Penn State players who covered him that night in the Fiesta Bowl. The Miami Hurricanes simply had the wrong game plan. Penn State was dropping back eight players and rushing only three. Run the football. Irvin didn't have to be the hero. Vinny Testaverde didn't have to be the hero. All the 'Canes had to do to win the game was give the ball to Alonzo Highsmith. Irvin figured he had caught his last pass of the night. It was a short completion on first down from the Nittany Lions' 10. The pass had gotten the Hurricanes to the five. They had a couple of timeouts left.

On second down, Irvin was surprised when Testaverde called another pass. The field was only 15 yards deep. It was going to be tough to find an opening in that kind of confined area. He said nothing. Tim Johnson sacked his quarterback. Lying on his back, Testaverde flicked his hands for a time-out. Irvin said, "At that point, I'm thinking, surely we're gonna run this sucker in. I *know* that Jimmy called a running play. I'm watching Vinny get into this discussion with him on the sidelines and I'm thinking, 'Oh no, he wants to throw it.' Sure enough, he comes back and calls a pass play. The problem was, I don't think anybody in the huddle except Vinny thought it was a good call. We weren't committed to it."

Two plays later, Miami lost the Fiesta Bowl. Irvin couldn't believe it. All the mess he had talked. All the bravado the Hurricanes had displayed. It blew up in their collective faces. Michael Irvin had never seen an evening in which he couldn't find a party. But not that night. The hours after Miami lost to Penn State, the Hurricanes' All-American receiver curled up in his hotel room and cried. "Don't nobody want to celebrate when you lose." Irvin didn't want to go near a club. Surely there would be fans out there, Penn State fans, most likely, who would want a piece of him, who would want to ask Miami's brash wide receiver, "What happened?" It was best that night to simply crawl into a hole, like a gopher, and not surface for days.

Michael Irvin's football career ended on the hard turf of Philadelphia's old Veterans Stadium, where he was slammed on his neck after making a catch. The impact jolted his spinal cord. That day, as Irvin lay motionless, Philadelphia Eagles fans cheered his injury, giving it back to the man who had for most of his career rubbed his bravado in their faces. The injury would force him into an early retirement.

The next year Irvin, the man whose career had been marked by drugs, adultery, and other troubles, who had nicknamed himself "The Playmaker" and had routinely parked his fancy sports cars in "No Parking" and handicapped zones at the Dallas Cowboys' workout facility, said he turned his life over to Christ. He accepted mentoring from former teammate Deion Sanders, a born-again Christian whose career had followed the same impish road as Irvin's.

In an interview published on a Web site called Pastors.com, Irvin said that he now routinely gives testimony speeches to church groups or athletes interested in his conversion.

"A lot of times I'll talk with players after the cameras are shut off and I'll be able to minister to them," Irvin said. "They all know I went through the ups and downs. I did almost every bad thing you could do, but it's through the power of God I can live this life."

10

WHERE LIONS LANDED

ONLY AN IDEALIST COULD LOOK at the 1986 versions of Penn State and Miami and determine that the Nittany Lions had better personnel. Yet, the Lions had maximized their opportunity, strutting their stuff on college football's biggest stage, upsetting the vaunted Hurricanes in the 1987 Fiesta Bowl, and enhancing their individual profiles among pro football scouts.

Ten of Penn State's twenty-two starting players in the 1987 Fiesta Bowl wound up being selected in the NFL draft, *not* counting punter John Bruno. All told, seventeen players who saw time that year were drafted, including juniors Stan Clayton (tenth round) and Pete Curkendall (eleventh round), who were taken in the 1988 draft, and sophomores Steve Wisniewski (second round), Quintus McDonald (sixth round), Gary Wilkerson (sixth round), Bob Mrosko (ninth round), and Keith Karpinski (eleventh round), selected in the 1989 NFL draft.

Shane Conlan would become the highest drafted Lion from the 1986 team, selected with the eighth pick in the first round by the Buffalo Bills. D.J. Dozier was taken fourteenth in the first round by the Minnesota

One of Penn State's most solid entities coming into the 1986 season was its kicking game. Placekicker Massimo Manca's numbers were slowly and surely moving up on the all-time Penn State charts to make him one of the most successful placekickers ever.

But in the early part of the 1986 season, Manca was struggling. He had only converted three of his first nine field goal attempts that year and couldn't figure out what he was doing wrong. In practice, he never missed. But once the game began, Manca just wasn't hitting the ball as solidly as he was used to.

Determined to turn the tables on his misfortune in Penn State's biggest game of the season thus far—at highly ranked Alabama—Manca responded by kicking three big field goals. But the following week, he missed two short attempts at West Virginia, causing Joe Paterno to give his kicker a short lecture on the sidelines.

"All right, that's it!" Paterno screamed at Manca. "No more. One more and you're done."

Manca made his next four field goals in a row.

Vikings. But offensive guard Wisniewski would become the Penn State player from the 1986 national champions who would last the longest in the NFL. Wisniewski, selected as the first pick in the second round in 1989 by the Cowboys, was then traded to the Raiders and wound up playing twelve seasons there, forging a Hall of Fame–worthy career.

After Conlan and Dozier were taken in the first round of the 1987 draft, the following Nittany Lions would be taken off the board: Tim Manoa (Browns) and Steve Smith (Raiders) in the third round, linebacker Don Graham (Tampa Bay Bucs) in the fourth, Bruno (St. Louis Cardinals) and offensive tackle Chris Conlin (Dolphins) in the fifth, Tim Johnson (Steelers) and Bob White (49ers) in the sixth, backup flanker Sid Lewis in the tenth (Jets), and Brian Siverling (Lions) in the eleventh.

For the most part, Penn State players from the 1986 team had pedestrian careers in the NFL. Conlan and Wisniewski were the only players who would make an All-Pro team. The 1986 Lions were a product of synergy—good college football players who bonded together for a couple of seasons to form a great team. And when their football careers were over, they went on with their lives just like everyone else.

MASSIMO MANCA, the Italian-born Penn State kicker who had made a bushel of key field goals for the Lions during the championship season, leads a simple life in bucolic Bucks County, Pennsylvania. He and wife, Suzanne, have a set of twins, a boy and girl, and he works in pharmaceutical sales, covering the Philadelphia area. He hasn't booted a football in years.

Manca came to Penn State from Reno, Nevada, by way of Sardinia, an island off the coast of Sicily. His parents, Maro and Nocileta, both of whom taught at the University of Sasseri, came to the western United States on a one-year stint as visiting professors teaching Italian at the University of Nevada–Reno. Young Massimo had been a soccer player in Sardinia and was drafted to kick a football for his Reno high school team his junior year, the one year he was supposed to be in the States. But Massimo was pretty good at it. When his parents were ready to return to Italy, Manca's coach asked Massimo to consider staying, that perhaps he could contend for a scholarship to a major college football program. His parents allowed it. With an uncle in Reno serving as a legal guardian, Massimo lived in a one-bedroom apartment with his two brothers, Marcello and Maurizio, whom his parents had also permitted to stay.

Manca had a great senior year. A Penn State alumnus happened to be at one of his high school games and sent word to the PSU football office that there was this semi-known Italian kicker in Reno who might make a good Nittany Lion. After seeing Manca on tape, the Lions coaching staff offered him a scholarship right away. By then, Nebraska and Oregon were also recruiting him heavily. Manca made a recruiting trip to State College. The colder weather was a far cry from what he had been used to in Sardinia and Reno, but there was something about the East Coast of the United States that he loved. And he could see that he might start at Penn State as soon as his freshman year. The Lions' starting kicker had graduated and the starting job would fall to either Manca or sophomore Ralph Gancitano, who hadn't kicked his freshman year. Manca had no ties to Reno other than his two years of high school there. So he took the Penn State offer.

The kid from Italy turned out to be one of the Nittany Lions' best kickers ever. After losing his job briefly as a freshman to Gancitano, Manca wound up scoring 186 points as a Lion, including 41 field goals, and he broke the Lions' career mark for consecutive extra points. But his senior year, the year the Lions won the national championship, turned out to a bit of a nightmare. That year, he got off to a three-for-nine start, missing three field goals in the Lions' win over Boston College in the second game of the season. Manca rebounded nicely, especially coming up big by kicking three field goals in Penn State's big win at Alabama that year.

The following week, against West Virginia, he missed his first two field-goal attempts, two chip shots that caused Paterno to rip into his kicker on the sideline.

"All right, that's it!" Penn State's head coach had screamed at him. "No more. Miss another one and you're done."

Manca responded by making his next four field goal attempts as the Lions shut out the Mountaineers, 19–0.

"If I have one regret about my career, it's that I didn't kick as well my senior year as I did my junior year," said Manca. "It was just a classic slump. All kickers go through them. Unfortunately for me, the slump happened in the most important year."

Massimo Manca, who after that season was Penn State's highest scoring kicker ever, wasn't drafted into the NFL. He signed as a free agent with the Bengals— who had recently cut longtime kicker Jim Breech—got cut during camp, but then was brought back to the team as a replacement player and lasted four games until the regular players came back. Manca signed with the 49ers the following season. They had promised to sponsor him for a green card, which would allow him to remain in the United States. But they, too, cut Manca during the preseason. To get the green card, Manca rushed into a marriage with his college girlfriend in a ceremony given by the mayor of her tiny town of Hatboro, Pennsylvania, in the living room of his soon-to-be in-laws. Two years later they married again in a church ceremony.

In 1989 Manca gave the NFL one last shot, by trying out to make the roster of the Dallas Cowboys. Jimmy Johnson was in his first year as Cowboys' coach, and he required his kickers to run 110-yard sprints with everybody else. Manca had come to camp seriously out of shape and after five or six sprints collapsed on the field.

"Get off the field, goddamn it!" Johnson screamed at Manca.

After practice, Manca, trying to cover up, lied to Johnson that he had asthma. So Johnson ordered breathing tests on the kicker, which revealed nothing of the sort. Johnson cut Manca the next day. He ended up kicking a season for the Barcelona Dragons of the World Football League. Jack Bicknell, the former Boston College coach who had watched Manca miss three field goals against the Eagles during the second game of the 1986 season, coached the Dragons. Manca made

$1,500 a game. But, by then football was out of his system and it was time to carry on with life.

"The thing I remember most about 1986 was the team unity," said Massimo Manca. "When I got involved in professional football, the one thing I realized was how separate kickers are from the rest of the team. I mean, the players just hate kickers. But at Penn State, kickers were as much a part of what was going on as anybody else. I was always grateful for that. I made friends for life."

ONE DAY DURING PRESEASON PRACTICE, Mike Russo just snapped.

The pressure had been weighing heavily on Penn State's starting nose tackle. He was coming off a decent junior year and as the Nittany Lions came into the 1986 season as again a contender for a national championship, Russo wanted to have his best season ever. He had designs on the NFL.

But something was missing in his play. Coaches hadn't been grading him out very well in preseason workouts. The coaching staff was on him. Russo was thinking he might lose his starting job to his backup, Aoatoa Polamalu. And that would have blown his whole gig, everything that he had worked for.

Russo's mind flashed on overload.

That day he just got up and walked out of practice. He went back to his dorm room and cried. Then, still wearing his Penn State gray matching practice T-shirt and shorts, a pair of sweat socks covering his taped ankles, no shoes, and carrying his wallet in a small gym bag, Russo walked to the State College bus station, bought a ticket, and boarded a Greyhound to New York City. He was headed to his father's home in the Bronx. Mike Russo was done with football.

"I don't know if you would call it a nervous breakdown or whatever," Russo says years later. "But it was something. I wasn't really in touch with reality for that small period of time. I had put so much pressure on myself that I just blew."

Sitting with Russo on the bus was a kid a couple years older. He told Russo his life story, a story that involved drug abuse and several failed attempts at rehab. It made the Penn State player feel terrible for the kid but a lot better about himself. His life wasn't nearly as bad as some others, he quickly learned. Russo gave the kid a crumpled Penn State jersey that had been in his bag. Arriving at Grand Central Station, Russo, still wearing only socks, hopped a cab to his locked-up family home and broke in. His dad arrived several hours later, stunned to see his son lying on the living room sofa, in total darkness, looking as worn out as he'd ever seen him.

"Mikey, what's wrong?" his father asked.

"I'm not sure I'm cut out for this, Pop," Russo replied.

The two men talked into the night. It was only a game, his father said. If you want to stay here, you can stay here. Russo slept a couple of hours, then had his father drive him back to State College, where together they went in to see Paterno.

"Mike, you're having a *great* camp; no one is down on you," Paterno said. "You have emotion. That's good. That's why this team is going to be good this year. You guys all *care*."

Russo went into the locker room. His teammates were all there waiting on him, waiting to give him a hug and a slap on the back. After all that, the season would be easy.

In many ways, Mike Russo had the most difficult job of any Penn State defensive player. In the Nittany Lions' 3–4 system, Russo had to occupy three players—the center and two guards—on nearly every play so that the Penn State ends, White and Johnson, could roam free and get to the quarterback and also so his linebacker, namely Shane Conlan, could wander around and get to the man who had the ball.

Russo was strong enough to do it, too. He was a monster in the weight room—he could bench press 500-plus pounds. In the off season Paterno allowed his nose tackle to join Penn State's powerlifting team. One of the team's meets was against the inmate team at nearby Rockview Penitentiary. The prison lifters who would compete in Russo's heavyweight division were huge; all they did all day was lift. Russo beat them that day and earned their respect. After the meet, he got into a conversation with one member of the Rockview team who told Russo that this was his third stint in the joint.

"Why do you keep coming back?" Russo had asked.

"Because you get three hots and a cot," the inmate replied, suggesting that three square meals per day and a nice place to sleep was more than he had gotten on the outside. After he heard that story, to Russo a difficult math test would seem like a piece of cake.

Mike Russo, playing the most difficult position to accumulate stats and recognition, nonetheless put forth a very good senior season for the undefeated Nittany Lions. Coming into the Miami game, he had accumulated three more tackles than Johnson and only one less than White. In the Fiesta Bowl on the play that resulted in Pete Giftopoulos's game-winning interception, Russo slipped through Miami's blockers on a stunt. Testaverde saw him in his peripheral vision and perhaps let go of the football a little early. It was one of those plays that had gone under the radar, but it was one of the most important of the game. Surely, the professional scouts had seen it. Russo thought he had a good shot to be drafted, especially after Penn State beat Miami on a national stage, but the NFL snubbed him.

Not getting drafted hurt Mike Russo badly. Half-heartedly, he went to a couple of NFL camps to try to hook on as a free agent. He wound up leaving camp with both Tampa Bay and then the Steelers. Nobody knew who he was. It seemed as if he had to scream for anyone to pay attention. Suddenly, football wasn't what he wanted anymore.

Life went on. Russo married Lynette, his college sweetheart from Pittsburgh, and that's where the Russos made their home with son Michael and daughter Alexa. Russo has a good job handling high-end accounts for a company that sells heavy construction equipment. And though he has some regrets that he didn't give pro ball a better shot, he isn't unhappy.

"Playing on that 1986 team was probably the most important time of my life," Mike Russo says. "How can you top something like that?"

WHEN HE ARRIVED AT his first NFL camp with the Tampa Bay Buccaneers in the summer of 1987, Don Graham noticed a few familiar faces.

Ray Perkins had just been hired as the new coach of the Bucs and he brought with him most of his staff from the Alabama team he had coached the year before. It was the same staff that had watched Graham and his fellow Nittany Lions linebacking corps wreak havoc on the Crimson Tide the year before as Penn State beat Alabama, 23–3.

Graham's party didn't end there. Sitting at a locker taping up his fingers for practice was none other than Vinny Testaverde, Tampa's bonus baby draft pick. Graham figured it was time for a little male bonding. He had his Penn State national championship ring with him. Graham slid it on the finger of his right hand, walked over to Testaverde, and stretched out his arm to shake Vinny's hand, making sure the quarterback saw the ring.

"Hey Vinny, how you doing; remember me?" Graham said.

Testaverde saw the ring first and then looked up and smiled. The two adversaries were now teammates.

"He was really a pretty nice guy," Graham remembered.

Don Graham didn't last very long in pro ball. He was cut in preseason by Tampa and then hooked up with the Bills, where he played sparingly that year. Late that season, dealing with a numbers problem on his roster, Bills coach Marv Levy told Graham that he needed to put the linebacker on waivers for a brief period, but promised he'd bring Graham back by the end of the year. The Jets claimed Graham on waivers, however, and he never got back to Buffalo, a team that would go to the Super Bowl the following year. Graham wound up playing one more season with the Washington Redskins before getting released again. With offers on the table from the Raiders, 49ers, and the Chargers, Don Graham, who by then was married and had a baby on the way, decided it was time to give up football for good and get a real job.

A hotel and restaurant major at Penn State with a minor in accounting and finance, Don Graham went to work as a comptroller with the Hilton Hotel chain. He bounced around in the industry and ran a sports and entertainment venue at Wrigley Field in Chicago before getting a job running the food and beverage operation for the Nashville Predators. He has made the Nashville area his permanent home, where he lives with his second wife and their two children. Graham also has two children living with their mother in South Carolina. In Nashville, he owns a couple of Dairy Queens.

Like Russo was to the Penn State defensive line, Don Graham was the grunt of the linebacking crew. While Conlan, Bauer, and Giftopoulos flew around the field with a little more daring and flash, Graham was the rock who stayed inside and took on every lead blocker that came at him.

"Shane always thanked me for taking guys on so he could make the tackle," Don Graham said with a laugh.

Graham and his buddies *loved* playing defense. What he remembers most was how competitive the Nittany Lions' practices were. Tim Johnson and Graham would take turns saying to each other as they broke their huddle, "Meet you at the quarterback." And they often did. In games the Lions defenders would ask each other, "All right, who's going to make the big play this time?" That's what they were saying just before Gifto intercepted Vinny to preserve the Lions' Fiesta Bowl win. Graham was in position right with Giftopoulos on that play. When Gifto caught the ball, Donnie Graham chased him from behind, yelling for him to get down and not to fumble but also to jump on him in celebration after the whistle blew the ball dead.

It had been the time of their lives.

ROBERT (DUFFY) COBBS, the cornerback who had thrown thunder into Michael Irvin the night of the 1986 Fiesta Bowl, gave up football after that season and returned to live a regular life in his hometown of Alexandria, Virginia, where he is a marketing representative. Cobbs didn't return telephone calls or e-mails when contacted for his views on the 1986 Penn State season.

JIMMY CEFALO, who was the color analyst of perhaps Penn State's most important game ever, became more of a superstar in broadcasting than perhaps he ever did playing football. Within a few years after the Fiesta Bowl, Cefalo sprung onto the national stage cohosting the 1988 Olympics for NBC in Seoul, Korea, then becoming the sports anchor on NBC News at Sunrise, and then getting a gig as a news correspondent for the Today show. Later Cefalo was chosen by Merv Griffin to be the host of Griffin's new game show Trump Card, a takeoff on the game show Jeopardy. The show only lasted one season, however.

Cefalo played for the Miami Dolphins from 1978 through 1984. A flanker in the pros, he caught 93 passes for 1,739 yards and 13 touchdowns.

Since 1992 he has been the nightly sports anchor for Miami's WTVJ-TV and owns several wine stores named "Cefalo's Wine Cellar" in the Miami area.

Cefalo did not respond to several requests to be interviewed for this book.

THE BIG JOKE GOING AROUND Penn State was that Brian Siverling was the Nittany Lions' third offensive tackle.

At least that's the way it was before Siverling, Penn State's starting tight end, got Jim Caldwell as a new assistant coach. Caldwell, a former Big Ten player who had brought some fresh ideas to college football as an offensive coach, was lured to Penn State from Louisville to coach the Nittany Lion receivers. He managed to spice up Penn State's offensive with a few more passing formations and plenty of pass plays to tight end Brian Siverling.

In 1986 Siverling led all Penn State receivers in catches. The tight end had twenty-one grabs that year—second to only D.J. Dozier—for 279 yards, an average of 13.3 yards per catch. He had caught only five passes the year before.

Memories of the Miami game remain fresh in Brian Siverling's mind. On the game's first play, the Lions, figuring Miami would come rushing hard, called for a screen pass. Stan Clayton, Penn State's left tackle, blocked the wrong guy and

Daniel Stubbs came flying unmolested at John Shaffer. After the series, which included another sack on Shaffer and resulted in a three and out, Siverling walked to the sideline and was met by his roommate, Mark Sickler. Sickler had been the Lions' starting left tackle until he got injured early in the year. Clayton, his backup, was inserted into the lineup and took the job for good even when Sickler was able to play. It hadn't sat well with Sickler.

"Sick says to me, 'Clayton missed the block, did you see that?' Siverling recalled. "I go, 'Not now, Mark. I've got enough to worry about.'"

Siverling has a picture on his office wall of him making a block that allowed Shaffer to dive into the end zone in the second quarter to get the Nittany Lions into a 7–7 tie.

"In the picture it looks like I'm clipping the guy, and anybody who ever sees it says, 'Hey, that's a clip.'" Siverling explained. "But in real time, it wasn't a clip. My body was in the proper position and it was a good block. But it's like I can't even get credit for the one good play I made in the game!"

Drafted in the eleventh round by the Detroit Lions, Siverling went to camp expecting pro football to be a penthouse of sorts, but when he got to the Silverdome, he thought it was a dump. He thought to himself, *No wonder you guys stink.* Pro football had been a thought in Brian Siverling's mind, but not a commitment. He wasn't having a great camp. He informed the Lions' coaches that he had to leave the second week of camp to be in his brother's wedding in Erie, Pennsylvania, and they granted permission for him to leave. But that Friday morning he started to have doubts about wanting to play anymore and cornered the Lions' tight end coach.

"I don't think I'm coming back," Siverling told the coach.

"Okay," the coach said.

Getting that response confirmed to Siverling he hadn't figured heavily in the Lions' plans anyway. He told a free-agent tight end he had befriended that he was leaving camp. The guy couldn't believe it.

"You're just quitting?" the player mused. "Jesus, I was driving a beer truck at this time last year. I'd do anything to stay here."

Siverling lives outside Annapolis, Maryland, with his wife, Wendy, and their two daughters. A civil engineering major at Penn State, he works now as an architectural engineer specializing in land development.

Back in 1986, Brian Siverling was one of four Nittany Lions—Johnson, Conlan, and Isom were the others—to be selected to play in the Japan Bowl, the college all-star game held in Tokyo the week after the Fiesta Bowl. Miami's Jimmy Johnson was the team's head coach. With Johnson sitting in the front of the bus that would take the team from its Tokyo hotel to the practice field and several Miami players scattered throughout the bus, Ray Isom broke into a rendition of Queen's "We Are the Champions."

Johnson, Conlan, and Siverling tried to suppress smiles, but they couldn't.

DAN MORGAN CAN REDUCE the thrill of playing football at Penn State to a single play.

It was the first play of the second quarter in the 1986 Alabama game. Penn State had the ball at the 'Bama 19-yard line, and in the huddle John Shaffer called for an off-tackle play to D.J. Dozier, which required Morgan, the Lions' left guard, to make a combination block with his neighbor, left tackle Chris Conlin.

The play was executed beautifully. Conlin knocked out the defensive tackle and Morgan pushed forward to bury the closing linebacker. Out of the corner of his eye, Morgan saw a flash of white move past him like a speeding bullet. It was Dozier. Penn State's star running back would take the ball to the end zone untouched for a touchdown.

"If you're an offensive lineman, it doesn't get any better than that," Dan Morgan would say years later. "The guy who scores the touchdown gets the glory. But when you make the block that gets him there, you get just as big a thrill."

Dan Morgan now lives in Lakeside Park, Kentucky, where he works in the computer industry as a network engineer setting up major systems for the likes of big companies such as General Electric. He and wife, Liz, have three young daughters.

Morgan came to Penn State from tiny St. Clairsville, Ohio, recruited as a tight end. Jerry Sandusky had been recruiting another high school player from Morgan's conference, but the Penn State defensive coordinator noticed this kid who played on the other team, this 6′6½″, 225-pounder from St. Clairsville High who could move pretty good. That night, Morgan caught a touchdown pass, scored another touchdown on an end around, and had 13 tackles from his defensive end positions.

UCLA had been recruiting Morgan hard. But once Penn State entered the picture, the kid from Ohio was coming to Happy Valley.

The Penn State coaches kept him at tight end his freshman year, where he battled in practice with incumbents Dean DiMidio and Siverling. But Morgan didn't play in a game that year, preserving his freshman eligibility. The following season he was moved to offensive line and saw playing time when starter Dick Maginnis was sidelined with injuries. It was clear that Paterno liked him. It just wasn't clear to the coaches where to play Dan Morgan.

He was a left defensive end the following season, starting ten games and making 26 tackles that season. His most memorable play was a crushing sack of Rutgers' quarterback Rusty Hochberg in the Lions' season opener that caused a safety. But the next year Conlin was hurt and out for a few games and Penn State coaches moved Morgan back to offense, where he would stay the rest of his career. His senior season, as the Nittany Lions chased another national championship, Dan Morgan was a swift, 270-pound offensive guard who was an anchor in blocking for John Shaffer.

Years later when Morgan signed with the New York Giants after getting cut by the Broncos, the team that had drafted him, the offensive lineman would liken his college quarterback's leadership skills to Phil Simms, the famed Giants quarterback who won a Super Bowl in New York.

"It was just the presence they both had," said Morgan. "Phil Simms didn't have a great arm, but he would get in that huddle and you would believe in the plays he would call. It was the same thing with Shaff."

STAN CLAYTON, Penn State's short-side tackle in the Fiesta Bowl, was a junior in 1986 who had gotten the starting slot early in the season after an injury felled Mark Stickler. Clayton made the most of his opportunity, keeping the job for the rest of his career. He wound up being taken in the tenth round of the 1988 NFL draft by the Atlanta Falcons and stuck around the NFL for several more seasons, ending up with the New England Patriots.

Clayton was the lone starting Nittany Lion that year to pursue a career as a college football coach. He began as a graduate assistant with Penn State in 1995 and then moved around to take coaching jobs at the University of Massachusetts, Alabama State, Kansas State, Princeton, and, most recently, the University of Toledo.

CHRIS CONLIN, as one of eight children, never much walked a solitary path, so it made sense that when Penn State won its national championship the night of January 2, 1987, Conlin had most of his home boys with him.

A large crew including several of Conlin's brothers, sisters, and friends from their old hometown hangout, the Colonial Inn in Oreland, Pennsylvania, just outside Philadelphia, came to Tempe to watch their buddy, Penn State's starting long-side offensive tackle. There was Richie and Boomer and Harry the Fly, and Ken Conlin, Chris's brother, who may have been the craziest of them all. That crew arrived in Phoenix two days before the game. On the way to their hotel from the airport, they stopped at the first 7-Eleven they could find, bought the convenience store out of their supply of bottled beer, and filled the bathtub in their room at the Holiday Inn with ice and brew. No one showered for three days.

Chris Conlin came along as the third child of the eight born to Mary and Joseph "Moon" Conlin. Chris had been born with fairer skin and lighter hair than Karen and Ken, the first two Conlin children. His hair was a reddish color, so they nicknamed him "Buckwheat." It was a name that would stick with Chris forever.

All members of the Conlin clan grew healthy and large. Brothers Keith and Kevin would also play line for Penn State later down the road. Brother Craig turned into a 6´6˝, 250-pounder who would become a basketball star at LaSalle University. Dinner at the Conlin house was a nightly banquet. It was routine for Mary Conlin to serve up two twenty-pound turkeys at one dinner sitting.

"You had to eat really fast if you wanted seconds," Chris remembered.

Conlin became a star at Bishop McDevitt High in Glenside, Pennsylvania, one of the building blocks of a major football program construction at the tiny parochial school that played out of the competitive Philadelphia Catholic League. With Conlin in the lineup, McDevitt managed to make the PCL playoffs for the first time in school history. Eastern football powers such as Penn State, Boston College, West Virginia, and Maryland noticed the big lineman, who was 6´5˝ and 255 pounds as a high school senior. But a spunky assistant from Florida State named Chuck Amato, who later would become the head coach at North Carolina State, recruited the East Coast for Bobby Bowden and really wanted Buckwheat Conlin. In the end, Conlin chose Penn State after playing in a Pennsylvania scholastic all-star game and getting to know several of the Nittany Lions' incoming freshmen, including quarterback Matt Knizner. Going to Penn State would also allow the Conlin clan to watch Chris play in person.

Conlin played right away at Penn State, seeing time at offensive line as a true freshman and then, to help out a banged-up defensive line, switching to defensive tackle for the Nittany Lions' Aloha Bowl game that year against Washington. He was back to offensive line for good his sophomore year and gained twenty pounds of muscle going into his junior year. That year, in the Orange Bowl against Oklahoma, Conlin was within direct earshot of Brian Bosworth, the Sooners' verbose linebacker who had taunted the Lions all game long.

"Look at all these fat-ass offensive linemen!" Bosworth was yelping.

Finally, by the third quarter, Conlin, normally a quiet and stoic offensive lineman who just paid attention to his job, had had enough.

After Bosworth made a tackle on D.J. Dozier after he had a five-yard gain, Conlin stood over the fallen Sooner linebacker and said, "Nice tackle, Boz. What's that, your first? You overrated piece of shit!"

The following season, Conlin would be conditioned for the taunting his team would face from Miami in the Fiesta Bowl, the game for the national championship.

Conlin most remembers that Joe Paterno stepped on the throttle hard in preparing for that game. He put the Nittany Lions through hell during their one month of practice leading up to the Fiesta. The Lions banged each other around in full pads three to four times per week. It was training camp all over again. It had been a long season. Paterno had had twenty practices that year for spring ball with nineteen of them in pads. As the Lions took the field for the Miami game, it dawned on Conlin that he had been immersed in football for almost one full year with very few breaks.

But he looked at this game as fun. The night the Hurricanes walked out of the barbeque, Conlin was unfazed, telling Dozier, "Don't worry about it; that's more food for us." Barely looking up from his plate, Conlin attacked his food, setting a new Fiesta Bowl record by wolfing down *seven* rib-eye steaks. Penn State was here for business. The Lions were here to win. Let the other guys make all the fuss. Let's just eat.

Coming into the stadium that night with Richie, Boomer, and Harry the Fly, Ken Conlin saw Vinny Testaverde's parents, Al and Rose, and a crew of their relatives and friends. They were wearing specially made T-shirts that on the front read "The Heisman Family." Chris Conlin's older brother remembered thinking the T-shirt gesture was so pompous. It fueled his rooting interest.

"I don't think there were any crazier fans in the stadium that night than me and my buddies," Ken Conlin says. "We wanted to win so bad we could taste it. By the end of the game, *I* was playing linebacker for Penn State."

On the final interception, just before Testaverde got the snap, Conlin reached down, subconsciously grabbed his buddy Richie's hand, and held it tight. He didn't realize what he was doing until the play was over and Giftopoulos was trotting down the field clutching the ball he had just intercepted. Conlin looked at Richie, realized he had been holding his friend's hand, and abruptly let it go. The two friends looked at each other in astonished embarrassment. Then they screamed a yelp of delight and hugged.

After the game Ken Conlin, Richie, Boomer, and Harry the Fly kidnapped Chris Conlin as he emerged from the Penn State locker room and took him on an all-night bender through Phoenix. They didn't get in until 5 A.M. It was the party of their lives.

Chris Conlin was drafted by the Miami Dolphins in the fifth round of the 1987 NFL draft six picks behind punter John Bruno and played three seasons there. He met his wife, Loretta, in Miami at a charity fashion show sponsored by Don Shula. The Dolphins released him in 1991 and he played two more years with the Colts. After a ten-year stint as an assistant coach with an Arena League team in South Florida, Chris Conlin is now a project manager for a construction company started by a couple of his old Dolphins teammates.

STEVE WISNIEWSKI KNEW he was destined to play football at Penn State even though he had grown up in Houston, Texas.

Wisniewski was only twelve years old when he came to Penn State to visit his older brother Leo, who at the time was a star linebacker at State. The Wisniewskis had originally been from Pittsburgh, but John Wisniewski, Leo and Steve's dad, moved the family to the southwest to take a sales job. Joe Paterno, wearing a Penn State coach's hat, had been giving the Wisniewski family a tour of the facilities when he suddenly took off his hat, placed it on Steve's head, and said, "One day, young man, I'm going to recruit you."

Steve Wisniewski never forgot that.

Years later, the kid would become a star offensive lineman at Spring High School in suburban Houston and would spurn offers from the Southwest Conference and Big Eight to become a Nittany Lion. He was the youngest starter on the team that would win the 1986 national championship; he was also the lightest offensive lineman that night.

A little-known fact the week of the 1986 Fiesta Bowl was that Steve Wisniewski had been suffering a serious bout of bronchitis and by game time had double pneumonia. The coaches, trainers, and medical staff knew Wisniewski was sick, but he kept the severity of his condition from them as best as he could. After practices and team meetings, the 6′4″ Wisniewski hunkered down in his hotel bed, piling himself with blankets.

"The day before the game I found a scale and weighed myself," Wisniewski recalled. "I was down to 238 pounds, but there was no way I was going to miss that game."

Battling such All-Americans as Jerome Brown and Daniel Stubbs, Wisniewski wound up holding his own the night Penn State beat Miami. His weight eventually returned. Wisniewski increased his workout regimen, and by the time he was a senior he had beefed up to 275 pounds and became a two-time All-American.

Drafted by the Dallas Cowboys, he was traded to the Oakland Raiders and made the Pro Bowl seven times as a swift and athletic 305-pound guard. He was named to the NFL's all-decade team of the 1990s.

Through his travels in the NFL, Wisniewski played with and against some of his best friends from the 1986 Penn State champs, including Shane Conlan, who became a star with the Bills and Rams.

"It's like the old cartoon you'd see on the Bugs Bunny show where the sheepdog and the coyote work at the same plant," said Wisniewski. "You clock in and you're all business, trying to knock your buddy's block off. And then you clock out and after the game it's like, 'Hey Shane, how's the family?'

"Shane Conlan was without a doubt one of the toughest guys I have ever seen. He wasn't that big of a guy, but he had the hardest head. It was well known around the league when Shane hit you, it was going to hurt."

Wisniewski also developed a reputation. An anonymous poll of players named the former Penn State star one of the dirtiest players in the league. He once racked up some $65,000 in fines from the league for dirty hits. Wisniewski downplays that reputation, saying that as an offensive lineman in the NFL you did what you had to do to survive. In an ultimate twist of irony, Steve Wisniewski recently became a born-again Christian and often speaks at The Well Christian Community Church in Dublin, California, near where he and his wife, Jeanne, and their three children live in the San Francisco Bay area. The church was founded by his former Raider teammate, running back Napoleon McCallum. He also works for a nutrition company.

Of all the thrills Steve Wisniewski experienced in his professional career—the Raiders went to two AFC championship games while he was there—nothing, he said, tops the feeling he had in 1986, when the Penn State Nittany Lions beat Miami to win the national championship.

"There's something about that bond with the guys you went to college with," he said. "I'm not sure whether it's because that college football is a little more innocent than the pros, or whether it's just that you're still growing up are a little more impressionable. But the night we won the Fiesta Bowl, I thought I was walking on a cloud."

ABOUT THE AUTHOR

M. G. MISSANELLI is a well-known media personality in Philadelphia who has worked for more than twenty-five years in the area of sports journalism.

A former varsity baseball player at Penn State University, Missanelli graduated from Penn State in 1977 with a B.A. degree in journalism. Mike spent ten years as a reporter with the *Philadelphia Inquirer* before becoming a popular radio talk-show host and television anchor in Philly. In 1983 while with the *Inquirer*, he was a member of a team reporting crew that was nominated for a Pulitzer Prize. In 1999 Missanelli won a Mid-Atlantic Emmy Award for his contributions to a sportscast on WPHL-TV. From 1992 to 1997 he served as editor-in-chief and co-publisher of *The Fan* magazine, a Philadelphia-based all-sports magazine. Previously, he authored a book entitled *The Transaction* on the life of a professional baseball player.

Mike is also a 1986 graduate of Delaware Law School of Widener University and is a licensed attorney. Currently, he teaches a class on sports and entertainment law at St. Joseph's University in Philadelphia.

KEVIN COURTER (Penn State '80) served as research assistant to the author and lives in Media, Pennsylvania, with his wife, Maria, and sons (future Nittany Lions), Michael and Eric. He is the founder of Playerz Ink, a firm that coordinates personal appearances and signing events for professional/retired athletes. Fall Saturdays will find him in Beaver Stadium joining thousands of others in cheering on the finest student-athletes in the history of college football. Kevin can be contacted at Kevin@playerzink.com.

NOTES

CHAPTER 1

D.J. Dozier interview. June 2005. Norfolk, Virginia.

page 5   "Dozier's about the only black kid": *Virginian-Pilot,* September 1, 1982 (Harry Minium).

page 8   "I'm trying to put together a team": *Centre Daily Times,* Special Supplement, January 7, 1986 (Ron Bracken).

page 11   "There was no doubt": *Philadelphia Inquirer,* October 26, 1986 (Ray Parrillo).

page 12   "For Miami, it turned out to be": Bruce Skinner interview. September 2005.

page 13   "Paterno said later that he thought Dozier": *Centre Daily Times,* D-1, October 15, 1986 (Jim Carlson).

page 16   "That's what Miami is going to expect us to do": John Shaffer interview. August 2005.

page 16   "They recruited me, but they told me": *Philadelphia Inquirer,* December 31, 1986 (Jere Longman).

page 17   "And then if that weren't enough": Jerry Sandusky interview. April 2006.

page 22   "In the locker room at halftime of the Fiesta Bowl": D.J. Dozier interview. June 2005.

page 22   "'Just be patient,' he told them": D.J. Dozier interview. June 2005.

CHAPTER 2

Tom Bradley interview. August 2000.
Trey Bauer interview. July 2005.
Shane Conlan interview. August 2005.
Tim Manoa interview. July 2006.

CHAPTER 3

John Shaffer interview. August 2005.

page 36   "Ray Perkins, the Alabama coach, compared Bennett": *Philadelphia Inquirer,* October 24, 1986 (Jere Longman).
page 40   "Miami cornerback Bennie Blades told a newspaper reporter": John Shaffer interview. August 2005.
page 40   "David Hartman, the host of ABC's *Good Morning America*: John Shaffer interview. August 2005.

CHAPTER 4

Jerry Sandusky interview. April 2006.

page 69   "As far as I'm concerned, Friday's game ": *Sports Illustrated,* January 12, 1987, p. 15 (Rick Reilly).
page 69   "Conlan covering me will be good for us": *Sports Illustrated,* January 12, 1987, p. 15 (Rick Reilly).
page 69   "You know what I think of John Shaffer": *Sports Illustrated,* January 12, 1987, p. 15 (Rick Reilly).
page 69   "[The Syracuse] receivers better tie their shoes on": *Philadelphia Inquirer,* October 18, 1986 (Ray Parrillo).

CHAPTER 5

page 73   "Penn State was leading the Tide": (written by author from game accounts).
page 74   "We should be better than last year": *Centre Daily Times,* D-2, August 16, 1986 (Ron Bracken).
page 75   "It's amazing the amount of friends I've made": *Centre Daily Times,* C-1, September 14, 1986 (Ron Bracken).
page 75   "I never had any trouble with confidence": *Centre Daily Times,* C-1, September 9, 1986 (Ron Bracken).
page 75   "I think their secondary could be a weakness for them": *Centre Daily Times,* C-1, September 8, 1986 (Ron Bracken).
page 76   "It was tough. I can't say that it wasn't": *Centre Daily Times,* C-1, September 24, 1986 (Ron Bracken).
page 76   "I don't care what John Shaffer thinks": *Centre Daily Times,* C-1, September 24, 1986 (Ron Bracken).
page 76   "The Hurricanes and Sooners are in a class by themselves": *Centre Daily Times,* D-1, October 2, 1986 (Ron Bracken).
page 77   "Stupid clips!": *Centre Daily Times,* D-1, October 5, 1986 (Jim Carlson).
page 77   "A guy hit D.J. and then knocked him down": *Centre Daily Times,* D-4, October 16, 1986 (Ron Bracken).
page 77   "Are you telling me how to coach the team?": *Centre Daily Times,* D-1, October 5, 1986 (Jim Carlson).

page 77   "I resent that attitude, calling them turkeys": *Centre Daily Times,* D-1, October
           8, 1986 (Ron Bracken).

page 77   "I had a bad day": *Centre Daily Times,* D-1, October 15, 1986 (Jim Carlson).

page 78   "That was the greatest moment of my Penn State career": *Centre Daily Times,*
           D-1, October 26, 1986 (Ron Bracken).

page 78   "Someone has to play awfully well to beat us": *Centre Daily Times,* D-1, October
           26, 1986 (Jim Carlson).

page 79   "Our money is in the bank": *Centre Daily Times,* C-1, October 28, 1986 (Greg
           Cote, Knight-Ridder newspapers).

page 79   "We're 9-0 and No. 3": *Centre Daily Times,* C-1, November 15, 1986 (Jim Carl-
           son).

page 80   "There were a lot of guys saying a lot of prayers": *Centre Daily Times,* C-1,
           November 17, 1986 (Jim Carlson).

page 80   "My mother told me not to say anything": *Centre Daily Times,* C-2, November
           16, 1986 (Jim Carlson).

page 80   "It's on their application, time and date": *Centre Daily Times,* C-2, November 23,
           1986 (Associated Press).

page 81   "I'm not going to let an hour go by": *Philadelphia Inquirer,* November 24, 1986
           (Ray Parrillo).

page 81   "Joe Paterno yelled at us that we have no class": *Philadelphia Inquirer,* Novem-
           ber 24, 1986 (Ray Parrillo).

page 81   "Before I ran across the field": *Centre Daily Times,* C-1, November 26, 1986 (Ron
           Bracken).

page 82   "I've been reading the last couple days": *Centre Daily Times,* C-1, November 28,
           1986 (Jim Carlson).

page 82   "I don't think Miami would have any problems": *Centre Daily Times,* C-1,
           November 27, 1986 (Bernard Fernandez, *Philadelphia Daily News*).

page 82   "I'll just run you over, then": *Centre Daily Times,* C-2, November 30, 1986 (Asso-
           ciated Press).

page 82   "Testaverde arrived . . . wearing a Penn State sweatshirt": *Centre Daily Times,*
           D-1, December 12, 1986 (Ron Bracken).

page 83   "I'm not the man I used to be": *Centre Daily Times,* C-1, December 21, 1986 (Jim
           Carlson).

page 83   "It's going to be a war out there": *Centre Daily Times,* C-1, December 29, 1986
           (Jim Carlson).

page 83   "They're overrated with all that nice guy stuff": *Centre Daily Times,* C-1, Decem-
           ber 29, 1986 (Jim Carlson).

page 83   "I could do it, but I think": *Sports Illustrated,* January 12, 1987, p. 15 (Rick
           Reilly).

page 84   "Ah, let them have fun": *Centre Daily Times,* C-1, December 30, 1986 (Jim Carl-
           son).

page 84   "I don't want to make more of this than it already is": *Centre Daily Times,* C-1,
           December 30, 1986 (Jim Carlson).

page 85   "It's kind of an unbelievable situation": *Centre Daily Times,* C-1, January 4, 1987
           (Jim Carlson).

page 85   "I'm kind of nostalgic": *Centre Daily Times,* January 18, 1987, p. 1 (Michael Arm-
           strong).

CHAPTER 7

Steve Smith, interview, August 2006.
Chie Smith, interview, August 2006.
John Bruno Sr., interview, September 2006.

page 117 "I really believe that Steve had this sick satisfaction": ESPN feature, "Silver and Black Fund, aired August 27, 2004.
page 128 "The Easter lilies stood around the altar": Jack Bogut, by special permission.
page 132 "We beat him up pretty good": Morris Smith interview. August 2006.
page 140 "He never asked, his wife never asked": ESPN feature, "Silver and Black Fund, aired August 27, 2004.
page 140 "Jackson said that . . . he didn't want to start crying": ESPN feature, "Silver and Black Fund, aired August 27, 2004.
page 140 "I was shoulder to shoulder": ESPN feature, "Silver and Black Fund, aired August 27, 2004.

CHAPTER 8

Ken Schanzer, interview, September 2006.
Bob Costas, interview, September 2006.
Sam Jankovich, interview, August 2006.
Michael Weisman, interview, September 2006.
Charlie Jones, interview, August 2006.
Andy Rosenberg, interview, October 2006.

CHAPTER 9

page 161 "We're better than Penn State": Pete Giftopoulos interview. August 2006.
page 162 "The loss was not a matter of us not moving the football": *Centre Daily Times,* C-2, January 4, 1987 (Greg Cote, *Miami Herald*).
page 169 "It was something that stuck with me": "Beyond the Glory," Fox TV sports feature, April 13, 2006.
page 184 "There was a story written about Dan Sileo": *San Francisco Chronicle,* March 22, 1997 (Susan Slusser).

CHAPTER 10

Massimo Manca, interview, September 2006.
Mike Russo, interview, October 2006.
Don Graham, interview, October 2006.
Brian Siverling, interview, October 2006.
Dan Morgan, interview, October 2006.
Steve Wisniewski, interview, October 2006.
Chris Conlin, interview, July 2005.